Protecting Children in Time

Child Abuse, Child Protection and the Consequences of Modernity

Harry Ferguson

palgrave
macmillan

First published 2004 by
PALGRAVE MACMILLAN
Houndmills, Basingstoke, Hampshire RG21 6XS and
175 Fifth Avenue, New York, N.Y. 10010
Companies and representatives throughout the world

PALGRAVE MACMILLAN is the global academic imprint of the Palgrave Macmillan division of St. Martin's Press, LLC and of Palgrave Macmillan Ltd. Macmillan® is a registered trademark in the United States, United Kingdom and other countries. Palgrave is a registered trademark in the European Union and other countries.

ISBN 1–4039–0692–0 hardback
ISBN 1–4039–0693–9 paperback

This book is printed on paper suitable for recycling and made from fully managed and sustained forest sources.

A catalogue record for this book is available from the British Library.

Library of Congress Cataloging-in-Publication Data
Ferguson, Harry (Thomas Harold)
    Protecting children in time : child abuse, child protection and the consequences of modernity / Harry Ferguson.
        p. cm.
    Includes bibliographical references and index.
    ISBN 1–4039–0692–0 – ISBN 1–4039–0693–9 (pbk.)
        1. Child abuse. 2. Child abuse – Prevention. 3. Social change. I. Title.
HV6626.5.F47 2004
362.76'7—dc22   2004045425

10 9 8 7 6 5 4
13 12 11 10 09 08 07 06

Printed and bound in Great Britain by
Antony Rowe Ltd, Chippenham and Eastbourne

To Claire and our children, Ellen, Katie, Ben and Susie

Constant revolutionising of production, uninterrupted disturbance of all social conditions, everlasting uncertainty and agitation distinguish the bourgeois epoch from all earlier ones. All fixed, fast-frozen relations…all swept away, all new ones become antiquated before they can ossify. All that is solid melts into air…

(Marx and Engels, 1888, pp. 53–4)

We always worked at a fairly cracking pace in north Tottenham.

(a London social worker in her evidence to the public inquiry into the death from child abuse of Victoria Climbié, cited in Laming, 2003, p. 184)

It seems to me that I would always be better off where I am not, and this question of moving is one of those I discuss incessantly with my soul.

(Charles Baudelaire, cited in Urry, 2000, p. i)

I am for an art that is political-erotical-mystical, that does something other than sit on its ass in a museum. I am for an art that embroils itself with the everyday crap and comes out on top. I am for an art that tells you the time of day, or where such and such a street is. I am for an art that helps old ladies across the street.

(Claes Oldenburg, cited in Berman, 1983, p. 320)

The knowledge of horrible events periodically intrudes into public awareness but is rarely retained for long. Denial, repression, and dissociation operate on a social as well as an individual level. The study of psychological trauma has an 'underground' history. Like traumatized people we have been cut off from knowledge of our past. Like traumatized people we need to understand the past in order to reclaim the present and the future. Therefore, an understanding of psychological trauma begins with rediscovering history.

(Judith Herman, 1992, p. 2)

Contents

Preface and Acknowledgements

For most of my working life – 25 years of it to be precise – I have been involved in doing but mostly studying forms of social intervention, especially child protection. In 1978 I left Ireland to become a social worker (then called 'Inspector') with the National Society for the Prevention of Cruelty to Children (NSPCC) in London. Like most social workers I witnessed first hand some horrendous cases of child abuse and neglect. Just a few that come to mind include: the terribly neglected three-year-old boy with a frost bitten penis caused by the bed he had wet freezing as he was locked for hours in a bedroom without heating; the two-year-old who was literally skin and bone and had eaten the plastic teat of the feeding bottle having been locked in a room and ignored for a week by his 'carer', his mother's boyfriend and pimp; the countless children with suspected non-accidental injuries, like the six-week-old baby with bruising to her face perpetrated it was suspected by her father; or the 15-year-old girl who had been so badly beaten by her mother that she needed hospital treatment, whose father was sexually abusing her, and who was removed into care never to return home. Then there were the countless less dramatic cases of mild neglect and low level risk to children living with vulnerable mothers and fathers struggling to care well enough.

Like the vast bulk of child protection, this kind of solid work went largely unrecognized beyond the confidential routines of the professional system. My research into child protection practice in the present has convinced me that this remains no less true today than it was in the 1980s. I have long believed that the routine achievements of social workers and other professionals involved in child protection have gone unheralded and that the sheer complexities of child protection work are deeply misunderstood, a situation that has been made much worse by the regular and often vicious public criticism of professionals for 'failing' to protect children. This book is, among other things, an attempt to put that right. Yet it is far from being some kind of unqualified celebration of heroic child protection. It is rather an attempt to critically analyse the meanings of child protection in modern societies, the forms it takes as a modern experience; its routines, creative possibilities and limitations.

On the basis of my practical experience I became deeply curious about why child protection took the forms that it did: where, for instance, fundamentally did its powers and practices come from? Why was home visiting such a key method of protecting children? And why was so much invested in the idea that children could and should be protected through such often tenuous practices? Opportunities for me to satisfy my curiosity arose first as an undergraduate at the University of Bradford (1983–7) and then through a PhD at the University of Cambridge (1987–90). I came to realize that an adequate answer to my questions would have to involve historical work and taking child protection back to its very roots. I was fortunate to discover a wonderful collection of historical case records and other documentary evidence in the archives of the NSPCC which went right back to the beginnings of modern child protection at the end of the nineteenth century, and to which I gained full access for my PhD.

Once securely embedded in academia, I began to formulate another, more theoretical, question: How might the complexities of child protection be better theorized and understood as an experience? The focus on *experience* felt important as it seemed to me to be the piece – the heart and soul, the smell even – that was left out of most analysis of welfare practices. I had begun to think about formulating the idea I call in this book 'the smell of practice' in the early 1980s when an experienced social work practice teacher told me that even her most enthusiastic and well prepared students were bemused and feeling failures on their first professional home visits having been rendered inert by the smells in their client's homes. Although I had no language for it then, I felt I knew very well what those students were experiencing: that radical dissonance that exists between, on the one hand, the bureaucratic and academic routines that go into producing files, theories, knowledge; and, on the other, of the immediacies, the shocks, all the profoundly *embodied* experiences and perceptions which register when professionals leave their desks and offices and those receiving services appear, quite literally, in practice. At the heart of this book is an attempt to think through the dimensions of such primal experiences in welfare and theorize the nature of this ambiguous space between files and visits, between objective knowledge and labouring in the messy actuality of people's lives that is exemplified by what we have come to know as child protection.

Marshall Berman's 1983 book *All That is Solid Melts into Air: The Experience of Modernity* introduced me to the notion of 'modernity' and had a profound impact in terms of how one might produce a narrative which is structured through experience, movement and the dynamic nature of human action in an (ever changing) modern world, as told through a dialogue between history and the present. I feel fortunate to have benefited from the explosion of work and debates in sociology concerning modernity/postmodernity, the body, gender, risk society and the sociology of mobilities. At the same time, I spent much of the 1990s researching current child protection policy and practices, including conducting a relatively large empirical study of how social workers and other professionals responded to child care and abuse cases and how they, children and parents experienced child protection work, all of which took some five years from conception to completion. Although I was fortunate to publish on historical and contemporary aspects of child protection, my aim had always been to one day produce a book which covered the broad sweep of historical and sociological analysis which I felt was necessary to reaching a full understanding of the nature of modern child protection.

Now that project, in the form of this book, is complete, I can only hope that it makes some contribution to deepening understandings of the complexities of child protection and advancing its capacities to protect children in time. The kind of theory and account of practice offered here won't resolve all of the contradictions and tensions that pervade child protection's modern character. But it might help students like those I referred to earlier to identify and understand the smell of practice for what it is; perhaps offering them some kind of necessary unity and strength from which to nourish and renew themselves, as they continue to step out of their offices, onto the streets and into their clients' homes, to face the torment, the paradoxes and the challenges that lie ahead.

Given that this book has been such a long time in the making, I owe a great debt to many people who have helped me along the way. At the University of Bradford in the 1980s, staff in the Applied Social Studies Department, especially Bob Ashcroft, Steven Collins, Nick Frost, Jeff Hearn, Eileen Moxon, Tony Novak, and Neil Small encouraged me to develop my thinking. At the University of Cambridge I was very fortunate to benefit from the extraordinary intellectual environment nurtured by Anthony Giddens in the Faculty of Social and Political Sciences and remain indebted to the influence of his work ever since. I am particularly grateful to Judith Ennew for her support in guiding my PhD. work. I am also grateful for the support of Mary Sheridan which was invaluable at this time.

I am grateful to the department of social studies, Trinity College, Dublin for the five years I spent there and to Robbie Gilligan and Ruth Torode in particular for the opportunities to teach and think about child protection. I cannot thank Fred Powell, Professor of Applied Social

Studies, the National University of Ireland, Cork, enough for the belief he showed in me, for creating the opportunity for me to spend five great years in Cork and for encouraging me to develop my theoretical interests in applied social science. Although our working relationship was relatively brief, I gained a great deal from my ex-colleagues in the Department of Social Policy and Social Work, University College Dublin and am especially grateful to Pat Clancy for his support and understanding. Into the present, I am grateful to Professor Robin Means, University of the West of England for his encouragement and support and to my colleagues in the Faculty of Health and Social Care.

I am very grateful to the NSPCC for providing me with prolonged and open access to their archives, to the many NSPCC librarians who have helped me over the years and the archivist Nicholas Malton. My research into current child protection benefited greatly from the unstinting support of Ger Crowley, while Máire O'Reilly and Michele O'Flanagan provided invaluable assistance with the research. I am particularly grateful to the professionals, children and parents who took part in the research and shared their experiences so openly.

I have discussed the ideas in this book with many groups of students over the years and have benefited from their feedback and challenges. Particular thanks go to a number of PhD. students with whom I have had the pleasure of working: Helen Buckley, Niall McElwee, Delice Osborne, Pat Kenny, Colm O'Doherty, and Michele O'Flanagan. A number of friends and colleagues have in various ways provided comment, conversations, support and inspiration which has benefited my work and I want to thank: Roy Boyne, Helen Buckley, Mick Cunningham, Jane Dalrymple, Brid Featherstone, Jan Fook, Anthony Giddens, Fergus Hogan, Paul Hoggett, David Howe, Stephen Hudson, Pat Kenny, Michael Kimmel, Scott Lash, Sarah Leigh, Ginny Morrow, Marian Murphy, Nigel Parton, John Pinkerton, Andy Portman, Nigel Richardson, John Urry and Stephen Webb.

I am very grateful to my editors at Palgrave: Heather Gibson who initially commissioned the book and gave it such enthusiastic support from the outset; and, latterly, Briar Towers for being equally inspiring, believing in the title and ultimately allowing me the space to express myself.

My mother Madge Ferguson has not only provided love and encouragement but gathered up countless press clippings, audio and video recordings and much else which have assisted my research. She and my late father Tom Ferguson have been endlessly supportive of my work and eccentricities, as have the rest of my family. My brother Ian Ferguson deserves a special mention for putting my overheads up so nicely at an international child abuse conference in Perth, Australia in 1998, for his inspiring feedback (I mean for an engineer) and his hassling of me over the years to publish this book.

Words cannot express my gratitude to my partner Claire Mackinnon for her love and support, while my step-children Katie, Ben and Susie, and my three-year-old daughter Ellen have taught me the most important lessons of all about just how precious, yet vulnerable children are.

Harry Ferguson
Bristol
November, 2003

1
Protecting Children in Time, or Failing To: Child Abuse, Child Protection and Modernity

There is a vitally important mode of modern work experience we know as child protection. It is to be part of a vast division of labour in a welfare state. It is an experience of time and space, of working simultaneously in public and private realms, of hourly home visits, office interviews, medical consultations, the working day, and weekends. Of being part of large faceless bureaucracies that have the power to enter people's lives, their homes, communities and to tear them apart by taking children into care, but only at the same time as it is to embody resources, initiatives and sources of strength which can also enable people, families and communities to pull together, to prevent them falling apart, to live to fight bureaucracy another day. It is thus an experience of power and control, but equally of caring and compassion: of helping and tending for others, of relieving the suffering of children and often their parents and other carers, many of whom no one else wants to know; of talking, listening, group meetings and often boring bureaucratic routine; of being blamed for the deaths of children or in other ways getting it wrong, and being made accountable and subjected to managerial guidance and control. It is pervasively an experience of mobility, of acting at speed to reach children, of the emotions and senses and intimate engagement with the sights, sounds and smells of other's lives and homes, their tragedy and pain, which threatens to become the worker's own; of pervasive anxiety, risk, danger and despair, but some joy and laughs too. Of being part of the pathos and courage of people's ordinary everyday heroic struggles to get through the day, at the same time as worker's may feel somehow courageous and heroic while making the chaos pay, acting at the interface between modern life's perils and possibilities. It is in total an experience of ambiguity, anguish and paradox in every action taken and decision made.

1

In this book I shall refer to this experience as the work and objective of *protecting children in time*. This is intended to capture two meanings which are central to the constitution of child protection and this study: the sense of (chronological) time as *history*; and of (acting in) time as *practice*. The central aim of the book is to explore the cultural roots and parameters of child protection as a quintessentially modern ideal and form of social practice and experience.

It seems to be characteristic of the experience of working at protecting children in time that child care professionals today are apt to feel that they are the first, and perhaps the only ones, to have experienced it as harrowing, elusive, tantalizing. Similarly, Western culture seems most at home believing that the problems which social workers and other professionals face have reached new and tragic depths, with an apparent desire to see their practices as plumbing similar depths of ineptitude. But as I want to trace it in this book, it is essential to understand that child care professionals have been going through this kind of experience for well over 100 years. To concede and understand this, or so I want to argue, has major implications for how social work practices in child protection are to be characterized, explained, defended and creatively developed. In fact it is only through such a historical conception that we can hope to fully grasp and explain what protecting children in time is all about.

Above all, this involves a (re)conceptualization of child protection as a quintessentially 'modern' social practice. 'To be modern', writes Marshall Berman, who has produced the definitive vision of 'the experience of modernity', 'is to find ourselves in an environment that promises adventure, power, growth, transformation of ourselves and the world – and, at the same time, threatens to destroy everything we have, everything we know, everything we are. ... To be modern is to be part of a universe in which, as Marx said, "all that is solid melts into air"' (Berman, 1983, p. 15). Using similar kinds of language and imagery, Bauman speaks of 'solid' capitalism and 'liquid' modernity. He regards 'fluidity' or 'liquidity' as 'fitting metaphors when we wish to grasp the nature of the present, in many ways, *novel*, phase in the history of modernity' (Bauman, 2000, p. 2, original emphasis). Urry, meanwhile, argues for a manifesto for sociology in the new millennium which has at its core a concern with movement and the notion of 'mobilities': 'that examines the diverse mobilities of peoples, objects, images, information and wastes; and of the complex interdependencies between, and social consequences of, these diverse mobilities' (Urry, 2000, p. 1). For Anthony Giddens, modernity introduces a dynamic experience of security and danger, chaos and control in our lives which he refers to as being like 'riding the juggernaut' (Giddens, 1990). This image captures well the sheer power of how technological innovation drives our lives yet our simultaneous inability to control what modernity has unleashed. What all these writers have in common is a concern with capturing and theorizing the uneasy relationship between the expanded capacities of global capitalism to modernize, revitalize as well as destroy people's lives, of nation-states in the context of a 'world society' to seek to regulate and exert control over those lives, and the movement, dynamism, flux, and uncertainty that characterizes the modern world we live in; how 'all that is solid melts into air'.

It is within this kind of 'modernist' ambience that the practices and ideals concerned with protecting children in time came into being, developed and must be understood and explored. The basic hypothesis of this study is that child protection has lost touch with its modern roots and fails to understand its own modern(ist) character. I will argue that this kind of understanding is required at the best of times, but in a climate of real and profound questioning of child protection systems due to 'failures' to protect abused children and especially to prevent them from dying, it needs this kind of modernism most, to show it where it has come from, what kind of practice it is and might be, and where it might try to go.

In this book, I want to examine the very constitution of the taken-for-granted notion which is implicit in all contemporary child protection discourse: that it is possible through social intervention to protect children from avoidable harm and even death – possible, that is, to protect children *in time*. Despite its centrality to contemporary society and social policy it is remarkable how little critical attention has been given to a full sociological interrogation of this ideal. Adopting a historical sociological methodology, the book studies the emergence and development of modern practices of child protection in the Western world, focusing in particular on empirical research from Britain and Ireland, but also giving attention to countries such as the United States of America and Australia. This book is not so much a detailed history and sociology of child protection in a single place, but an analysis of the emergence of a particular idea and its enactment in modern times: the ideology that it is possible to prevent children suffering from child abuse, neglect and especially death; that professionals not only can but *should* protect children in time. The focus, then, is on the emergence of a global idea and ideal of child protection, one which has come to have an immensely powerful hold in the Western world today.

The book has three main aims. First, it is intended as a contribution to theoretical knowledge, elucidating the sociological character of modern child protection. Second, it seeks to advance historical as well as contemporary knowledge of child abuse and protection and the state's attempts to intervene to prevent children's suffering, as well as regulate childhood, parenting and family life over the past 130 years. Third, the book aims to provide insights which can contribute to the development of more effective child protection policies and practices.

At its most basic, this book seeks not only to re-examine issues like child death from a historical perspective, but to explain sociologically what child protection workers do, why they do the things they do and the (changing) meanings attached to child abuse. While there are differences in the specifics of how child protection is delivered from place to place, a standardized child protection process exists across the Western world, involving the identification, investigation and management of child abuse. The socio-historical approach adopted here provides a means to setting out how it came to pass that child protection work goes on in the way that it does. The home visit by a social worker and medical examination by doctors are perhaps the two key rituals in modern child protection. Yet, as this book shows, while they have always been beset with problems in terms of difficulties in getting to 'see' children and make sense of their experience, they did not always carry the meaning and power they have today and examining how they came into being and to have such a pivotal role in child protection can enable us to see in a new way the limits and possibilities they contain.

Despite the extraordinary level of contemporary concern and the vast amount of conceptual rethinking that has gone into child protection since child abuse re-emerged as a major social issue over three decades ago (Nelson, 1984; Parton, 1985), surprisingly little historical and sociological investigation has been carried out into the nature of child abuse as a social problem and child protection as an institutional practice. With only a few exceptions (Gordon, 1989; Jenks, 1996; Corby, 2002; Hendrick, 2003), the formative influences of modern child protection are traced to events since the 1960s and major developments since the work of Kempe *et al.* (1962), and legal and administrative changes since the 1970s (Kempe and Kempe, 1978, p. 15; London Borough of Brent, 1985, chapter 1; Dubowitz and Newberger, 1989; Zigler and Hall, 1989). However, contrary to what is commonly assumed today, problems like the deaths of children in child abuse cases are far from new. As I show in this book, how to protect children from avoidable harm and death has exercised the minds of child protection agencies in a profound way since their modern beginnings in the late-nineteenth century. Up until the middle of the twentieth century, literally hundreds of children were dying every year in child protection casework. The social construction of child survival as a technical problem about which something can and should be done is in fact quite a recent phenomenon (Scheper-Hughes, 1987, p. 2), and in this book I trace it as it emerged in the late-nineteenth century and developed across the twentieth century into the present.

Life and death politics: the contemporary state of child protection

For three decades now across the Western world the issue of the deaths of children in child protection cases has hung like a dark shadow over the professions who work with child abuse, and especially social work. In Britain, children such as Maria Colwell, Jasmine Beckford, and Victoria Climbié; in Ireland, Kelly Fitzgerald; in the United States of America, Danzel Bailey, are just some of those whose cases have gained national and even global notoriety because they died from child abuse despite the attentions of child protection professionals. Media, academic and front-line professional interest in such child protection failures is truly international as the dead children form a litany to which we constantly return (Stanley and Goddard, 2002). The sheer scale of the problem can be seen from the fact that although the cases of most children who die despite being known by professionals to be at risk never gain national let alone international prominence, at the local level they still cause enormous distress and often public outcry about the (in)effectiveness of child protection systems. An internet search of child protection case deaths in the United States provides many typical examples.

In Arizona, 20-month-old Liana Sandoval 'was already dead on 27 September 2001, when a state Child Protective Services [CPS] caseworker closed the file on the little girl, writing off allegations as "unsubstantiated" that her mother's boyfriend was abusing her'. The night before, he confessed to police that 'he tied the 20-month-old girl with a heavy wire to an 18-pound chunk of concrete and sank her body in a filthy canal'. The child's mother had driven to the canal with Liana's body wrapped in a blanket on her boyfriend's lap, while Liana's three year old sister, Isabella, was (alive) on the back seat. A CPS investigation into the case and a civil lawsuit taken against CPS by Liana's non-resident father suggested that social worker's had investigated allegations of abuse but concluded that three year old Isabella's disclosure that her mother's boyfriend, Juan, had inflicted the injuries she and her sister had, arose from the child being coached because she used the same wording as her aunt who had reported the case. Meanwhile, a breakdown in communication between the police and social workers meant that the police never got involved in the case. Two weeks later, Liana was dead (*The Arizona Republic*, 12 January 2003, at www.azcentral.com/ specials/special46/articles/0112liana12.hml).

The appalling violence and suffering perpetrated on children in such extreme cases is an obvious feature of the scandalous quality such events and public disclosures now contain. A number of mechanisms have been developed by nation-states to manage such child protection 'failures': from a detailed focus on the circumstances and practices surrounding individual cases, either through high profile independent public inquiries – in which the UK particularly excels (see Reder *et al.*, 1993) – or through routine case reviews of child death cases (Reder and Duncan, 1999); to large-scale reviews of of child death cases and the inadequacies of the system's responses to them (on Australia, see, for instance, *The New South Wales Child Death Review Team Report*, 1997; on the United States of America, for instance, the report of the *US Advisory Board on Child Abuse and Neglect*, USABCAN, 1995). What all countries have in common is the construction of child protection in terms of 'scandal politics', which refers to the pattern of increased stress on public disclosures of welfare failures and revelations in news media that are shaming for public figures and services (Chaney, 2002, p. 116; Lull and Hinerman, 1997). Since the 1970s every conceivable aspect of child protection and welfare services has been subjected to controversy and placed under intense public scrutiny. I use the general notion of 'scandal' to refer to this process of aggressive media reporting of child protection case 'failures' and increasing demands that the state be accountable for preventing them happening again.

The effectiveness of entire child welfare systems has come to be viewed through scandal politics and the prism of child deaths, despite their being only a very small minority of all investigated cases. Again the Arizona situation can be used as a typical example. Liana Sandoval was among 28 children in the past five years whose cases were known to Arizona Child Protection Services, 'but died of abuse or neglect anyway' (the *Arizona Republic*, 12 January 2003). In all, 74 Arizona children died of mistreatment, of whom 38 per cent had some contact with CPS, which was more than double the national figure of 15 per cent for 2000. While the local Governor, Janet Napolitano, 'promised a complete review of CPS', the head of the state's Child Fatality Review Team which reviews all child deaths in Arizona, argued that 'putting additional pressure on CPS caseworkers won't prevent deaths' and that larger numbers of children die without having had contact with CPS. Staff were carrying excessive caseloads due to problems in recruiting and retaining people to do such stressful work, with an annual staff turnover rate of 20 per cent, and an increase in referrals of 21 per cent in the past two years (at, www.azcentral.com/specials/special46/articles/ 0112cpskids12.hml).

Across the developed world, such pressures of stress, staffing problems and increased demands on child protection services due to more referrals appear commonplace. So great have these problems become for social work in the United Kingdom that following a recent very high profile inquiry into a child death, the profession was pronounced to be 'in terminal decline' (*The Times*, January 29, 2003). While the death of a child is far more important than the death of a profession, the future safety of many children is at the same time inherently linked to the well-being and effectiveness of social work as the primary statutory child protection agency. It is no exaggeration to say that the very future of social work itself rests on reaching deeper understandings of the nature of child protection.

A striking feature of such scandal politics and administrative procedures, like public inquiries or internal case reviews, are their reforming ambitions and the underlying assumption that children could have been and should be protected in time. In Britain alone, since 1974, well over 50 major inquiries have taken place into individual cases in which known 'at risk' children died as a result of abuse while under the protective supervision of state professionals (DHSS, 1982, 1991). Through the 1970s and 1980s, these inquiry reports were unequivocal in their condemnation of the communication and co-ordination breakdowns of the child protection system and the individual professional practice which it is argued resulted in the children's deaths (see, for instance, London Borough of Brent, 1985, p. 287; London Borough of Greenwich, 1987, pp. 216–17). In the United Kingdom, the murder of eight year old Victoria Climbié, who died a horrific death despite the attentions of social services, health professionals and the police has plunged the issue back into the public eye. Her case can be seen as an exemplar of how child protection issues are addressed in scandal cases across the Western world. Victoria died in February 2000 with 128 separate injuries to her body after suffering months of torture and abuse by her great aunt, Marie Therese Kouao, and boy friend, Carl Manning, who are now serving life sentences for her murder. Victoria was brought to London by Kouao from the Ivory Coast less than a year before she died. Her parents hoped this would give her the opportunity of a better education and life, yet Kouao never ever enrolled Victoria in a school. She was starved, beaten, scalded, burned with cigarettes and left in a freezing bathroom trussed up in a bin bag strapped into a bath. The inquiry report argues that a massive system failure occurred, with an estimated 12 bungled occasions when Victoria could have been rescued.

The inquiry into Victoria's death conducted by Lord Laming illustrates how such scandals and the investigations that are central to them are now extraordinary cultural phenomena in their own right. The inquiry's web site (www.victoria-climbié-inquiry.org.uk) received around three million hits in the period 30 September 2001 to 30 September 2002 and the average visitor session was for 20 minutes (compared to an internet average of three minutes), which shows that people were reading material rather than merely surfing (Laming, 2003, p. 21). The thirst for knowledge about such tragic cases can also be seen from the fact that in the first week following the publication of the 400 page report in January 2003, 110 000 copies were downloaded from the internet. However, despite casting its net wide in terms of examining key issues and events, the Laming report ultimately exemplifies the limitations of such texts in how the dominant approach to understanding child protection is a rational bureaucratic one, with the primary emphasis on the need for better management and accountability. This has its place but, as I argue in this book, it is only one aspect of what needs to be grasped as a multi-dimensional social practice.

This can be illustrated by its approach to the emotions and the body. A key reason why her injuries were never properly acknowledged and responded to by health and social workers was because Victoria was diagnosed early on in the case as having scabies. Two social workers (independently of one another, and from two different teams) and a police officer were explicit about the fact that they decided not to visit Victoria at home because of the health and safety risks from the scabies. Despite this and the fact that everything about the case smacked of marginality and professional fear, these issues are not critically examined in the report. The underlying process here concerns how, because of their marginality, abused and neglected children raise fear and disgust. This, as I shall show, has a long history. There is an underlying generative structure to practice, a structure of feeling and meanings which the historical and sociological evidence I present here will show meant that not only parents but abused children have been constructed as an excluded, dangerous 'Other', a contaminating presence which required exclusion. It is here that we find the cultural roots of contemporary problems professionals have in getting close to children.

In addition, scandals have been concerned with apparent 'over'-intervention and misdiagnosis of child sexual abuse and children being wrongly taking into care, as in the UK Cleveland Affair of 1987 (Butler-Sloss, 1988) and comparable situations in places such as the Netherlands (Edwards *et al.*, 1994); controversies over false-memory syndrome (Kitzinger, 2003) and, latterly, with the abuse of children accommodated in care by the state (Kirkwood, 1993; Stein, 1993; Corby *et al.*, 2001). The prominence these kinds of system failures have gained across the globe is evident in a wide range of cases which have contradictory implications. In places such as the United States of America and Ireland, the failure of the Catholic Church to stop so called 'pedophile priests' who were known to be offending has caused uproar and greatly damaged the moral legitimacy of the Church (Ferguson, 1995). Similar outcomes have followed disclosure of the failure of the Church and State to protect children from sexual and physical abuse in residential care institutions in the United States of America, Canada, Australia and Ireland, among others.

The case of Ireland exemplifies yet another pattern in how high profile failures by social workers, police and health professionals to protect children from prolonged sexual violence by fathers has led to major reforms of the child care system, the state being sued by adult survivors and the emergence of a survivors movement of significant power (McGuinness, 1993; Ferguson, 1996; Sgroi, 1998). What all this adds up to is something much more significant even than the ubiquitous talk of a 'child protection crisis'. Ongoing disclosures of child abuse over the past 30 years have been fundamental to the (reflexive) modernization of Western societies, challenging traditional power structures, processes of identity formation and creating the conditions for the protection of children in new times.

At the heart of this book is the question of why is it that across the Western world within so many nation states the death of a single child can elicit such public outcry and demand for reform? On one level the answer is painfully obvious: that in Western society children are valued highly and such avoidable harm and suffering to them is unacceptable. Yet, on other levels, this answer is inadequate. To begin with, Western societies quietly tolerate all manner of exploitation of children. Second, viewed historically, there is something quite remarkable about the social reaction to such failures. Not that long ago the deaths of children in child protection cases were a routine occurrence and not the subject of public outcry at all. Such deaths were, in fact, once a sign that child protection systems were actually working *well*, not badly, that children at

risk were being reached, albeit too late. Such high levels of public concern about the deaths (and lives) of children arises in a particular social
context which is highly ambiguous. It is essential to grasp this ambiguity.
The central paradox of contemporary concern about child deaths is that
it arises at a time when children have never been safer, when child protection systems have, on balance, never been more effective. This does
not mean that they are good enough, only that in general they have
never been better.

The overwhelming response by welfare states to child deaths and other
system failures has been to seek bureaucratic solutions by introducing
more and more laws, procedures and guidelines. The more risk and
uncertainty has been exposed, the greater the attempts to close up
the gaps through administrative changes. While these are valid concerns
the problem surrounds the one-dimensionality of the approach and the
relentless focus on new forms of organizing child welfare work and
instrumental rationality as the key to solving problems. Here, practice is
regarded as little more than rule following. The space between organizations and lay people, the agency and the child's home, the case-file and
the visit has been very poorly theorized indeed. Safety for all children
from abuse and death, meanwhile, continues to be as elusive as ever as all
those solid laws and guidelines melt into air.

I will argue in this book that a fuller historical and social analysis of
child protection work and its relationship to 'modernity' shows that it
needs to be grasped as a three-fold typology. Not only is it constituted by
forms of instrumental reason embedded in administrative power and the
law, but by an *aesthetic* sensibility and an *expressive* dimension. These
arise from how child protection is fundamentally a social practice based
on movement and relationships, involving engagements with time and
space (such as the client's home) and acting in and through the body, the
emotions and the senses. Child protection is a form of what I call *bureaucratic modernism* and can only be properly understood in terms of how its
legal and organizational imperatives and procedures have been built on
the dynamic socio-cultural space of modernity. A more complete understanding of the character, limits and possibilities of protecting children
from abuse requires getting back in touch with what I call in this book
the 'smell of practice' and conceptualizing child protection as an embodied form of social action.

Researching child protection, past and present

The past 20 years have witnessed an explosion in books and debates
about the nature of 'modernity' and 'post-modernity' and there are

now a number of ways of approaching the topic. My focus in this book is on child protection in terms of the experience of modernity or, more accurately perhaps, the experience of engaging in child protection in conditions of modernity. This involves trying to render what gets done in practice from the perspective of the practitioner who is in the office, the hospital, out there on the street, in the homes of clients. This is not to ignore the perspectives of agency clients, managers, or the influence of organizational cultures and strategies of governance by nation-states, all of which will be given considered attention in what follows. It means rather approaching people's lives and practice from a phenomenological perspective that understands child protection work as it unfolds through action, meanings and what Giddens (1991) calls 'fateful moments'. What is needed to promote real learning about child protection is to show where its contemporary ideals and practices came from, why they take the forms they do, and how practice intervenes into the flow of life, identifying how professionals have (struggled to) work creatively with and within structures to carve out actions which make a difference to children and their family's lives.

The empirical sources I draw upon to do this take two main forms: Chapters 2, 3 and 4 draw on historical case records and agency reports which document actual child protection work (in the United Kingdom and Ireland) from its beginnings in the late-nineteenth century through to the mid-twentieth century (see Appendix 1); while Chapters 5, 6 and 7 draw on a comprehensive study of contemporary child protection work based on detailed quantitative and qualitative analysis of 319 cases dealt with by three social work teams (in Ireland) (see Appendix 2). Historical case records provide exceptionally useful, if neglected, sources through which to construct a socio-historical analysis of institutional practices such as child protection. As Linda Gordon shows in her important history of American child protection work, such sources provide evidence which has the advantage that it is not subject to the later reinterpretation of memory (Gordon, 1989, p. 214). Nor is it subject to the kinds of distortion of myth and untested assumptions that underlie much historical commentary on child protection, such as the notion that the dominant response to children in the past has been to 'rescue' them by removing them permanently from parental custody (for instance, Holman, 1988).

The problem here lies partly in the reliance that has been placed on prescriptive sources and a failure to differentiate what agency reports, inquiries, rules and laws have prescribed in principle, and the ways in which child protection powers have been turned into practices and given meaning through action. The core methodological and conceptual problem with most analyses of child protection is that it constitutes a form of objectivist social analysis and a legalist approach which Bourdieu characterizes as 'the tendency ... to describe the social world in the language of rules and to behave as if social practices were explained merely by stating the explicit rule in accordance with which they are allegedly produced' (Bourdieu, 1990, p. 76). What is at issue is the need for adequate social analysis of the relationship between the law, procedures and social practices in child protection in terms of process, outcomes and meanings. Thus little attention has been given to the actual numbers of abused children taken into care in the past (see Parr, 1980), and even less to the reasons why and the practices through which the removal – or not – of children from their homes by professionals actually happened. One of the key reasons for removing children was in fact to try and stop them from dying. Yet, despite the extraordinary presence of concern about child death in child protection today, matters of life and death for 'abused' children in the past have no history. This exemplifies how consideration of how the meanings of child abuse and protection practices have been constructed over time at local, national and international levels has been almost completely ignored (see, however, Jackson, 2000). Key aspects of modern child protection, such as referral processes, gaining access to children, examining and working with them and their parents, modes of inter-agency working, and the nature of state–community relationships are largely without sociological histories.

Similar themes are explored through the contemporary data on child protection practices. A more sophisticated knowledge base about contemporary child protection practices is emerging based on qualitative studies of the work as it is being done (Farmer and Owen, 1995; Ferguson and O'Reilly, 2001; Buckley, 2003; Scourfield, 2003). My approach here to contributing to knowledge about how practice goes on today is particularly through analysis of statistical data on 319 cases reported to three child protection teams and the use of intensive case studies which draw from interviews with professionals, children and parents involved in the same cases (see Appendix 2). Crucially, this data enabled me to compare and contrast contemporary practices with what went on in the past, locating the insights from research into the present within a broader historical and sociological framework.

The development of what I call intensive case studies involves interviewing as many stakeholders as possible involved in the same cases to provide for as complete an insight as possible into the nature of intervention practices, which seeks to do justice to the multilayered character of child protection by analysing what gets done by the range of professional and lay actors to produce a universe of events, experiences, meanings and outcomes. The cases in question were chosen through a theoretical sampling method which enabled key themes to be addressed concerning responses to particular forms of abuse and intervention practices (see Appendix 2). This enabled the cases chosen for inclusion in the book to not only stand as examples of interventions in their own right, but to represent general issues and themes in relation to how practice today goes on. Taken together, the empirical sources I draw on provide the basis for an analysis of the emergence and development of the actual practices of 'modern' child protection and concepts of child abuse over the past 130 years, and for a detailed theorization of their relationship to and experience of modernity.

Theorizing child protection and modernity: 'solid' and 'melting' visions

By way of further setting the context for the analysis presented in this book, it is important to clarify further the theoretical resources that are required to engage effectively in studying the relationship between child protection and modernity. As I have already pointed out, it is my contention that a three-fold typology is required which understands child protection and the 'modern' in terms of: administrative power/instrumental reason; aesthetic rationality/action, movement through time and space; and the expressive domain of the psychological, emotional and symbolic. Each of these requires attention to distinct lines of social theory. I want to focus first on the aesthetic realm because it is such a significant yet neglected feature of child protection. If there is one archetypal voice who must constitute a point of departure for characterizing modernity it is Charles Baudelaire, for whom:

> Modernity is the transient, the fleeting, the contingent; it is one half of art, the other being the eternal and the immovable.

In expressing these sentiments in a piece called the 'Painter of Modern Life' (Baudelaire, 1965), for many commentators Baudelaire is recognized as the originator of a conceptualization of 'modernity' and 'modernism'. Baudelaire gave birth to and expressed the scope of 'modernite' in relation to the aesthetic realm of artistic endeavour. However, a recognition that his vision has a wider relevance to understanding the character of 'modern' life has been around in social theory for some two decades (Berman, 1983; Frisby, 1985), although it has been completely ignored in the social policy and social work literature. Not only contemporary arts but social practices more generally can be understood in terms of modernism (Lash, 1987).

The links to social work and child protection are apparent in how child protection clearly moves on a 'space' where it is indeed, in Baudelaire's sense, 'eternal and immovable' in character in the way it embodies 'solid' formations of laws, rules, power, control and bureaucratic objectives. Equally, however, the nature of this space is fundamentally one of the 'transient, the fleeting, the contingent' in how these solid visions materialize themselves in practice: through action, leaving the office, taking to the streets and going into the homes of those we know as clients; through transient and fleeting face-to-face transactions with those people which invoke ideologies and experiences of helping and caring – which emerge right in the midst of 'control' itself. The operationalization of social work's 'solid' visions gives to the experience its essential ephemeral and elusive quality, its 'melting' visions, we might say.

Yet the visions inherent to most child protection discourse are decidedly solid. This applies equally to official texts like inquiry reports into children's deaths and to critiques which emphasize child protection as a form of state-sponsored social control of (marginalized) families (Thorpe, 1994; Scourfield and Welsh, 2003). We need to melt this entire highly influential way of viewing things, theoretically, into air. It is the mobile, slippery, liquified nature of the social relations of welfare that demand conceptualization, not (just) their solid rational forms. The importance of insisting on an aesthetic conception of child protection is that it enables us to begin to conceptualize the space upon which laws and other bureaucratic procedures are turned into actions. This space is fundamentally 'artistic', first, in the sense of the creativity and capacities it requires to act and construct 'casework' and, second, in the form that child protection takes as a practice that is fundamentally based on movement and experiences of time and space.

Social science has begun to produce what Scott Lash and John Urry (1994, p. 254) a decade ago called a sociology of travel or mobility and indeed a key deficit in theorizing child protection is the failure to grasp the dynamism of its practices in terms of *movement*. The notion of 'sociological modernism' attempted to capture the movement, flux and dynamism that is at the core of modern social practices (Lash and Friedman, 1992). Urry's more recent work places the notion of 'mobilities' at the centre of his manifesto for a new sociology for the twenty-first century (Urry, 2000, 2003). At the top of his list of 'new rules of sociological method' is the requirement 'to develop through appropriate metaphors a sociology which focuses upon movement, mobility and contingent ordering, rather than upon stasis, structure and social order' (Urry, 2000, p. 18). This needs to go hand-in-hand with other rules, such as the need 'to embody one's analysis through investigating the sensuous constitution of humans and objects', and 'to describe the different bases of people's sense of dwelling, including their dependence upon various mobilities of people, presents, photographs, images, information, risks and so on'. These practices and processes require exploration in terms of the ways they are shaped by 'how class, ethnicity and nationhood are constituted through powerful and intersecting temporal regimes and modes of dwelling and travelling' (Urry, 2000, pp. 18–19).

In adopting these new rules of sociological method in the context of an upsurge of work on mobilities – which Urry (2003) characterizes as a 'mobility turn' in the social sciences – this book argues that if we are to properly understand the modern character of child protection it is crucial that we begin to conceive of its practices as they are practised: on the run. Without movement, someone getting up from their desk, leaving the office and *doing* something, there is no protection. In Chapter 3, for instance, I show how child protection was shaped within the twentieth century culture of modernism and took on new meanings through advances in travel, science and technology – like the invention of the bicycle, motorbike, motor car – which transformed the speed with which practitioners could cross space and reach children and literally gave meaning to protecting children in time. Child protection simply cannot be adequately grasped without theorizing its relationship to social action, to what happens when all the solid laws and procedures that it represents are literally acted upon. Bureaucratic modernism refers to the 'transient, the fleeting, the contingent' encounters in which child protection professionals engage in the course of putting laws and agency functions into practice, and I will show how this came to be and the late-modern forms it takes today.

In tracing the 'cultural roots of the present' (Frykman and Lofgren, 1987, p. 4) the book begins from the assumption that underlying contemporary discourse on child abuse and child protection there is a deep 'generative structure' at work (Stallybrass and White, 1986). Studies of custodial and welfare institutions have been an important point of convergence between history and sociology (Cohen and Scull, 1983), seeking out the origins or, more fashionably, the 'birth' of disciplinary practices of penology, medicine and social work by 'excavating' their 'master patterns' (Cohen, 1985, p. 85). To characterize child protection in terms of aesthetic modernism as I have begun to do here is to fly in

the face of what has become the most popular approach to such histori-
ography in the form of the work of Michel Foucault and his followers.
Visions don't come much more solid than Foucault's, for whom any
attempt to understand penal-welfare practices such as child protection
must come to terms with the nature of power in modern societies.

He is critical of conceptions of power which try to define power-free
zones of rights. The 'repressive hypothesis' assumes that power works
negatively repressing subjects, and identities; that it just says 'no' to
what are defined as illicit acts and desires, through such operations as
interdiction, censorship and denial (Fraser, 1989, p. 27). The adoption of
what Foucault calls a positive conception of power leads to a recognition
of the ways in which disciplinary practices 'produce' subjects, differentiate populations, individualize and work to reform the 'offender'. The
socio-historical method which Foucault calls 'genealogy' provides a
means to excavating how persons and bodies of knowledge become
'subjects': how social administration and practice came to define certain
types and persons as 'cases'; how modern power works through a hierarchical surveillance, the 'gaze', the examination and their connections
to the socio-political domain and the formation of strategies of 'gover-
mentality' of a given society (Dean, 1994).

For Foucault modernity is constituted pervasively through a new kind
of power he calls 'discipline'. He describes a historical transformation in
the mode of governing Western societies that was marked by 'the movement from one project to another, from a schema of exceptional discipline to one of generalised surveillance' (Foucault, 1977, p. 209). The
shift to a generalized surveillance rested on 'the gradual extension of the
mechanisms of discipline … their spread throughout the whole social
body, the formation of what might be called in general the disciplinary
society' (Foucault, 1977, p. 209). Disciplinary power is distinguished
from its predecessor in the classical age, what Foucault calls 'sovereign
power'. The latter was a system of power related to the central role of the
body of the sovereign as the focus of law, disciplinary practice and justice. It was a system which worked negatively according to tactics of
exclusion and was spectacular and highly visible in form. The
vengeance of society was literally carved out on the offender's body
(Foucault, 1977). It was a juridicio-political form of classical power
established through the monarchy in which the principle which held
was that law had to be the very form of power which 'must be exercised
in accordance with a fundamental lawfulness' (Foucault, 1979, p. 88). In
the transition to modernity, the relation between the law and social
practices was transformed through a shift to a modern discursive

'normalizing' form of power. This refers to a modern practice of state regulation in which the 'policing' of individuals, families and neighbourhoods is primarily conducted not by means of punishment or coercion but instead by the normalizing agencies of social welfare – social work, education, insurance, child care and so on (Donzelot, 1979). From this complex of agencies of social investigation and scrutiny the penal option (while in classical jurisprudence the first) is the last of many, the coercive end of a much broader continuum. The modern, reconstituted domain of the 'social' allows 'a new mode of social administration which was underpinned and sanctioned by law but whose effects were not limited by it' (Garland, 1981, p. 39). The practical consequence of this transformation was a new 'moral therapeutics' which opened up a correctional system (probation, juvenile courts, after-care) which permitted personal contact and policed not crimes but characters.

While Foucault's periodization of modernity focuses on the post-enlightenment eighteenth and early nineteenth century, I am arguing that the key time for the birth of child protection is the 1890–1914 period, for which similar transformations in governmental strategies have been described for the United States of America and as well as Britain (Rothman, 1980; Garland, 1985). It was at this time that agencies like Societies for the Prevention of Cruelty to Children emerged which were in many respects classic bearers of disciplinary power, pioneering new institutional practices and the birth of a 'modern' form of child protection. As I show in Chapters 2 and 3 their primary focus was on gaining access to and literally seeing children and families, closing up gaps in time and space, stopping the movement of recalcitrant families; on categorization and producing a scientific knowledge of child abuse – precisely the kind of 'productive' use of power to which Foucault alludes.

This is, however, but one part of the story. Foucauldian and post-structuralist work on the nature of the 'social' has been influential in analyses of professional interventions into child welfare and protection (Harris and Webb, 1987, pp. 66–86; Rojek *et al.*, 1988; Frost and Stein, 1989; Parton, 1991; Thorpe, 1994). However, while contributing some important insights, the approach focuses on just one aspect of the constitution of modern society: the development of administrative power and modernity as instrumental reason. What is offered by the (post) structuralists is a vision of asymmetrical networks of flows of power, bureaucratization and regulation which focuses on the development of procedures, laws, and an entire state apparatus in the definition of 'child protection'. Although the genealogical approach seeks to conceive of culture as practices, it leaves out cultural processes and the subjective experience of practices altogether. For Foucault modern forms of surveillance are constituted by a 'disembodied gaze' in which the 'psy' professional is basically a functionary caught in the midst of a power–knowledge complex with little or no discretion to act and where no meaningful face-to-face interaction goes on between worker and client. 'Discipline', Foucualt argues, has the effect of rendering bodies 'docile', but his 'docile' bodies, as Giddens remarks (1984, p. 157), 'do not have faces'. Foucault is too rejecting of the possibility that there is something to be gained from an appraisal of so called 'surveillance' as a nuanced, subjective experience of embodied perception and *action* (Jay, 1986) – which is precisely what I am arguing is needed in child protection studies.

Having already indicated how the creative and mobile aspects of the aesthetic dimension must be seen as always both potentially strengthening and undermining of the 'solid' forms of administrative power in child protection, what I am calling the 'expressive' dimension renders it still more ephemeral and unpredictable. This requires a theory of practice, or of 'situated social action' (Thrift, 1983) which can get 'inside' the institutional system and show how practice is experienced and given meaning – by workers and clients while acting in time and space. Because the Foucauldian sociology of knowledge and disciplinary practices overdetermines the power and control features of modern disciplinary practices it lacks an understanding of welfare as fundamentally *social* practices in the sense emphasized by Durkhiem (Garland, 1990a,b) and psychodynamic commentators like Freud (Hoggett, 2000; Froggett, 2002).

Durkheim's characterization of disciplinary practices is much less instrumental than Foucault's, seeing punishment as, above all, a product of public sentiment, a 'collective representation' of society's conscience. Punishment is an *expressive* institution. It is an authentic act of outrage against behaviour which offends social norms. 'Passion' and social sentiment constitute the 'soul of penality' (Durkhiem, 1964, p. 90). What is emphasized here is the emotional aspect of punishment, its social origins and the impact it has beyond the relationship between the state and the offender/client. Durkhiem emphasized the ways in which the expressive dimensions of punishment played a part in shaping penal institutions, and the form as well as the force of social interventions. This position has the great virtue of recognizing the fact that the values and sentiments that are intrinsic to social relations form the broad context within which legal punishments and welfare practices operate (Garland, 1990a, p. 8). Durkhiem, however, goes too far in the degree to which he emphasizes the expressive functions of punishment and the law and overlooks administrative power. An adequate framework of inquiry into the sociology of disciplinary practices must therefore include aspects of both the power perspective derived from Foucault and the cultural dimension in the work of Durkhiem. Child protection, like punishment, 'is what might be called a symbolically deep event, that is to say an event which has profound cultural resonance. It is a matter of real seriousness, involving not just the state, but also the wider community in matters of ultimate common concern...and as such it evokes powerful sentiments and a rich symbolism' (Garland, 1990a, p. 10).

This points to how child protection is constituted in terms of a symbolic system. The emotional, expressive dimension is deeply constituted by the issue of boundaries and the human body and fears of pollution and contamination by the marginal, neglectful families who came to dominate its practices (Douglas, 1966). Dirt and smell came to be child protection's key modern metaphors in a context of marginality where service user families have been treated as the excluded 'Other'. In Chapters 2, 3 and 4 I trace the roots of this to key cultural processes that developed from the late-nineteenth century and the formation of child protection within conceptions of 'high' and 'low' culture (Stallybrass and White, 1986). This led even abused children to be viewed as a contaminating presence and treated with fear and kept at a distance – a system of meanings which the tragic experience of children like Victoria Climbié (Laming, 2003) suggests persists to this day.

The 'expressive' dimension concerns the psycho-social dynamics which are always present in child protection practices because it is deeply embedded in *relationships*. Encounters between workers and users of services are mediated through the emotions, senses and the body in ways which give rise to complex forms of reciprocity and resistance to agency intervention by clients. From a Freudian psychoanalytical perspective, this can be interpreted in terms of processes such as transference and counter-transference and reflects the multifaceted ways in which professionals and service users experience intervention (Mattison and Sinclair, 1979). As I show throughout the book, and in Chapter 7 in particular, these struggles are invariably quite literally fought out on client's doorsteps or inside their homes and are central to the contingent, unpredictable nature of interventions. It is only in making this move from the office into the homes of children and families that the full multidimensional nature of child protection comes into being.

This connects these psychosocial-symbolic 'expressive' dynamics to administrative powers, the time–space concerns of aesthetic modernism and the sociology of mobilities, and means that child protection has to be understood as a form of embodied action. The primal step that professionals have always had to take in realizing child protection is out of the office into the street and (via the car or some other form of transport) across the threshold into the homes of children at risk. Time–space sensitivities are crucial to unravelling the situated character of cultural practices. Giddens argues that alongside a concern with 'moral education' that is inherent in the surveillance practices of the modern state, it is important to understand the timing and spacing of human activities. Time and space are constitutive of the lived contexts within which cultural practices unfold. Context is constitutive of social action and not merely a background to its unfolding (Giddens, 1984, chapter 2, 1985, pp. 46–7). This book shows the centrality of the 'poetics' of the space (Bachelard, 1969) of the client's home to the nature of child protection as an embodied practice.

The issues addressed by Foucauldians at the objectivist level of 'governmentality' and 'social' politics are recast by Giddens in terms of subjective experiences of trust, risk and expert systems in conditions of modernity (Giddens, 1990, 1991, 1992, 1994a,b). This offers a theoretical perspective which enables links to be made between the themes of power, the state, space, temporality and practical action and consciousness in child protection and makes it possible to focus on the constructive and enabling elements of the rules and conventions that govern social practices. Modern social intervention, he argues, is deeply bound up with the management of risk and a concern to promote mechanisms of trust amongst lay persons in expert systems such as child protection. Unlike post-structuralism, this places the knowledgeable reflexive human agent at the centre of the constitution of social practices and institutions.

The position I am adopting in this book therefore differs in some key respects from post-modernist theorizing. Post-modernism depicts the loss of 'grand narratives', of a single unitary way of describing social phenomena. A multiplicity of voices are now recognised as needing to be heard as constituting the complex nature of 'truth'. All discourses and practices are seen to be run through with power. Unlike modernism, which was essentially a dialogue based on post-enlightenment rationalism, optimism and hope, postmodernism is sceptical of ideas of progress and constantly asks at what and to whose cost? The work of Giddens and other 'late-modernists' – such as Ulrich Beck – do not deny that the world has become much more fragmented and lacking in universal truths. Their notion of 'reflexive modernization' argues that there no longer exists a central authority to which we can resort to for resolving disputes about expertise and truth-claims. The emphasis here, however, is on the 'knowledgeable human agent', the self's agency and its reflexive reworking of the body and structures as holding the potential for a revised social order (Bryant and Jary, 2001, p. 115). This does not mean that people can know everything about why they act as they do while doing it, as I argue in Chapter 7 (see also Hoggett, 2001). Yet this is a very different way of viewing individuals and the social world compared to the 'decentred subjects' portrayed in post-modernism, mainstream structuralism, or in Foucault's accounts of 'disciplined bodies'. For Giddens 'the self is more than just a decentred site of intersecting forces, it is the site of an active, reflexive self-identity which can shape and redirect personal and social events' (Bryant and Jary, 2001, p. 116). Thus while I accept the emergence of postmodernist cultural forms, rather than speaking of postmodernity I use the language of late-modernity and/or reflexive modernity. This is because of the distinctive analytical focus such a paradigm provides for studying social action and embodied human agency in the context of institutional practices and a commitment to reconstructing social theory and practice (Beck *et al.*, 2003).

Having shown in Chapters 2 and 3 how the modernity of child protection was well and truly established by the first decades of the twentieth century, the remainder of the book examines the nature of continuity and change in constructions of child abuse and child protection's modern character. Chapters 4, 5 and 6 draw heavily on the work of Giddens and Beck and map out the changing nature of child protection within a shift from 'simple' to 'reflexive' modernity – the same transition that Bauman (2000) characterizes as a passage from 'heavy' to 'liquid' modernity. Having had a high public visibility through to the 1920s, knowledge of child death was repressed in simple modernity, only to return to public debates again with a vengeance since the 1970s with the emergence of reflexive modernity.

A key dimension of this concerns changes in the nature of risk which mean that professionals have to live with the knowledge that, despite itself, no expert system can guarantee safety, that it won't fail (Giddens, 1990; Beck, 1992). These chapters show how in conditions of late, liquid or reflexive modernity trust, risk and expertise have become radicalized in ways that do not lead to a uniformly pessimistic scenario for the future – unlike that painted by some theorists of (post)modernity. Alongside and against the 'top down' pressures of legalism, bureaucratization and managerialism there is, I shall argue, evidence of a different and quite radical other set of developments which have been under-theorized in the literature of social work and child protection. The same individuals who are

increasingly subject to, and the subjects of, social regulation have simultaneously become increasingly critical and *reflexive* with reference to them
(cf. Lash and Urry, 1994, p. 4; Fook, 1999).

This is exemplified by the emergence of child sexual abuse as a social
problem and of knowledge of serious physical violence against children
(and women) which represent genuine advances in the quality of life for
children in general. This, I suggest, arises from a loosening of traditional
boundaries around the family, processes of 'individualization' and a
broad democratization of family relations which has gone on since the
1970s and created conditions where children (and abused women) are
seen as entitled to live a safe life of their own (Beck and Beck-Gernshiem,
2002). Yet, the consequences of modernity are such that significant problems remain in the capacities of child protection systems to identify and
reach abused children in time. A key source of struggle surrounds the
growing intensity in late-modernity of the relationships between professionals and service users, many of whom are at best ambivalent and at
worst involuntary clients of child protection. It reflects also the nature of
practice in terms of symbolic actions and the complexity of what happens when professionals step across the threshold into the 'other world'
of clients' lives and homes (see chapter 7).

The book shows that many of these complexities and difficulties are
inherent to the very nature of child protection and are a normative
rather than exceptional feature of its practices. The heightened impact of
the aesthetic and 'expressive' dimensions illustrates the extent to which
psychosocial and symbolic dynamics are at the heart of late-modern
child protection practices and how it is constituted by the emotions, as
well as reason; by unintended consequences, as well as rational planning;
by the unconscious as well as the conscious; by the senses and the body
as well as the mind; by mobilities, movement and the ephemeral, the
fleeting and the contingent, as well as the static and apparently eternal
and immovable structures of the law and procedures.

What we are witnessing at the beginning of the twenty-first century
through the public upheavals in child protection are genuine transformations in social relationships, expertise and knowledge. It is because of the
dynamic nature of the experiences of security and danger, chaos and control that modernity introduces and radicalizes that those involved in child
protection must 'ride the juggernaut' (Giddens, 1990), knowing that all
those solid laws and procedures they embody melt into air in ways which
enable them to protect many, many children while agonizingly failing to
help others in time. It is hoped that the analysis presented in this book can
serve to deepen our understandings of these dynamic processes and help
to advance the protection of children in the best possible times.

2
Taking it Onto the Streets: The Discovery of Child Death and Birth of Child Protection, 1870–1914

Making sense of the protection of children in particular times has to involve an analysis of the relationship between the social practices that went on in particular historical *periods* and the concepts of risk, childhood, time and space and technological resources available to enable children to be reached in *practice* in particular times. Compared to the mobilities that constitute effective child protection and the speediness with which children are reached today, nineteenth-century social practices were decidedly static and plodding. Yet, it is only by going back to these formative years in the construction of child protection that we can begin to fully understand it as a modern social practice.

In the winter of 1873, in a New York neighborhood called Hell's Kitchen, a church worker called Etta Wheeler was told about a case of child cruelty to a little girl named Mary Ellen Wilson. Etta Wheeler was determined to see through the rescue of the abused child, however the absence of specific child protection laws and agencies meant that social reformers resolved to bring the child before the court under anti-cruelty to animals legislation. The manner in which Mary Ellen was successfully protected and removed from parental custody led in 1875 to the creation of the first dedicated child protection agency in the world, the New York Society for the Prevention of Cruelty to Children which was organized in response to a law passed in that year by the New York State Legislature authorizing the establishment of branches of this child-welfare organization in each county of the state (Ross, 1980; Pleck, 1987, pp. 69–87). The Mary Ellen case was the first known child protection case of its kind in the world to be investigated and dealt with in what would become recognizably 'modern' forms and heralded the birth of an international child protection movement. In a little over a decade, for example, a similar movement, agencies and laws had been established in the United Kingdom and Ireland (Behlmer, 1982).

In tracing the origins of the very idea that through social intervention children can be protected in time from avoidable harm and death, an important starting-point is to locate a pre-modern world where no such ideology existed. It is conventional to trace the construction of child protection to the post-war welfare state and the 1960s 'discovery' of child abuse, when its essentially 'modern' forms began in fact to be constructed much earlier. This chapter explores the protection of children in Victorian times and how dramatic new constructions of security and danger and child cruelty emerged with the birth of modern child protection over the 1870–1914 period, at the heart of which were new concepts of risk, mobility, space and temporality in practice. As I begin to show, what emerged by the 1920s was not simply a social and professional ideal, but a type of practice, a way of going about the work, an experience of child protection and modernity which remains constitutive of practice to this day.

Child protection in pre-modern times

I shall begin by considering the forms of responses to child cruelty which existed in the United Kingdom and Ireland in the years prior to the establishment there in 1889 of a dedicated child protection agency and legislative framework. In July 1879, Richard Moore, a 'puddler', was brought before a Police Court in Stockton in the north-east of England under a warrant issued by his mother-in-law. He was charged with committing an 'aggravated assault' on his son, James, who was 'of a tender age, of some six or seven years'. James told the court that his father whipped him with a belt because he looked out of a window after he went to bed and subsequently threw pillows out of the window. There and then in the courtroom:

> The lad's clothing was here removed, and his body exposed to the Bench. It showed evidence of severe ill-treatment; his back, limbs, and side were covered with bruises, and were much discoloured.

On being apprehended by the police, Moore confessed that he did it, but insisted that 'it was not punishment; it was correction'. Moore had previously been convicted of wife beating. There was also a younger child whom he had beaten who was 'little better than this'. The Bench committed Moore to Durham Gaol for one month's hard labour without the option of a fine (reported in the *North Eastern Daily Gazette*, July 1879).

Ten years later the courtroom was still the site of the spectacular display of children's injuries. In September 1888 a Catherine Kendall was convicted by the Middlesbrough Stipendiary of 'assaulting her little boy'. Eight-year-old Robert, who was the complainant, told the court that his mother 'scratched his face and thumped him'. The following day she 'leathered him on the arm' with the poker. His mother turned him out of the house and a neighbour took him in. In the courtroom: 'the boy stripped up his shirt sleeve showing the livid marks on his arm'. There were previous convictions for assaults against the woman. In sentencing her to two months' imprisonment the Stipendiary termed her 'a cruel, brutal woman, saying she must have broken the boy's arm by her illtreatment' (*North-Eastern Daily Gazette*, 3 September 1888). As there was now no one in the community to care for him, Robert was taken to the Workhouse 'pending efforts to get him into an industrial school'. Four days later the police brought him back before the Middlesbrough Bench, described him as a 'neglected waif', and he was sent to an Industrial School for six years.

These cases illustrate that Victorian society clearly did have some conception of the maltreatment of children before specific anti-cruelty societies were established in localities, in response to which the public, even in the most deprived neighbourhoods, showed its concern by bringing cases forward. This evidence supports Pollock's (1983) contention, also arrived at through an analysis of newspaper reports, that for at least 100 years *before* the passing of the Prevention of Cruelty to Children Acts in the late-nineteenth-century child cruelty was condemned by the judiciary, punished by the state, and regarded as socially aberrant (Pollock, 1983, pp. 92–5; see also Demos, 1985; Jackson, 2000). Pollock lambastes a generation of historians (for instance, Pinchbeck and Hewitt, 1969; Shorter, 1976; Stone, 1977) for their preoccupation with radical breaks in parenting practices to the neglect of continuities in parent–child relations over time. Here the history of childhood was characterized as a catalogue of unrelenting parental cruelty and societal disregard for children, as 'a nightmare from which we have only recently begun to awaken' (deMause, 1974, p. 1). The 'history of childhood was virtually reconceived as the history of child abuse' (Wolff, 1988, p. 62), a pattern that was allegedly only broken by the mobilization of humanitarian impulses which led to the formation of Societies for the Prevention of Cruelty to Children (SPCC). Commentators on child abuse in our own times have offered similar visions of a history of nightmares and shift from cruelty to enlightenment (Bakan, 1971; Gilmour, 1988, p. 7).

Such correctives as Pollock's, however, remain partial. It is nominally true that children have always been the victims of some 'cruel' behaviour, but if not followed through into detailed analysis of the *kinds* of social regulation of childhood and families and conceptions of 'cruelty' that prevailed historically, cultural practices are emptied of their very content and meaning. It is not sufficient to show that 'cruel' parents have been punished for child maltreatment in the past. Punishment itself and social intervention more generally need to be placed in the context of the social functions and meanings of social regulation in particular times and places.

My research suggests that the scale of social regulation of parent–child relations prior to the 1880s was not extensive. No more than a handful of child cruelty type cases were brought before the courts each year.[1] As the typical cases profiled above show, expertise barely penetrated into the core of domestic relations at all. While the police were the state regulatory agents of physical and sexual violence toward children and the Poor Law authorities brought cases of 'neglect', there was an absence of professional mediation into parent–child relationships to an extent that the courtroom itself was the site upon which injuries to children were literally made visible, and in which knowledge of the family was gathered. The emergence of SPCCs spelled the beginnings of new forms of social regulation and expertise which began to reconstitute the meanings of child maltreatment and relations between the state, parents, children and civil society. It is the nature of the changing forms of social regulation as they intersected with lay perceptions, trust relations and cultural norms that require illumination, rather than some notion of 'child abuse' and 'protection' as having a reality which pre-existed those forms.

Taking it onto the streets: child protection's modern roots

At the heart of child protection's modern character is order and movement; chaos and regulation, and any account which seeks to outline what child protection is must do justice to its multifaceted nature which arises out of its origins. Child protection as a modern social practice began to emerge by the last quarter of the nineteenth century in the guise of philanthropy. It appeared within historically specific social processes of capitalist development in which 'masses' of people were brought together into vast cities which grew overnight and which from the mid-nineteenth century became the dominant social form (Williams, 1973). This is the same ambience within which Baudelaire's vision of modernism was conceived: of rapid and explosive transformations in human experience of space and time, of consciousness, home, work, social relations and the state. As Marx understood it, the compulsive beat of an expanding capitalist economy had turned every corner of the earth, space, time and even human beings and labour power into saleable commodities. These processes of bourgeois modernization, the industrialization of production, the tearing up of social space, of communities, of people's lives, is the climate in which, in Marx's words, 'all fast-fixed frozen relations are swept away' and 'all that is solid melts into air' (Marx and Engels, 1888, pp. 53–4).

On the one hand this ushers in a celebration of modern life and the sheer scope and dynamism of what it had opened up. Each creative possibility, opportunity for growth and adventurous moment of modernity was offset and tinged, however, with the despairing depths of its radical antithesis: the many and tragic human and social problems of the vast moral, social and psychic abyss that bourgeois creativity opens up. As Helen Bosanquet, one of the major nineteenth-century protagonists in the founding of social work wrote of British experience, 'It was a common-place of the time that over a million poor persons had to be turned out of their houses within a period of ten years by railways and improvement schemes, while fresh accommodation had been provided for only 20,000' (Bosanquet, 1973, pp. 14–15). Waller (1983) estimates that in Britain alone over the second half of the nineteenth century, at least *five million* people were cleared out of the way to make way for 'progress'.

In these kinds of social processes, so basic to capitalism, nothing 'solid' is safe, least of all the vulnerable human beings who became mangled up in how, as Berman (1983, p. 99) writes, 'everything Bourgeoise society builds is built to be torn down' – if it means more profit, more growth. These same processes appalled and infused such urban writers as Engels, who noted how in 1844 Manchester builders were tossing up houses built to last only 40 years (Engels, 1969). Fifty years on, in York, the great social reformer Seebolm Rowntree (not normally known for his modernism) noted the same frenetic metamorphoses within the late-Victorian city where 'Old dwelling houses are constantly being pulled down' (Rowntree, 1901, pp. 4–5). In her study of Victorian prostitution in York, Finnegan also observes something of the social consequences of how in the 1880s such modernization unfolded in this city:

> With the Improvement Scheme, however, which not only plunged the new street through the upper portions of the Lanes but considerably widened the lower parts of both Middle Water Lane and Friargate, some of the most dilapidated slums in York were demolished, and infamous beerhouses and brothels, the dingy and dangerous nests of vice which were the haunt of criminals, prostitutes and thieves, were razed to the ground. (Finnegan, 1979, pp. 35–6)

Writing of the impact of similar modernization processes in the creation by Haussman of the Parisian Boulevards, Berman suggests that Haussman, 'in tearing down the old medieval slums, inadvertently broke down the self-enclosed and hermetically sealed world of traditional urban poverty [where upon] ... the misery that was once a mystery is now a fact' (Berman, 1983, p. 153). Through a brilliant modernist reading of Baudelaire's prose poem 'The Eyes of the Poor', Berman evokes the horrific immediacy with which these 'criminals, prostitutes, and thieves', but less dramatically, the poor, the homeless, the vulnerable, appear on the streets having crawled through the holes that modernization made, to confront the prosperous classes, and modernity itself. The eyes of these poor now stare into the eyes of those lovers, *flaneurs*, 'moderns' so free to enjoy the new public spaces on offer. The epiphany, however, flows both ways. The poor, as well as being seen, were able to see: they too could join the race for the bright lights. Faced with such stares, as well as the threat of being literally touched by the 'dangerous' classes, a major social, moral and political dilemma opened up concerning how to deal with the poor. The decisive Bourgeois response was to contract out – mainly to social work – the dirty work of dealing with the 'refuse' of modernity in order to try and sanitize these new spaces and seal up these wounds that modernization was creating.

Bourgeois fears of social disorder, of a threatening 'mass' or a 'mob' were fuelled by how the 'disreputable' lumpen-proletariat were often merged in popular imagination with the 'respectable' labouring classes who were increasingly well organized and politically active as the nineteenth century wore on. Through fears of popular revolution and a world-view which blamed the poor and vulnerable for their own demoralization, the prosperous classes was driven into defensive action by donating relatively huge amounts of money to charities to redistribute to the poor (Stedman Jones, 1971). This, however, created its own problems in that indiscriminate alms-giving and receiving were deemed to undermine initiative, the work ethic and spawn the amorality of the 'clever pauper'. Charitable giving and 'helping' would now be more strictly mediated through charity organization societies and the embryo of complex welfare institutions and roles and in particular social work. 'The problem could be resolved, the spirit of community reasserted, and the poor remoralized through personal influence exercised in a structured and responsible way' (Fido, 1977, p. 210; Woodroofe, 1962).

The crux of the problem was not simply the confrontation with the poor and increasing segregation of social classes brought about through such urbanization processes (Stedman Jones, 1971), but the manner in which these traditional divisions were breaking down. As Harvey argues, 'It is the sense of proprietorship over public space that is really significant, rather than the all-too-familiar encounter with poverty. ... The more space had to be opened up physically, the more it had to be partitioned off through social practice' (Harvey, 1985, pp. 204–5). The central dynamic was to attempt to control the poor, the dangerous, through rendering them visible through social intervention. In a post-enlightenment discourse which positioned sight at the top of the hierarchy of the senses (Urry, 2000, p. 94), 'seeing' the poor was regarded as equivalent to 'knowing' them and surveillance as the means to inculcating civility and acceptable behaviour. In the process 'the city of touch is turned into the city of visibility' (Urry, 2000, p. 95).

We need to go even further to recognize the central dynamic between public and private space in these processes. The work of urban historians and human geographers has begun to show that the home has undergone significant changes in how it has been constituted and is just as important an arena for sociological and historical analysis as the office, the street, the city, or any other part of the public domain (Daunton, 1983; Williams, 1987). At its most basic, the home is, after all, where the vast majority of children at risk live. Yet it is remarkable how little socio-historical attention has been given to how professionals have accessed children, engaged parents and generally experienced the child protection task in the homes and spaces of others. Social scientists have had to, as it were, discover the home. As a leading urban historian has put it: 'the concentration among geographers on segregation by areas has led them to neglect how space was used within working-class districts, or within individual dwellings, a scale of experience possibly more relevant than was the distance of working-class from middle-class districts' (Dennis, 1984, p. 294). In its concentration on organizations, rules and regulations, child protection has similarly been subject to 'the overso-cialization of the public sphere' (Gamarnikow and Purvis, 1983; Sheller and Urry, 2003).

A key practical vehicle for this 'partitioning' of space was social work and a variety of moral reform movements organized through the state and especially philanthropic organizations. None were more proactive in it than the child protection movement. Following on from the pio-neering creation of the NYSPCC in 1875, in Britain and Ireland the first such society was established in 1883 in Liverpool and was quickly fol-lowed by the formation of one in London, from which the national organization began in 1889 (Behlmer, 1982). The NSPCC eventually came to cover England, Wales and Ireland. The Liverpool Society main-tained a separate status until 1953, while the Republic of Ireland Branches remained within the NSPCC until 1956 when the Irish Society for the Prevention of Cruelty to Children was formed (Allen and Morton, 1961, p. 26). Scotland never became part of the NSPCC's juris-diction, and its child care legislation and services remain separate to this day. The SPCC movement had two broad aims: to pressure for the reform of the criminal law surrounding child cruelty and the social reg-ulation of parent–child relations; and to develop a social practice for the purpose of investigating suspected cases. In England, Wales and Ireland, the 1889 PCC Act created new offences of child cruelty and enabled children who had been cruelly treated to be removed from the custody of parents and given by order of the court to designated persons or institutions.

As soon as they hit the streets, SPCC workers – who were all men and known as 'Inspectors' – confronted the immediacy of how not only sight, but every other sense was brought to bear on practice, especially smell and touch, and the reality of how vulnerable children and families actually lived ... and died. The death of children in casework was a rou-tine part of child protection work from the outset of the practice. In 1893, for example, while on a routine visit to a case, an Inspector dis-covered a 15-month-old boy 'laid out on a brick floor in the kitchen with only a rag to cover its nakedness. It was covered with filth and ver-min, much emaciated, and suffering from bronchitis. It appeared to be very hungry and was gnawing a piece of chalk.' The child's mother was in the house 'but was too drunk to give a rational answer to ... questions, and the husband was asleep on a dirty mattress'. The Inspector immedi-ately took the child in his mackintosh to the Society's Children's Shelter, where he got him some food. The boy was found to be eight pounds underweight, weighing only 13 pounds. Both parents were convicted of child neglect and committed to prison, and custody of the child was terminated and given to the Society. Despite this intervention, 'after a painful and lingering illness', the child died some weeks later.[2]

The Children's Shelters operated in most urban areas between 1891 and 1903 and played a crucial role not only in protecting children against cruelty, but also against loss of life. Children admitted to the Shelters were the suspected victims of all types of cruelty: from the most serious cases where life itself was at risk; to those children who were brought there simply because they were on the streets – what the Society called 'cruelties of the street'. In addition to the 'ill- used and neglected' child, the Shelters also catered as a Place of Safety under the 1889 Act for the child 'found on the streets begging and hawking until it is ascertained why they are thus employed' (*North Eastern Daily Gazette*, 1 October 1891). On admission, children were examined by the Shelter's elected Honorary Medical Attendant, a function seen as particularly important and urgent with regard to young children, where keeping the child alive was often the first priority. Within five months of its opening in 1893, the Matron of the Middlesbrough Shelter gave evidence at an inquest into the death of a two-year-old girl whom she had fed and tried to resuscitate in the Shelter the day before the child died. The Shelters were also given a pivotal role in interventions that prevented death, like in a 1894 case where a child, once recovered, was 'handed back to its mother' (HDAR, 1894). Faced with criticism that they were duplicating the work of the Poor Law Union in workhouses, it is little wonder that the NSPCC claimed that the 'improved condition of the child is greater in our Shelters than in the Workhouse' (STAR, 1892, p. 7). They had living proof of the matter.

As I shall continue to show, proprietorship over public space was an important aspect of this new social work, particularly in 'clearing' the streets of evidence of endangered (and endangering) children. But a core aim was not to stare into the eyes of the poor in public, but expressly to do so in *private*. It seems paradoxical, but the more that public space was opened up, the more private became the social practices of partitioning. Once grasped in this manner we begin to get a sense of a high point of possibilities here. Inspectors were not the first to visit the homes of the poor (see, Bosanquet, 1874). But they were among the first to do so equipped with significant new statutory powers to regulate the lives of children and parents. These first social workers newly empowered to ferret around in people's homes didn't quite know what had hit them.

Here a York Inspector describes what he found in 1899:

> This family occupy two rooms in ... Smithfield. The downstairs place is always in semi darkness, damp and filthy. There is an old table, a pail, and a railed seat only for furniture. Upstairs is a kind of loft which contains straw bundles and loose straw, but no covering whatever. This place is filthy and smells foul.

Feeling the cold, haunting seriousness in these lives and spaces, they describe every artefact, every sensation. They evoke the sheer olfactory despair, sympathy, fascination and disgust embodied in their encounters with human misery, abject poverty, death, cruelty, decay (can people REALLY live like this?). They grope for a language and a means through which to make sense of it all and are acutely aware of the times and spaces of other people's homes and all that dwelled within them. Here an Inspector describes what he found in a 1898 case:

> With the man's permission we went upstairs and found all the family have to sleep on one bed which was in a wretched dirty state ... back upstair room absolutely empty.
> In a cradle laid a baby Ralph fourteen months old – since dead – in a very ill condition suffering the wife said from pneumonia. The child's face was bedaubed with mucous and dirt, whilst the back door was open exposing the child to a draft. The morning was particularly cold. ... A few days later the child died.

These are primal modern scenes of child protection in how they involve embodied practices which are fundamentally focused on moving within people's lived time and spaces, including even their bedrooms and the most intimate corners of their lives and selves. Yet, as I shall show in this book, these embodied practices have developed different meanings over time. In the final years of the nineteenth century, child protection was in equal measure a public and private experience in how it involved actions to protect children on the streets as well as in people's homes. This meant that these early domestic encounters had not gained the intensity that came to characterize their twentieth-century forms. In important respects institutions like the Children's Shelters – which closed in 1903 – provided transitional spaces between public and private in which the very notion of 'child protection' was given meaning.

Some 55 per cent of admissions to the Shelters were in relation to 'cruelties of the street' (cf. STAR, 1899), a category that was mostly made up of older children who were able to roam the streets and be taken in. The proportion of younger children involved in casework was relatively low as 15 per cent of all children investigated in child cruelty cases between 1884 and 1914 were classified as 'infants', or those who, after 1908, were classified as 'babies under two years of age'. The Shelters acted as immediate Places of Safety in emergency situations under the 1889 PCC Act and were also used in longer-term casework as a form of provision for children sent to them by magistrates, often for many weeks and months. As the Clerk to a Borough Court put it in 1892 in one of the first cases of its kind, in which a mother was convicted of 'systematically' neglecting her eight-month-old daughter, 'the case was adjourned for a while to give the woman an opportunity to improve her conduct, whilst one of her children was sent to the NSPCC Shelter'. The function of the Shelters within the child protector's strategy, therefore, was as institutions which could enable children to *remain* in parental custody. For as the NSPCC emphasized: 'Whilst other Societies house, feed, protect, and care for children, this Society requires the housing, feeding, protecting and caring for to be done by the parent' (NSPCC AR., 1895, p. 32; also 1896, pp. 51–2).

The literature on child welfare is replete with erroneous claims and assumptions about the ways in which state powers to remove children from households have been used in the past. As this conventional story goes, from the late-Victorian period right up until the 1950s, children were invariably 'rescued' from (cruel) parents and destined, more often than not, never to return home (see, for instance, Holman, 1988). Gordon concludes from her American study of child protection work that 'By far the most common outcome of agency action was not prosecution and jail sentences but the removal of children' (Gordon, 1989, p. 219). However, she does not examine systematically the numbers of children who were removed from parental custody, the reasons why such actions were taken, or whether the children returned home or not. In her analysis of the work of the Pennsylvania SPCC, Elizabeth Pleck suggests that in the late-nineteenth century three out of every 10 cases 'led to placement of the child outside the home'. While she observes that not all children were kept in care permanently, no indication of the numbers who returned home, and why, is given (Pleck, 1987, pp. 84–5). A deeper analysis of the evidence suggests that in fact only a fraction of the children who came to the attention of child protection agencies at this time were permanently removed from parental custody.

In a typical locality as many as 17 per cent of the children investigated by the NSPCC were taken from their homes and placed in care, in

Children's Shelters run by the agency. At first sight, this appears a very high proportion of child removals, and given the historical context in which such practices began, it was unprecedented. But these figures are relatively meaningless unless examined with regard to longer-term outcomes, patterns and meanings of the uses of state powers. Some 94 per cent of these children were quickly returned to parents, either immediately in the case of a court action not being pursued; or usually within three months in the case of one or both parents being imprisoned. Only 6 per cent of the children who were admitted to the Shelter did not return home, which means that just 1 per cent of the 5112 children dealt with by this typical Branch in the 1891–1903 period were *permanently* removed from parental custody.[3] Thus while over 80 per cent of children involved in cases were never taken from home under any condition, for the overwhelming majority of those who were removed the experience was self-consciously temporary, fully justifying the official definition of the shelters as 'Temporary Homes for Children' (STAR, 1891). In 1902 it was estimated that during the 13 years of its existence as a national organization at least 20 000 children had been placed temporarily in institutions by the Society whilst their parent(s) were in prison. Of these, it was 'found necessary to permanently remove' less than 600 (NSPCC AR., 1902, p. 14).

During the Shelter years, 1892–1903, some 69 per cent of cases were classified as 'neglect'. A further 15 per cent were designated 'ill-treatment and assault', 5.6 per cent were to do with 'begging and improper employment', a further 3 per cent involved 'exposure', 2 per cent 'abandonment' and 4 per cent came under the category 'other wrongs'. A final 1.7 per cent were classified under 'immorality', the category that included sexual offences against children. The child protectors repeatedly claimed that one of the primary roles of the Shelters was to facilitate the protection of those children whose abuse at home might not otherwise come to light but for this opportunity to disclose it. 'To mention only one case' they wrote in 1893:

> had it not been for a home such as this, we should never have learnt the sad story of tiny G 's [sic] cruel ill-treatment, and her tormentors would have gone unpunished. She was brought with her brothers to the Shelter, and after a time the kindness received here unsealed the boys lips, and we were able to prepare the case for court. If they had remained where they were, this would have been quite unacceptable. (STAR, 1893, p. 16)

It is not made explicit just what these boys disclosed that helped reveal the story of their sister's abuse. Such euphemism pervades the entire discourse on children's 'disclosure'. What was critical about this process was that the site of children's disclosures had shifted from the courtroom to institutions like the Shelters. Space and time had been created for (abused) children which was built around professional mediation. Its effects were complex. Since so many of the serious cases brought to the Shelters were pre-verbal infants, the idea of their disclosure was mostly irrelevant. If these children were to be heard to speak at all by welfare practitioners, it had to be, as it were, in a different voice: through their bodies. More accurately, the Shelters were historically novel institutional spaces within which the body of the mute child was made available to welfare practitioners to be read off for signs of what was classifiable as child maltreatment in social practice.

There were systematic limits to the forms of victimization that it was deemed possible for children to speak about, or for adults to hear and inspect. Cultural historians have begun to show the extent to which the human body has a history, and perceptions of children are no exception (Steedman, 1992). Legitimate boundaries to child protection and perceptions of 'vulnerable margins' (Nettleton, 1988) to children's bodies vary across time and place. Child sexual abuse is now widely accepted as being historically the least visible form of child maltreatment (Gordon, 1989), such that it has had to rely heavily on the testimony of children in order to be discovered and validated. Thus one might expect such Shelters to have provided ideal safe spaces in which professionals could seek out the physical signs and verbal disclosures necessary to bringing sexual abuse into the open. However, the entire discourse suggests that the perceived possibilities for disclosure of abuse by children had little, if any, meaning in relation to sexual crimes.

'Cruelties of the street' and 'neglect' were different matters. By the 1880s, philanthropic and political concern for the vagrant and street child were familiar motifs of respectable society. Such children provoked fear as well as pity. Middle-class sensibilities regarded such children as 'arabs', 'urchins', 'guttersnipes', as a 'wild race', 'nomadic', 'a multitude of untutored savages' – labels which identified them as heathen and uncivilized, alien to order and progress (Davin, 1988, p. 3). Middle-class ideology held that children belonged in protecting families, an ideal which placed the street and home in total opposition. 'The street stood for danger and corruption, and no child with a proper home would be freely allowed there' (Davin, 1988, p. 3). The reform campaign surrounding the 1885 Criminal Law Amendment Act proved a watershed in the social and legal construction of childhood (Gorham, 1978; Walkowitz, 1980; Weeks, 1980, pp. 87–89; Brown and Barrett, 2002). Middle-class concern about the sexual exploitation of girls conceptualized them as in need of protection by criminalizing the men who exploited them. These provisions had a greater effect in protecting a guardian's right to control a girl's sexuality (the law on this concerned only them) than in seeking to prevent harm to the girl. The child was conceptualized as 'the helpless victim of adult lust' (Davin, 1988, p. 6), an image that emphasized the importance of childish innocence in late-Victorian middle-class ideology.

By the 1880s and 1890s parents who left their children to roam the streets were vulnerable to being viewed as neglectful or exploitative and failing in their parental duty. They were subject to new codes of social regulation that extolled the sanctity of the (civilizing) home and the dangers of the street. The NSPCC embarked upon a strategic effort to 'clean up' the streets. Evidence from case materials and agency reports helps us to understand what was at stake here and how 'cruelties of the street' came to light in two ways: through the contingent spotting by Inspectors themselves of possible victims of cruelty on the streets, or others who reported such cases to them; and in the determined surveillance of lower-working class districts by Inspectors. Over time the Society focused ever more discriminatingly on what was referred to as the 'low part' of their districts (STAR, 1899, pp. 32–3). But they were equally concerned with more affluent neighbourhoods and removing children from what one Branch called 'our most fashionable promenade' (HDAR, 1892, p. 11).

This practice of taking children from the streets illustrates most acutely the combination of reform and control in child protection work: indeed, *reform as a means of control* in disciplinary practices (cf. Weeks, 1980, p. 89). The suffering of children was not the only question at issue. Also relevant were struggles surrounding the values and survival strategies of the poor and the autonomy of working-class culture. By clearing the city's high and low areas of the pitiable, offensive and threatening evidence of childhood corruption and parental indiscretion, Inspectors must not only be seen as 'protecting' children, but the quality of life of the bourgeois philanthropic supporters of child protection agencies was also enhanced: as agency representatives and ordinary citizens they could protect children and at the same time gain the freedom to walk the streets with ease.

Protecting children in late-nineteenth-century and early-twentieth-century times

The importance of being clear about what did happen to children is not simply to produce more accurate history, but to ensure more grounded theorizing of the nature and development of child protection practices. In an important sense, the spectre of SPCC Inspectors dashingly conveying starving and neglected infants to places of safety can be taken as an evocative image of the emerging character of 'modern' child protection, with its emphasis on concerted action and movement. I am arguing that these pioneering child protection practices embodied the spirit of their time in how they were both caught up with and helped to give birth to modernist forms of social practices which nourished themselves on the vagaries of industrial capitalist development. Yet, the precise meaning of such interventions in terms of what professional culture deemed it possible to protect children from requires careful judgement. Although child protection workers did indeed protect child life in some such cases, it would be misleading to over-invest these practices with a professional belief that regarded the deaths of children as ultimately preventable and avoidable through social intervention, although at the same time such an ideology was taking shape.

Between 1884 and 1914, the pattern was one of continual growth in the numbers of cases coming to attention. By 1910, over 50 000 cases were being investigated annually in England, Wales and Ireland, which was double the 1898 figure and five times greater than the cases handled in 1892 (see Table 2.1). This is partly explained by the acquisition of more social workers as it took until the turn of the century for the child protection movement to reach its goal of becoming truly national, in the sense that the entire geographical area was covered by fund-raising and management committees and an Inspectorate conducting actual child protection practices. Ironically, the more that casework developed the *more* children were dying in child protection cases. Between 1884 and 1914, no less than 13 613 children were classified as having died in NSPCC cases (see Table 2.1).

A good reason for this lies in the fact that as it first encountered 'abused children', child protection work intersected with broader and very serious social problems of poverty and infant mortality. As the classic poverty studies of the period showed, in the most socially deprived areas of cities as many as one in every three children born did not live beyond the first year of life (Rowntree, 1901). Infant mortality rates were higher in 1899 than at any other time in the nineteenth century (Dyhouse, 1978). This suggests that the children who died in these first cases were children who were probably *dying anyway* and who became caught up in the new powers and classifications of child protection. This does not mean that all such parents were now labelled as child murderers, but what were previously seen as deaths explainable by disease and

Table 2.1 NSPCC cases ending in the death of children, 1884–1914 (from NSPCC AR, 1914)

Year	Total cases	No. of children affected	Cases ended in death
1884	95	175	1
1985	147	327	5
1887*	258	899	6
1888	284	599	19
1889	737	1 165	16
1890	3 947	7 463	74
1891	6 413	13 955	78
1892	8 324	19 802	118
1893	11 336	27 637	123
1894	15 679	37 642	272
1895	19 156	47 212	258
1896	20 739	52 871	233
1897	23 124	61 625	204
1898	25 170	68 008	204
1899	28 165	75 732	199
1900	28 758	75 872	222
1901	31 725	85 506	246
1902	32 787	88 829	306
1903	34 946	95 560	445
1904	37 490	104 301	556
1905	38 036	105 926	617
1906	38 705	108 225	619
1907	40 433	115 002	799
1908	46 212	134 252	970
1909	49 092	144 234	1 100
1910	52 670	154 061	1 070
1911	54 123	158 206	1 229
1912	54 118	156 639	1 255
1913	54 514	159 407	1 143
1914	54 772	159 162	1 226
TOTAL	812 682	2 260 294	13 613

* Fifteen months figure.

hazardous social conditions began to be re-framed in terms of a new conception of parental responsibility in child welfare. To SPCC agencies all child deaths were suspicious. In 1900, for example, a York Inspector wrote: 'I found the baby dead laid out on the bed. I asked [the mother] when it died and she replied that morning at 9.50 am.' The worker, who had been involved with the case for well over a year, was surprised to find the eight-month-old baby dead, noting that he had visited two months earlier and 'at that time I noticed nothing in the condition of [the] baby to excite my suspicions' (York NSPCC case record, 1900).

The annual rate of children who died in protection cases was still in fact low relative to the total number of children worked with – even if by today's standards it was astronomically high. Between 1907 and 1914, the death rate was consistently between 0.7 and 0.8 per cent of all children involved in cases (NSPCC *Annual Report*, 1914, p. 29). These rates were still considered high by the society as 'cases ending in death' had a high symbolic importance and information about the problem was routinely made public. In 1898, for example:

> The number of children whose interests were involved in all these cases was 68,008. On behalf of 204 of these the Society's intervention came too late; the violence or neglect they had endured ended in death. (NSPCC AR, 1898, p. 38)

And in 1912:

> Unfortunately, cases of brutal cruelty are more numerous this year by 346. Probably for that reason the death-rate is higher.
>
> In 1,255 cases children succumbed to their injuries; this is 26 more than last year, and the largest recorded total for any year. There is more food for reflection in this paragraph than in any other throughout the whole of this report. (NSPCC AR, 1912, p. 14)

From the perspective of present day sensibilities, a remarkable feature of the representations of this time was the way in which the Society actually used statistics on child deaths to assert the *value* of its work. In its 1897 annual report, for example, the NSPCC compared the proportion of cases in which children died in the earlier and in the later periods of its work. In the first three years of the Society 'a child died in 15 per cent of cases'; in the last three years (1895–97) 'only 1.5 was dead'. Its conclusion was that this 'makes it certain that the Society is telling on the life of children' (NSPCC AR, 1897, p. 38). Child death was viewed with dismay, but high death rates in casework were a vital *resource* for child protection organizations. Information about the deaths of children was used as a sign that the practice was working *well*, not badly; that children were being reached and preventative work was *succeeding*, not failing.

This reflects how conceptions of risk to children which held in professional ideology and practice prior to the 1900s were simply not

sufficient to make children *predictable* subjects for preventative intervention. Before circa 1900, 'there seems to have been a powerful disposition
to see infant death as normal and to assimilate it into natural processes of
decay' (Wright, 1987, p. 108). The deaths of children were generally
placed in a context of meaning and explanation in which they were
associated with concepts like sin, natural wastage and seasonal rhythm.
The meanings of the protection of children were derived much more from
tradition and providential fortuna (Giddens, 1990) than through any
notion concerning the effectiveness of the expert system of child welfare.

The prevailing ideology of child welfare accounts in large part for
the temporality of practice. At its most tangible, prior to the 1900s,
the temporal structure of interventions was mediated by the length of time
parents were given to improve their standards of child care, rather than
from a concept of risk to children as such. This can be seen from a case
study[4] which illustrates the general pattern of intervention across the
years 1889–1903 and which led to the ultimate removal of children
from parental custody. The 'James' household had first come to the
Society's attention in December 1890 when Mr James complained of his
wife's heavy drinking and neglect of their three children who were then
aged seven, four and fourteen months. Mrs James, who already had convictions for drunkenness, was committed to prison for one month, and
subsequently prosecuted by the NSPCC on four more occasions during
the 1890s. As the decade passed, the committals to prison became pro-
gressively longer in duration: in 1890 she served one month with hard
labour; in 1893, two months; 1894, three months; 1896, four months;
and in 1899 the sentence was for five months with hard labour. On only
one of these occasions was her husband prosecuted with her, in 1896
when the case against him was 'dismissed'.

A remarkable feature of the casework of the 1890s and early 1900s was
the persistence with which parents such as these were disciplined.
Whatever autonomy NSPCC and other institutional practices like the
School Board may have had to determine the destiny of their casework,
during these years it had to defer to a judicial system that maintained
and exercised a direct degree of local control over decision-making
and outcomes of cases. Thus in 1893 the case of child cruelty against
Mrs James was not resolved immediately, but went through four adjourn-
ments, two of four weeks, one each of three weeks, and two weeks
consecutively, before she was finally committed to prison for two months.
On the occasion of the reconvened hearing, matters were more explicit
as to what the objective of this socio-legal procedure ultimately was. She
was given this chance on the strength of the NSPCC Inspector's report

back on what had proceeded since 'the case had been adjourned for a month to permit defendant's reformation'. During the 'month's probation', the court were told that Mrs James 'had been twice drunk, and had managed to get two black eyes and a cut lip'. But the Inspector's view was that the three children 'had-been somewhat better cared for'. Mr James offered the opinion that his wife 'had conducted herself very well'. Finally, at the end of June 1893 she was committed to prison for two months on the original charge of cruelty to children. She was viewed as 'guilty of gross neglect of her maternal duties' and after some 13 weeks of supervision by the Society carried out under the direct auspices of the courts, Mrs James was finally sent to prison.

As the years passed, Mrs James had more children, and the presence of those vulnerable infants increased the likelihood of her being viewed as neglectful. In 1896, the parents 'were charged with cruelty to their four children, but more especially toward their youngest child, which was eight months old'. A Police Inspector gave evidence to the effect that he knew the family well and that, 'It was not long ago since the woman was locked up for being drunk, and her baby had to be taken to the Shelter'. Mrs Berryman, the Matron of the Stockton NSPCC Shelter, told the court that 'when the child was brought to the Shelter it was in a very dirty condition, and its clothes had to be burned'. There had already been inquests on three children of the James's.

The case culminated in 1899 when Mrs James was committed to prison for five months with hard labour on a charge of serious neglect. Although there were now four children, the offences were 'only in respect of two, of the ages of ten and four', whose siblings were now aged 16 years and 13 years. By this time (June 1899), Mrs James had 'been convicted 16 times previously, including four times for cruelty to children'. The NSPCC had reached the view that, by now, 'the woman almost seemed past redemption'. Just a week after her committal to prison in 1899 the Society applied to Stockton Police Court for the custody of the two children aged ten and four years and it was granted. Out of a total of 409 children involved in cases in that locality that year, the James children were among 13 taken into care permanently. Six of these children went to Dr Barnardo's Homes, three to Roman Catholic Homes and four to 'other training institutions' (STAR, 1900, p. 13). Mr James was brought before the Police Court on four subsequent occasions for failing to comply with the order for contributions towards the maintenance of his children in care, the last being in November 1904 when he was committed to prison for two months. This was almost exactly 14 years after he had, ironically, first called the Society into the case.

What stands out is the extraordinary lengths to which the entire penal-welfare community – the NSPCC, courts, police, school board, doctors – went to in order *not* to remove abused children from parental custody. In every case where children were removed to 'Places of Safety' during the 1891–1903 period they were returned to parents at least once following the latter's imprisonment and/or the restoration of the child to health. Children were never permanently removed from the custody of mothers and fathers without the latter experiencing at least two committals to prison for child cruelty, or many adjourned appearances before the courts in the judicially based supervision of their case.

On the rare occasions that it did happen, the permanent removal of children was grounded in the histories that were established between parents, professionals and the local state in casework. It was a child welfare system centred upon the judgements of the judiciary and which had a deep symbolic resonance. In their representations, the child protectors were convinced that prosecutions had a significance far beyond the contours of the individual lives they so drastically tried to affect:

> We feel that the success of the work in our district is very largely due to the exemplary sentences which have ever characterised our magistrates' sense of a child's wrong. In the Appendix are given details of some of the cases dealt with in the past year, and also a list of the convictions obtained. (STAR, 1893–94, p. 14)

Punishment as represented here was designed to effect retribution through the deprivation of liberty and the physical endurance of hard labour. It worked to induce fear in local citizens and thereby deter through a spectacular display of the retributive power of the local state (Foucault, 1977). This in turn had a moral aspect to it as offenders were expected to reflect on their wrongs and reform. Casework strategies based on 'exceptional discipline' were motivated by the elements of 'deterrence', 'retribution' and 'moral reform' which went to make up Victorian penal-welfare strategies (see Garland, 1985, chapter 2). In this sense, penal-welfare practices demonstrated a negative use of power that sought to exclude child abusing parents from society. This was both symbolic and real as they were incarcerated in total institutions placed on the edge of society.

Although it had a reformative aspect to it, the nature of this practice was relatively undifferentiating. No special interest was shown in responding to recalcitrant parents as 'child abusers' as such. They were part of a generalized population of criminals and 'rebels' responded to in a uniform way by the penal law, social practice and the judicial process of this Victorian period. The grounds on which children were removed into care on a permanent basis had as much to do with the perceived inability of the disciplinary apparatus to deal with recalcitrant parents, as with attempts to protect children in some authentic sense from risk of abuse, or even death. This did not reflect a lack of concern for children as such, but in its own time and place a particular experience of space, temporality and mobility and professional ideology in terms of expectations of what was involved in protecting children in time.

Changing strategies of practice: bringing child protection into the home

Against this background, it becomes possible to see more clearly how, from the first years of the twentieth century, the modern practices and discourse of child protection truly began to take shape. As the children involved in casework became 'cases', and the practice evolved within an emerging modernism, a new conception of risk and optimistic professional belief began to be constituted which held that these deaths could be prevented and reformation of deviant parenting effected through social intervention. Despite having unrivalled powers in the history of state–family relations (Percival, 1911), up to 1914 permanent removals of children remained at much less than 1 per cent of all children investigated (NSPCC AR, 1912, p. 16). In the United Kingdom and Ireland, for instance, further PCC Acts in 1894 and 1904 were consolidated in the massive 1908 Children Act, which further clarified the nature of child cruelty offences and powers to prosecute cruel parents and remove children to safety and detain them in care. For instance, under former Acts an Inspector could not remove a child on his own but had to be accompanied by a policeman or a Poor Law relieving officer. Inspectors were now empowered without seeking the aid of another person and on obtaining the authority of a Justice of the Peace, to remove a child (Allen & Morton, 1961, p. 33). In addition, the Punishment of Incest Act 1908 made incest a criminal offence, punishable by imprisonment. The modern basis of the administrative powers' social workers needed to protect children had been put in place.

What had changed was the *form* that practice in general and the removal of abused children took and the concepts of risk on which such decisions were taken. The Children's Shelters closed in 1903 as a result of national policy imposed on localities (STAR, 1903, p. 12). From 1904, child protection practice guidance formalized the agency rule that workhouses, Poor Law Cottage Homes for children and hospitals – especially the Children's Hospitals which were built around this time (Weindling, 1992) – should be used in cases where children needed emergency protection in 'places of safety'. In crucial respects, however, the key site of medical as well as social work practice in child protection was now not institutions but the home. Increasingly after the closure of the Shelters, doctors were brought on visits to examine children on NSPCC invitation in their homes. As late as 1910, doctors continued to defer to the judgements of social workers in the designation of emergency cases. This occurred regardless of the severity of the abuse, be it neglect [e.g. CR 19103262], physical abuse [e.g. CR 19083011], or incest [e.g. CR 19093204]. This was soon to change.

Medical practices had a growing impact in child protection which reflected the growth in medicine's professional power and the emergence of a new 'mentalité' through which a way of seeing a child as in need of emergency intervention unfolded. By 1910, medical reports on case-files had a new sophistication and level of detail which included percentile charts (e.g. CR 19103289). Not only were hospitals now being used as places of safety in some emergency cases [e.g. CR 19154420], but in a general way the examination moved to the centre of child protection practices. A process of *medicalization* during the years around the First World War was crucial to the construction of the child as a social object. As Hendrick has written:

> through its ability to describe normal growth and the obstacles erected by immoderate toil, medicine gave children a *physical* and *material* identity. This may be described as a form of *medicalization*, a *mentalité* which internalised an understanding derived from medicine (and psychiatry and psychology). The inherent awareness of this *mentalité* with respect to children was 'real' in two senses. The child as a maturing person, observable to the eye, who could be physically damaged – the idea objectifies the child (and annexes its body) – by stress and strain; and, second, it saw the child (or childhood) as a phenomenon which in part could be understood only by reference to medicine, and other categories of 'expertise'. The identity bestowed upon children was one which confirmed their special 'nature,' whose existence nineteenth-century opinion had first conceded, however ambiguously and ambivalently. (Hendrick, 1992, p. 64, emphasis in original)

A further key indicator of shifts in casework and how child protection as a 'modern' form of practice and 'mentalité' came into being was a dramatic transformation in the use of penal practices. Prosecution rates dropped from 15 per cent of cases in 1901 to just 3 per cent in 1906, having been as high as 18 per cent in the early 1890s. The prosecution rate did not decline in relation to a static amount of casework, as some 40 per cent more cases were being investigated in the 1900s. When measured in terms of the increased possibilities to bring cases before the courts, the scale of the decline in prosecutions was very great indeed. A superficial assessment of this shift might take it to represent a straight-forward liberalization of attitude toward the punishment of cruel parents. However, the decline in prosecutions must be seen in the context of the 'substitute for imprisonment' (NSPCC AR, 1905, p. 9).

The prison ceased to be the central institution and the predominant sanction in social practice and became one institution among many in an extended network of practices which now descended on the homes and lives of vulnerable children and families. This is epitomized by the UK Notification of Births Act 1907 that laid down requirements for the notification of births and regular visiting of working class households by 'lady Inspectors' who became known as health visitors (Lewis, 1980). These visits had 'the aim of preventing the formation of habits in regard to the management of the child'. Hereafter, in cases where 'bad habits' had been formed 'where serious neglect of children was observed, inter-vention by the Society of the Prevention of Cruelty to Children was enlisted' by health visitors (Stockton MOH, 1910). The supervision of parent–child relations in their own homes was an important aspect of SPCC work from the outset. It had to be. Invited or not, the extension of disciplinary powers and practices into this spatial context was a fun-damental prerequisite to gaining access to suspected abused children and regulating parental conduct.

However, as I have shown, during the 1880s and 1890s child protec-tion was given meaning in terms of a determinedly public focus in the eradication of 'cruelties of the street'. Thus, it was only from 1895 onwards that systematic classification of the numbers of supervisory home visits began (STAR, 1985, p. 17). By 1914, what was now referred to as the 'Society's system of supervision' had been institutionalized and was 'being carefully carried out, both in the towns and the country dis-tricts, with very gratifying results' (STAR, 1914, p. 7). From the 1900s 'Supervision visits' began to be categorized separately from home visits made on 'original inquiries' into allegations of cruelty (MDAR, 1910, p. 8). The crucial shift was in the *intensity* of supervision on a case-by-case basis. Between 1899 and 1904, a typical Inspector made 3036 supervi-sions in 946 cases, an average of 3.2 per case; from 1905 to 1910, 4766 supervisions went into 1192 cases, an average of 4 per case; while between 1909 and 1914, 6228 supervisions were made in 1325 cases, a case-by-case supervision rate of 4.7. The latter represented a 32 per cent increase in the rate of supervisions compared with the equivalent period (1899–1904) ten years earlier.[5] 'Supervisions' changed in their intensity and meaning, having a function that was distinct from the investigation and becoming the *modus operandi* of child protection.

Through this shift, it was the principle of moral reformation of parents (and children) that defined the core goal of these reconstituted practices. The goals of deterrence and retribution remained within the system, but in contrast to the legalist and highly symbolic processes which characterized the 1889–1903 years, 'disciplinary practices are henceforth to place their emphasis upon the positive incentives of "hope", with its possibilities of moral regeneration instead of the negative conformity produced by fear' (Garland, 1985, p. 30). The core child protection casework strategy changed from that of the punishment of parents to reformation through the supervision of parent – child relations in their own homes. As they became caught up in these processes of change, the lives of householders in child cruelty cases were being reconstituted as a modern social and administrative child protection system was set in place. Indeed, they had *become* individual 'cases', which is not something that should simply be taken for granted. Such administrative processes as the maintenance of case-files are central to all modern 'disciplinary' procedures and practices.

The effects of this were not only administrative but highly practical: 'child abusing parents' were no longer 'rebels' but social deviants who could be *reformed* according to modern standards of competent parenting and 'good' citizenship that were defined through the socio-political process of which these transformations were a central part. Power was now being used positively. It began to individualize and mobilize recalcitrant parents who were now routinely labelled as social deviants and either institutionalized or (much more frequently) supervised around a rehabilitative ideal that sought to correct them *as parents*. The primary objective continued to be not to relieve parents of the care of their children, but rather to enforce their responsibilities as newly conceived for them by the state, although the means to achieving this had changed.

From the turn of the century, for example, the child protectors were writing in terms of 'inebriate mothers and their reform' and some women were being sent for individualized correction to newly established inebriate reformatories for up to three-year incarcerations (e.g. CR 19134521). 'While in the retreat', it was stressed, 'it is for us to see that she never forgets that she is a *mother*. We recognize that she is where she is in order that she may be restored to her honourable place in the world of mothers' (NSPCC AR, 1903, pp. 13–14, emphasis in original). Inebriate reformatories symbolized one way in which women – or 'neglectful mothers' – became the subjects of new forms of persuasion and discipline oriented towards their education and reform.

However, incarceration in reformatories and prisons now happened in only a minority of cases, reflecting national trends in what the Society referred to as 'Modern tendencies towards a less harsh treatment of offenders against the law' (NSPCC AR, 1911, p. 19). In Foucauldian terms, child protection practice was now constituted by surveillance rather than exemplary sentences and ceremonies (cf. Foucault, 1977, p. 193). The movement from one project to another, from a schema of exceptional discipline to one of a generalized surveillance (Foucault, 1977, p. 209), was complete. Looking beyond the solid Foucauldian language of 'surveillance', as we must, in real terms what this meant was that child protection came to depend on what practitioners were able to achieve on home visits. A form of social work practice was born here which, far from the implied solid, penetrating gaze, was essentially mobile and much softer and 'liquid' in nature given that what was seen of children and families in their day-to-day lives and family homes was fragmented, ephemeral, fleeting and contingent – a point I return to at length in Chapter 3.

Prompt local action: the protection of children in new times

A case record, which documents one of the first interventions in which the new form of child protection was clearly evident in practice, will help to bring the shift that I am arguing about into clearer focus.[6] In May 1913, 'Mrs Smith', a 46-year-old widow and lone-parent mother of three dependent children aged eight, five and two and a half years, was reported to the NSPCC because her children 'were said to be dirty and sadly neglected sleeping on the kitchen flags with nothing to cover them and Mrs [Smith] said to be drinking having sold her home up to obtain drink'. The Inspector made the investigatory visit to the home at 5.50 pm on the day he received the complaint, taking a police sergeant with him. He 'obtained Mrs [Smith's] permission and in her presence ... saw the three children who were well nourished, but superficially dirty, unkempt, untidily and poorly clad, bootless and all were more or less verminous (both body and head lice). They looked dejected and poorly.' He made a similar close examination of the home – a downstairs backroom, which was judged to be dirty and poorly furnished.

Inquiries among the neighbours elicited a statement from one woman who lived in another part of the same house, and felt that because Mrs Smith drank heavily and neglected the children, she was 'not a fit and proper person to have the care and custody of her children'. The Inspector had known Mrs Smith for over two years. He had warned her in the past for neglect and for sending her children begging. She was presented unfavourably throughout the file as a marginal individual who 'goes on tips and gathers scrap and earns a precarious living'. She had recently spent a month in prison for theft of scrap metal. On the present investigation the Inspector confronted Mrs Smith with his concern 'showing her how such is neglect and explained to her how to remedy the same by going into the Workhouse as she had twice previously on my visiting her and I warned her'. Mrs Smith insisted that she had 'never neglected' her children. 'I am going to get work and will soon get straight but I won't go into the Workhouse', she insisted.

The Inspector called in a doctor who 'advised that the children be removed to the Workhouse as soon as possible' and a warrant for a removal order was granted to the Society at the Police Court, the children were removed to the Cottage Homes, and Mrs Smith arrested. The police sergeant's view was that 'If properly attended to, in my opinion they would soon become fine children.' Mrs Smith was subsequently found guilty under the 1908 Children Act of cruelty to children and sentenced to six months imprisonment with hard labour. Mrs Smith had spent periods in Stockton Workhouse on three occasions between 1911 and 1912: one period of five weeks; one of two weeks; and a third, which lasted almost five months. On each occasion the children were admitted to the Cottage Homes and were returned to their mother when she left the Workhouse. The effects of this latest intervention were very far-reaching, as the children remained in care in the local Children's Homes up to the 1920s. Two of them were discharged from the Homes as late-teenagers into 'service' while the third child was emigrated to Canada at the age of 15, having been placed with Dr Barnardos. This was the first recorded instance of a child in the research sample admitted to care due to child maltreatment being migrated abroad to an outpost of the empire, an aspect of the history of child welfare which has only recently been fully told (Bean and Melville, 1989; Raftery and O'Sullivan, 1999). As late as 1924, Mrs Smith was still recorded as living in the locality.

The novelty of the case was also apparent in the structure of the emergency intervention which led to the removal of the children in

1913. The Inspector wrote that he had made the application for the removal order 'as directed', but this 'direction' did not come from the NSPCC's legal department, or the courts, as traditionally happened, but from the doctor who had examined the children at the Inspector's request. The doctor wrote in his report:

> On Friday May 30th about 6pm, at the request of Inspector H I visited [the home address], where Mrs [Smith] and her family occupied the back downstairs room. The furniture consisted of a couch, one chair, a pushchair and some bedding and on the mantel shelf, a lamp and a clock. There were three children aged 8, 5 and 2 years and an old woman, Mrs [Smith's] mother. Mrs [Smith] was toxicated. The children were fairly healthy but dirty and verminous.
>
> There was no bed and no bed coverings. The beddings stretched on the floor was the only place for them all to sleep on. Under the circumstances I recommended the removal of the children to the Workhouse, as their neglected condition was prejudicial to their health and character. Signed Dr____

The form that the protection of children took had changed. As the NSPCC Legal Department wrote after seeing the case-papers: 'Thank you for sight of papers herein in which it was necessary to take prompt local action without reference to us. We fully confirm the steps taken and have pleasure in recording the case and conviction and now return report.' The degree of assessed risk to some children was now at a level that the relatively drawn out, time consuming administrative procedure which had been in place since the practice began in the 1880s was no longer viable if children were to be protected in time. Professional assessments such as that of the doctor above – 'The children were fairly healthy but dirty and verminous' – give important clues as to the concept of 'manufactured risk' (Giddens, 1994a) that now held in practice, its relationship to dirt, marginality and notions of order, and child protection as an embodied work experience, all of which I shall analyse in further detail in the chapters that follow. What can be said at this point is that the power to protect was now not in the hands of local child protection administrators, or even the courts, but rather in those of the professional practitioners who had come to surround the child. The law remained important to the practicalities of protecting children, but in 'emergency cases' the newly established children's courts would act merely to rubber-stamp the prompt local action already taken to protect children in time.

A paradoxical outcome of the new construction of child protection was that the deaths of children in casework gained further systematic recognition. Changes in NSPCC discourse signified the new meaning that protecting child life and death now had to professionals. When it was noted, for instance, that four children had died in the Middlesbrough district in 1912 'while their cases were under investigation', the Committee added that this was 'surely the most urgent appeal for early information of children's wrongs. Delay may be fatal' (MDAR, 1912, p. 8). These representations reflected the new concept of risk and time-consciousness intrinsic to the modern mentalité of child protection. As the scope of child protection developed and its character changed, the conviction grew that death was avoidable if children could be reached *in time*.

In exploring developments during the first phase in the construction of modern child protection between 1870 and 1914, this chapter has detailed the complex ethical and practical problems that had begun to emerge in attempts to protect children. Central to the fulfilment of the growing desire to protect children in time were the development of administrative powers and refinements in the scientific expertise of medicine. Through these developments I have shown how the two most important rituals in modern child protection, the home visit by a statutory social worker and the medical examination by a doctor, were created and routinized in practice. I have shown how the Children's Shelters which existed between 1889 and 1903 reflected the social basis the power professionals had over the lives of children and the prohibitions and permissions surrounding the child's body and reading of signs which constituted maltreatment. Thereafter, professional power came to be engaged with the (abused) child and family through the home visit. By 1914, negotiations in social work had become inexorably private. Cruelties of the street had by now disappeared as a category altogether. The deeper meanings and experiences of these changes in terms of the full modernity of child protection can now be explored.

The consensus view underpinning the literature of child care today that the experience of most, if not all, suspected abused children of this period was to be 'rescued' by the state and taken from parental custody has been shown to be a myth. It has led to a total neglect of analysis of vital questions concerning concepts of trust and risk and the grounds on which decisions to remove children were taken, and the increasingly mobile practices of child protection through which such interventions were effected. Myths of rescue belie the complexity that every era must face in confronting the difficult social obligation of protecting abused children. And such myths close off attention to the temporality of practice, the concepts of risk, safety and danger and the actions professionals have taken which must be carefully analysed if we are to reach a deeper understanding of the meanings of protecting children in particular times.

3
The Smell of Practice: Child Protection, the Body and the Experience of Modernity

The importance of the account I am seeking to offer in this book is that it does not only constitute a socio-historical argument and corrective to standard accounts of the history of child protection. It paves the way for a grounded theoretical account of how modern child protection is constituted, based on more accurate representations of the emergence and development of its practices. I have shown how, by the first decades of the twentieth century, child protection came into being in terms of the emergence of administrative powers to protect children and the manner in which those practices began to focus upon a concept of risk to children. These powers were enacted in a manner which gave child protection professionals a new autonomy to act in discretionary ways in protecting children.

Yet, child protection was (and is) constituted as a practice not simply through the law and administrative powers, but in terms of the cultural and social domains and my focus in this chapter is on the emergence of what I call a modernist culture of child protection. Child protection was here constituted in terms of a particular experience of modernity, of time, space and causality, as a form of *bureaucratic modernism*. The 'bureaucratic' part of this conceptualization refers to the centrality of administrative powers and the welfare state in determining agency function, while the 'modernism' dimension concerns the socio-cultural influences which are equally important in defining what child protection is. This is especially in terms of the ways in which such powers are enacted through movement and mediated by the body and the senses. I shall show how child protection's modern character came to be constituted by the aesthetic and expressive realms, as well as by administrative powers. I use the notion of 'the smell of practice' to reflect both key elements of the emergence of modern child protection's substantive concerns with dirt and disorder and the (domestic) space of others, and as a metaphor for it as an embodied, sensuous, fleshy, ambiguous experience of mobility and modernity. The ephemeral, invisible yet deeply affecting nature of the sense of smell aptly reflects the aesthetic and expressive properties of child protection in terms of how, despite its rational objectives, (some) families have always eluded (total) regulation and control.

Yet, despite this fluidity, as it took shape in the first years of the twentieth century, child protection did have a 'solid' basis to it in how it was held together culturally by a distinctive classification system, forms of risk management and relationship between expert systems and lay people. At the heart of this was the emergence of a particular conception of the human body, which I show took on new meanings in response to developments in the 'social' body. These classification systems structured definitions of child abuse which persisted right through to the 1970s and which account for the dominance of child neglect and the virtual disappearance of child sexual abuse as a social problem. This arose in an era characterized by what Bauman (2000) calls 'heavy' capitalism and a form of social order where class, gender, age and ethnic roles and identities were clearly defined, people came to know their place and child protection workers intervened to make sure they didn't forget them.

Child protection, mobility and the culture of modernism

The notion of 'prompt local action' and new time consciousness that at the end of the last chapter I suggested typified the new parameters of 'modern' child protection arose out of the expanded capacities of practitioners to cover space and reach and supervise children; changes in the nature of time; processes of medicalization, and a new belief in the transformative capacity of state intervention to reform deviant citizens. Prompt local action embodied the three key dimensions that I shall continue to argue constituted modern child protection by the first decades of the twentieth century: the application of new administrative and disciplinary powers to protect children arising from the law and agency functions; a new time and risk consciousness and temporal structure to social practices which arose from scientific and technological innovations within an emerging culture of modernism and new conception of risk to children, heavily derived from medical discourse; and an expressive, symbolic order at the heart of which was conceptions of the body, and powerful notions of purity and danger that gave to child protection a particular quality of bodily, psychological and emotional experience. In delineating these three dimensions of influence and experience, I shall begin with mobility and experiences of time and space.

From the turn of the twentieth century, the new time consciousness that entered child protection was fundamentally shaped by new technical resources and modes of modern communication – cabs, railways, buses (cf. NSPCC *Inspector's Directory*, 1904, p. 53, 1910, p. 86) – to which professionals had access that enabled them to cover space and reach children in time. Prior to the turn of the century, while child protection workers used their legs and transport on trains to reach children, child protection was a relatively static affair in that the technology did not exist to get them around more quickly. Changes in the tempo of practice reflected, quite literally, changes in the meanings of protecting children in time. 'As to "emergency", in all cases the interests of a child are superior to rules', the NSPCC advised from 1904 onwards (NSPCC *Inspector's Directory*, 1904, p. 21, 1910, p. 34). Fundamental to the shift under consideration here was the manner in which the 'interests' of abused children were redefined according to a new concept of risk, danger and 'safety' necessitating immediate social intervention.

The birth of modernism at the turn of the century and transformations in time and space were transforming cultural practices generally and led to the birth of what can be characterized as a modernist culture of child protection. Inventions such as the telephone and the bicycle transformed people's experiences of time and space, leading Kern (1983) to characterize this late-Victorian-Edwardian period as the 'culture of time and space'. NSPCC inspectors began using the bicycle in the late 1890s and it had an enormous impact. Increases in detection of child cruelty cases did not only arise from more efficient administrative organization in outlying areas, but were 'partly owing to the provision of a Cycle for the Inspector, who has thus been enabled to visit Rural Districts otherwise less accessible' (STAR, 1900, p. 14).

The social impact of the bicycle was huge (Kern, 1983, pp. 111–13), radically changing the *spatial* dimensions of practice, enabling more ground to be covered and greater numbers of suspected abused children to be reached. Changes in speed of action led to the 'shrinking' of geographical boundaries and a new spatiality (Soja, 1985) of cultural practices which in turn transformed the *temporal* structures of child protection. As children could now be reached *physically*, so it became thinkable that they could be seen more *quickly*. A new phenomenology of time and social action and transformed time-consciousness entered practice which became a fundamental defining feature of the modernity of child protection. Protecting children in time literally took on a crucial aspect of its modern meaning.

Thus hand-in-hand with transformations of concepts of space went key changes in the nature of time itself. Prior to the nineteenth century, time had gone largely uncoordinated at a national and international level and was deeply embedded in local activities. Most towns kept their own time zones and stagecoaches, for instance, which emerged from 1784 required their guards to adjust their timepiece to cope with these different zones. From the early nineteenth century time had begun to become more fully 'disembedded' from the social activities which had previously structured it. The development of the railways from the 1840s and especially with the carrying of mail, meant that the problem of coordination of time became more important (Thrift, 1990). By around 1847, national timekeeping was begun by the railways, the Post Office and many towns and cities as they adopted Greenwich Mean Time (Urry, 2000, p. 111). Clocks and watches suddenly became common. The first watches that were entirely machine-made were produced in the USA in the 1830s, and it was Henry Ford (of motor car fame) who first devised a mass production system in the 1880s for the manufacture of clocks (Lash and Urry, 1994, p. 228). Cross-Channel and then cross-Atlantic telegraph services contributed further to the need to coordinate time internationally. The establishment in 1913 of 'world time', with the first signal from the Eiffel Tower sent across the globe, was the culmination of the increasing coordination of time between European countries and between Europe and north America that had gone on from the second half of the nineteenth century with regard to standardization of time measurement (Urry, 2000, p. 112). With these developments, 'clock-time' spread into almost all aspects of social life and came to play 'a singularly powerful role in western societies' (Urry, 2000, p. 107). Hereafter a core tension in child protection would surround the different temporal rhythms and experiences of welfare organizations and workers (increasingly governed by clock time) as it intersected with agency clients (lived time).

The child protectors were quick to celebrate the technological scope of their new capacities to protect children in time:

> a tramp woman and her three children were traced from place to place and found after about 100 miles cycling, with the result that the mother was sentenced to two months' imprisonment for cruel neglect, and the care of the children given by the Magistrates to Dr Barnardo. (STAR, 1901, pp. 14–15)

This was one of eight 'tramp' cases investigated by the Branch that year, 1901, constituting 5 per cent of the case load (STAR, 1901, p. 14). In the same year the society remarked on how 'a large number of the cases' were now 'in towns and villages scattered over counties, and have involved travelling of Inspectors from the centres at which they are stationed over not less than 1,000,000 miles' (NSPCC AR, 1901, p. 5). The dynamic at work here can be related to the process of 'time–space compression', which is characteristic of the capitalist world. The time horizons of both private and public decision-making shrink, while the development of sophisticated communication systems and declining transport costs made it possible to spread those decisions over ever wider and variegated space (cf. Harvey, 1989, p. 147). As a consequence, both time and space appear more and more compressed.

The desire to spread their practices all over the country and to homogenize child protection was an important objective of the child protection movement from the outset. As I showed in Chapter 2, this connected to a powerful desire by social reformers and the upper and middle classes to bring the poor under control by making them *visible*. This was not simply a matter of a self-serving organizational desire to expand and grow, but was intrinsic to the kind of relationship between power, space and literal seeing of people – the 'will to power' (Foucault, 1977) – that was inscribed within the child protector's vision. As Foucault writes of such disciplinary power, 'Discipline is an anti-nomadic technique':

> discipline fixes; it arrests or regulates movements; it clears up confusion; it dissipates compact grouping of individuals wandering about the country in unpredictable ways; it establishes calculated distributions. (Foucault, 1977, p. 219)

A complete national network of Inspectors was regarded as essential to creating conditions where it would be possible to enforce parental responsibility by closing off the gaps through which recalcitrant and evasive parents could slip. In the early 1890s local reports even had a category of 'decamped' families in their returns, for example in one place involving three out of the 66 cases investigated that year (STAR, 1891). As the child protection movement grew in size and experience, it adopted an increasingly self-confident view of its ability to render visible even the most transient and elusive households. Although it had been in principle a national Society since 1889, it was over a decade before the organization could claim to have covered its boundaries in actual *practices*. As it was observed in 1893, 'four-fifths of the country is still outside the Society's operations. Its true nationality cannot be realized until its agency extends throughout the length and breadth of the land' (STAR, 1893, p. 17). By around 1897 we are told for the first time that, 'the advantage of the national character of the Society has been marked in several instances in tracing and supervising removals' (STAR, 1897, p. 16). From 1899, annual reports began to offer the first of what became routine sample cases of 'Branch Inquiries', which related to households that had moved out of one locality only to be traced by the resident Inspector in the area to which they moved, irrespective of how far away it was. This extended to places as far as the United States where 'defaulting' fathers, in particular those who went there in search of work – Ireland being the most common example – were traced and made to provide for their families, thus reflecting the practical operations of a truly national and international movement (see, for instance, Dublin Branch NSPCC Reports from 1889–1955). From the child protector's point of view the gaps that once existed in the geographical network had been closed off, 'decamping' families now had nowhere to hide and the gaze of child protection was believed to be impenetrable.

Thus by the beginning of the twentieth century the child protectors came to believe that no one could escape them, and were astonished if anyone now managed to do so. 'The most peculiar thing about this case', an Inspector wrote of a serious neglect situation in 1909:

> is that the family have lived in this house 13 years and yet the neighbours never complained and although the County Court Bailiffs have been going to the house regularly for years, a complaint has only first been made. When I spoke to the neighbours, all I could get out of them was that they were a queer family and rarely seen lately and the doors always kept locked.

Any time since 1896 this family could have been reported in this street for neglect [CR 19093163]. To have avoided the gaze of one's neighbours and the state was now unthinkable. It was to be without a history in the annals of social administration and in the cultural domain to be judged 'queer'; it was to be seen as living beyond the margins of rationality, citizenship and sociability. We see being institutionalized here the fantasy of total transparency of family life which constitutes perhaps the most powerful single assumption underpinning the discourse and psyche of modern child protection. And the more the twentieth century develops, the more it and the underlying power of the visual, of a 'hegemony of vision' (Rorty, 1980) to modernity and child protection was bolstered by science. The possibility that children could not now be seen in some predictable fashion, and that their parents could transgress the inscribed boundaries of practice had become unthinkable within the professional ideology of protecting children in time.

This shows how fundamental scientific and technological advances lay behind the shaping of cultural meanings and professional ideologies in child protection. A socio-cultural 'space' had been opened up which meant that the 'culture' of child protection took on a new dynamic from the culture of modernism in which it was being constructed. Twentieth century innovations in transport, such as the motorbike – which social workers used from the 1940s – the automobile – which they began using in the 1950s, in telecommunications, with the popularization of the telephone, the fax machine, and latterly the internet and mobile phone; and in child health technologies, such as the x-ray machine, show how the socio-cultural space that was opened up here has been utilized and we have developed the mobilities and technology to protect probably more children in time today than ever before.

Child protection as the fleeting, the ephemeral and the contingent

These developments and the culture of modernism had two, quite contradictory, effects on child protection: on the one hand rendering it more open; on the other, leading to processes of boundary marking and 'closure' which created real clarity as to its forms and processes. There emerged, in effect, a particular combination of solid and melting visions, heavy and soft forms to child protection. Relative to the risk anxieties that pervade child protection today, in the era of simple modernity prior to the 1970s, there was a deep certainty to what its practices were meant to be about. The paradox of this certainty was that it concealed all manner of insecurities, not least with respect to child death. I shall deal first with the contingent, uncertain dimensions before moving on to consider the more solid, bounded forms that child protection now took.

In practice, child protection was a much more risky, vulnerable and fateful endeavour than the grand assumptions and claims that were routinely now made for it. The core problem was getting to see and know enough about children and how they were cared for to ensure their protection without having to take them into care, a response which remained a minority practice throughout the twentieth century. After the First World War, the number of child removals and prosecutions of parents remained tiny relative to the number of children involved in casework. The *modus operandi* for this was home visiting, which involved encounters between laypersons and professionals that were periodical and transitory in form. By around 1908, case-files exude a sense of the increased tempo, urgency and intensity of visiting that now characterized child protection. In 1909, a School Board Officer reported the mother of four children aged between 12 years and a baby of three weeks for their 'neglect'. Their father was working abroad and had called on the Inspector before going away, gave him a calling card and 'asked me to watch his children if I received a report about his wife drinking'. On investigation of the report that did eventually come, the mother, who 'looked ill', admitted that she had been drinking and neglecting the baby by leaving her unattended for several hours. She promised to do better. The Inspector 'warned' her and told her he would 'call again'. Counting the number of subsequent supervisions in the narrative of the case-file, in the nine months following the first investigation he made 29 visits, a period that included '14 days leave of absence' [CR 19093170]. In effect, the weekly or fortnightly social work visit had begun and a distinct *rhythm* to protecting children in time had been established.

Here we see the powerful influence of clock-time in how a bureaucrat-ically framed temporal structure to practice in terms of the periodical home visit was imposed on the 'lived time' (Lefebvre, 1991) of the family lives of agency clients. Following the routinization of the home visit, social worker's engagements with client's lives became fleeting, transi-tory and contingent. The practices of child protection became consti-tuted through encounters with client's homes which were concrete, immediate and intimate: with space as fleeting – moving between town and country, from street to street, home to home, room to room; with time as transitory – moving into and through other's time and rhythms for short durations, of weekly home visits, and hourly interviews; and of causality as fortuitous or arbitrary – visiting only certain people through set legitimated procedures which gave a contingent basis to how persons become clients and the kinds of things that were, or were not, seen on investigations and home visits.

These modernist forms that child protection now took require forms of sociological modernism to make sense of them and in particular the insights of social theorists of modernity who have emphasized the fleet-ing, fragmented character of modern experience and for whom access to the 'totality' is seen as simply not available. Thus we find Simmel, whose own life and modernist sensibility spanned the (late-nineteenth and early twentieth century) historical transformations mapped out here, seeking out the 'fortuitous fragment' of social reality, the 'fleeting image' of social interaction (Frisby, 1982, Chapter 4; Whimster, 1987). Simmel wrote and practised widely the art of capturing 'snapshots' of modern life from the 'whole colourfulness and unity of this so evident and so puzzling life of society' (quoted in Frisby, 1985, p. 55). For Benjamin, the fragment now remains the gateway to the totality, rather than the latter shedding light on the former (Benjamin, 1973; Frisby, 1985). Benjamin developed the photographic metaphor into a critical concern with the whole medium as an art form and with the ontological status of the photograph. For him, with the appearance of the camera around this time, 'a touch of the finger now sufficed to fix an event for an unlimited period of time. The camera gave the moment a posthumous shock as it were' (Benjamin, 1973, p. 132). 'Passing moments' we have come to know as child protection investigations and social casework were similarly conceived in social work terms through the 'posthumous shock' of the knock on the door, the visit and the case-file as it were. The paradox of these snapshots is that although they constitute only fleeting images of their subject's lives, they must be made to endure (adapted from Frisby, 1982, p. 82).

Child protection had become a professional life on the run as social workers always had to act through movement to protect children and so often had to chase the most marginal families around trying to bring them under 'control'. Once located, the next challenge was to gain access to their homes. In 1909, for instance, an Inspector wrote of a lone-parent mother of five dependent children aged from 12 to two years:

> I have known this case since June 1908 on and off and to my knowledge they have been in 9 houses. She gets a house and stays in free until things get hot and then she moves. She has 3 children in Industrial Schools for stealing. It is one of the most difficult homes to get into and many a time I have gone three or four times and been unable to get in. She is a terror to landlords and the children are a bother to the S B O [School Board Officer] and the police. I have told her that she will be getting into my net someday. She said, no fear I'll watch that. I will supervise again.

Despite (and indeed because of) her best efforts to avoid it, three months later this mother fell into the disciplinary 'net' of child protection. She was brought before the courts on a charge of neglect and the network of agencies had grown to include the Poor Law (the children were in the Cottage Homes) and a Probation Officer who, as a result of the court proceedings, was supervising an older girl of the family. Under strict conditions, the mother and the other children remained under the supervision of the Society. As the Inspector wrote: 'The case ... was adjourned for 3 months and unless she allows the children to remain in the Workhouse I have to bring the case forward again.' The mother refused to accept intervention on these terms, removed the children from the Homes and went on the run. She was apprehended and the children were taken into care permanently. One of the children subsequently died, in part it was thought, due to the hardship of living rough to avoid the authorities. Such human tragedy spoke volumes for the complex relationships and paradoxes that now lay at the centre of child protection: the very efforts made by the state and this mother to protect this child (albeit on very different terms) had contributed to the child's death [CR 19093243]. Thus despite its orientation to control and increasing belief in total protection, the expert system had to learn to live with its own failures; and, more poignantly still, with how it came to actively constitute its own tragedies, most vividly in terms of the deaths of children. Such dynamics were central to the nature of 'manufactured risk' (Giddens, 1994) now at the heart of these processes.

An important dimension of the role of child welfare professionals was to intervene into the lived time and flow of domestic life to change parental expectations and practices surrounding child survival. As this book has already begun to show, child protection now focused on women in a way that both reflected, and helped to constitute, their cultural role as primary child carers. In 1913, for instance, it was asserted that: 'Much suffering is often caused through sheer carelessness and ignorance on the part of the mother, in the way children are nourished, and in all such cases forms are distributed dealing with the proper way to feed and bring up a child, much good resulting from the advice given therein' (STAR, 1913, p. 7). This outlook of maternalism was shared by other state agencies, such as health visiting (see, Stockton MOH., 1912, p. 10; Lewis, 1980, pp. 97–108), constructing motherhood as crucial to child health.

In 1909 a York Inspector intervened into a 'neglect' case following the death of a baby. He had known the family since 1907, and two other children had died. The mother, he wrote, 'is seldom in her own house, and has been in the habit of leaving the children at home alone with an unprotected fire. The deceased baby has been left for 3 or 4 hours at a time lying in bed alone and awake.' Finding the woman in a neighbour's house, the Inspector accompanied her home to see the baby.

We found it upstairs in bed alone and awake. I told Mrs _____ that the child looked starved, and she replied that it was consumptive, adding: 'It is going as the other two did.' I said she had no right to assume such a thing, and to take it to a doctor.

The mother duly took the child to the doctor who 'examined it' and informed the Inspector 'that the child needed nourishment and fresh air. ... I saw the doctor several times who assured me that he was looking after the mother'. Such casework reflects well the great efforts that were put into promoting child life by these early child care professionals, how they invariably had to decide what constituted abuse or wilful neglect or simple ignorance in the context of dire poverty and disadvantage, and how this was accomplished in terms of a discourse that was pervasively gendered.

There is a whole aesthetic proportion available here which emerges precisely in this space and time on the relationship of such social work and child protection practices to day-to-day life, on how they touch only 'passing moments' of a child and family's densely lived day. In this light it is hard to believe that social work, child death inquiry processes, the state and general public could ever harbour such solid visions of societal totalities in relation to what can be known about how people live and such fantasies of total transparency of family life. Yet these case examples also illustrate the high consequence risks for children of professionals *not* getting it right and the emerging desire that they must and *should* protect them in time.

The smell of practice: child protection as embodied action

A key consequence of this was that it was the body of the practitioner moving from place to place that was the conduit through which the rules, regulations and cultural norms of practice passed. A crucial gap had opened up between organizational dictates, the case-file and the visit. This arose from a mixture of an instrumental rationality derived from the state and developments in science and technology, and symbolic and cultural processes. The project of spreading child protection within national and international borders brought a deep concern with *boundaries* which worked its way into the most intimate dimensions of practice. And the more solid forms that these practices took over the period arose from how these boundaries related to strategies of governance which sought to regulate age, class, gender and ethnic relations.

Within a remarkably quick time a new 'order' had entered the practice of child protection in terms of the social, administrative and symbolic, as well as spatial and temporal boundaries which surrounded its practices.

By 1904, agency rules made it clear that: 'No Officer should overstep his own Branch boundary except under urgent necessity, and then only under the instructions of his Honorary Secretary' (NSPCC *Inspector's Directory*, 1904, p. 21). Clearer emphasis was given to the boundaries of citizen's rights within the private domain and to the fact that Inspectors had no legal right of entry to houses – however much they suspected that abused children were inside (NSPCC *Inspector's Directory*, 1904, p. 35, 1910, p. 55). Once inside houses, the examination of children's bodies was a focal point of new directives on face-to-face practices. In a remarkable passage from the 1910 NSPCC *Inspector's Directory* (pp. 42–3) under the heading 'Cleansing of the Hands' workers were advised of hygiene rules:

> To avoid risks to the health of himself or other persons, an Inspector should at all times, in cases where there is any likelihood of there being any disease of an infectious or contagious nature, and also after handling a dead child, take precautions for the thorough cleansing of the hands. It is best to use a carbolic soap for washing the hands after dealing with such cases. The hands should always be well-cared for, and any cuts or abrasions have suitable dressing applied in order to keep the wound free from the chance of contamination. The nails should be kept clipped quite short, and no dirt allowed to accumulate under them. (NSPCC *Inspector's Directory*, 1910, pp. 42–3)

This passage had been inserted since the 1904 edition of the *Directory*. Such a coalescence of anxieties around dirt, boundaries and pollution was highly significant in the context of the wider social and political concerns about the performance of the economy, the fitness of the race, social defence and the globalization of capitalist markets (Davin, 1978; Lash and Urry, 1987). This was a crucial period of nation-building within which the good family was defined as a clean, orderly household, with a devoted mother and housewife and hard working bread-winning family man.

As the work of Mary Douglas (1968, 1970) shows, such contamination fears and pollution beliefs articulate crucial aspects of the symbolic parallel between the body and society in the way that the body hovers ambiguously between the world of nature and moral facts. Adopting a structuralist approach derived from Durkhiem, this is to regard the body as a cultural product which cannot exist prior to our classification of it. Douglas follows Durkhiem in emphasizing the collective nature of human existence, and the centrality of questions about moral order, and how rituals dramatize that order. Her work reveals a general concern with classification schemes, and with the patterns of cultural systems that give symbols their meaning and which are reaffirmed in cultural practices. Through such processes, I will suggest that at this time dirt and its embodied corollary, smell, became the key symbol of modern child protection.

Here we have the social construction of the 'dirty', 'dysfunctional', 'neglectful', 'problem' family as the marginalized, dangerous 'Other' and a category of 'neglect' case that dominated twentieth century child protection and which continues to have a powerful presence to this day. By 1914 and after, in the region of 80–90 per cent of cases were classified annually as 'neglect', 'ill-treatment and assault' accounted for around 7–10 per cent; while less than 1 per cent of cases were classified annually as 'criminal assault' or 'immorality', the category that included sexual offences against children (NSPCC, 1914 and selected Annual Reports thereafter).

The impact of these classifications and new dynamics of child protection as an embodied social practice can be seen from a 1909 case of 'alleged neglect' of four children aged 13, 10, 3 and 1 year, which was reported by a County Court Bailiff. The Inspector visited the 'Green' family home immediately:

> The woman and two youngest children were at home, but for more than twenty minutes she refused to open the door, she simply cheeked me through the window. But, when she did open it and I went inside the hot musty and dirty stench drove me out again and I had to have the back door open too. The woman and two children were as black as tinkers.

Just like in the late-nineteenth century, every corner of the house, piece of furniture and artefact possessed by the family is described.

> The back kitchen windows [were] broken and filled up with sacking and paper in a filthy state. But, the pantry was the gem of the lot, the shelves were so thick with dirt and grease you could peel them off. Then to mend matters, she had swept the kitchen and other place up and instead of taking it up, she simply shut it up in the pantry on the floor. It must have gone on for some time by the look of the heap.

Up the stairs all thick with dirt and dust. The bedrooms were really shocking. The front room contained broken furniture, bedstead and bedding. The window was broken and then stuffed up with paper. The place could never have been swept of [sic] months perhaps years. The bedding was wet and rotten and falling to pieces and small portions littered the room. The covering consisted of dirty cast-off clothing.

And so it goes on. But, by now, the register of the description has changed. Disgust, horror and incredulity about how people lived had always been part of social worker's descriptions from the outset of the practice in the 1880s, but now it had become more personal and laced with additional fears – not only for the children, but for workers themselves. What they now feared was contamination. As the Inspector wrote:

When I got home I had caught 26 fleas. I had to have a bath and change all clothing. I even had a flea in my hair. I did not see any other class of vermin on the children.

The contamination of the worker is directly connected by him to the contaminating state of the children. Other workers were similarly appalled. The County Court Bailiff gave a statement saying he had known the family for about three years and 'The smell of the house is so disgusting that I am compelled to smoke to keep the taste out of my mouth.' According to the doctor who visited to examine the children: 'the stench was abominable and I had to ask the Inspector to try and open the window'.

In analysing such discourses, it would be pointless trying to deny the reality of the smell. What matters is what the odours and the perceived dirt mean and symbolically represent. It is through the use of sight, sound, smell, taste, touch that we literally make sense of the world. As Constance Classen (1993) points out in her cross-cultural investigation of the senses, and especially smell, a bodily threshold around intolerance of smell seems to be present in all societies, but how that threshold is drawn varies from place to place and is socially constructed (see also Classen *et al.*, 1994).

My research shows that, while prior to the end of the nineteenth century, social reformers and social workers were concerned about the unpleasant, acrid smells or poor home conditions they observed – or sniffed – these were not of themselves taken as a sign of moral failure as a parent. As I showed in Chapter 2, children were never removed from parents on the basis of neglectful home conditions alone. Invariably it was the failure of parents to reform, classically to stop drinking, which resulted in the removal of children. As Alain Corbain shows in his olfactory history of France, *The Foul and the Fragrant*, even up until the late-nineteenth century dirt could be seen as having positive qualities, as a protective resource for the poor. A cake of dirt on the baby's head protected the fontanel, for instance. The poor resisted aspects of public health reforms and sanitation measures because of a 'loyalty to filth' (Corbain, 1988).

But here in the first decades of the twentieth century, dirt and smell took on new meanings and became key reasons why children began to be removed from home and were even excluded from their communities. It is worth stepping back for a moment to trace the meanings of this transformation in practices. From its beginnings in the nineteenth century social workers have ferreted about in the most unsavoury and dangerous places in society. The investigative brief of child protection workers meant that they were at the forefront of such techniques, going into the slums to root out the evil of child cruelty. As I showed in Chapter 2, the background context was one of industrialization and the development of cities and huge public health problems. As an NSPCC Inspector wrote in 1898:

> When patrolling various slums, I discovered the four children of Thomas P.... They were all sickly, pale faced and greatly distressed in appearance.... I examined them and found their clothing swarming with monster lice, their clothing was also filthy and bloodstained. Their bodies a mass of bites and full of eruptions. The house (two rooms) [sic] was foul and filthy with dirt and the only bedding was a shakedown.

Geoffrey Pearson has elegantly charted the metaphorical flow of such nineteenth century perception in how:

> Sewage and drains were the guiding metaphors for those who depicted the deviants of the time. 'Foul wretches' and 'moral filth' lay heaped in 'stagnant pools' about the streets. When they moved they were seen to 'ooze' in a great tide... their houses were depicted as cess-pits. (Pearson, 1975, p. 161)

Pearson is exceptional for his concern to place social work in a context of the space and time of modernity. He shows to great effect how the metaphor of the sewer 'speaks to the nineteenth century about its dangerous moral and material condition'. He is referring to how the prosperous classes grew to fear the emergence of large communities of slum dwelling poor, at a time when the organized labour movement began, regarding the respectable worker as indistinguishable from the 'mob'. The sewer and management of human excrement were central metaphors of the Victorian age, speaking to the fears of contagion of respectable labour by the under-class 'residuum'. The metaphor of the sewer, Pearson argues, arises in the context of the 'creation of a stable working population within the rising domination of a factory system of labour', and reflects essentially political fears and questions involving 'the crucial task of training urban man [sic] to be orderly in his habits' (Pearson, 1975, pp. 165, 176). While valuable, this characterization stands in need of development and revision because Pearson fails to carry it through into its twentieth century forms. It is a public vision of what, by then, must be understood as deeply private, domestic practices.

The introduction of an industrial economy and systems of factory labour in the nineteenth century had seen the creation of a 'trained urban man' (Schoenwald, 1973), a disciplined individual, with a new sense of time, work habits, and also new personal habits as he learned to go on the toilet (rather than the street) – in effect a new human nature (Thompson, 1967). By the early twentieth century this disciplined working man/citizen was taken for granted as a new social order had been created. In the process, the focus of social intervention shifted from men to women, or more accurately, to mothers and children and involved a literal shift of focus from the public to private domain. As the nineteenth century runs into the twentieth, the key metaphor becomes dirt, reflecting political fears and questions involving the training of women as housewives and mothers to have clean and orderly homes and children. In short, the problem of child cruelty and the threat it posed to the social body had been *domesticated*. It was now firmly behind closed doors and the key encounters in social work and child protection took place in the home, which had gained a kind of sacred status in the symbolic ordering of everyday life. The metaphor of dirt and obsession with smell speaks to the twentieth and twenty-first century about its fears of contamination by the underclass of excluded 'problem families' and the individualized 'Other'.

In modernity, then, the smell comes to represent something else: disease, social danger and (dis)order. By 1914, not only social workers, but doctors were rushing around examining suspected abused and neglected children in their homes. Foucault has described the examination as the core ritual and procedure of disciplinary practices in modernity: 'in this slender technique are to be found a whole domain of knowledge, a whole type of power'. The examination is highly ritualized because 'In it are combined the ceremony of power, and the form of the experiment, the deployment of force and the establishment of truth' (Foucault, 1977, pp. 184–5). However, the literal and metaphorical power of the examination must be understood also in terms of social factors. Medicine's role in constructing the new form of child protection practice was facilitated through what Peter Wright has called 'a generative metaphor', which in this case was germ pathology. The basis of a new medicalized conception of the child and baby had been laid within the medical profession from the turn of the century, after which barriers to its adoption were cognitive rather than institutional (Wright, 1987). Something more than a reconstituted 'medical gaze' in the administrative sense was required.

Again, following the perspective of Durkheim and Douglas (1966, 1970), the extra dimension was *social*. It was supplied by germ pathology which gained cultural power as a form of explanation in a context of the wider social and political concerns about the competitiveness of the economy, the fitness of the race and social defence that I have referred to. The result was an early twentieth century culture deeply concerned about the drawing-up and maintenance of *boundaries*. It was in this context that a major preoccupation with germs and dirt and a dread of internal pollution found its way into child protection discourse. Its key symbol was the obsession with dirt and smell and redefinition of 'neglect' as an essentially *domestic* problem – 'cruelties of the street' having been eliminated, as Chapter 2 showed. In their expressions of disgust, fears of contamination and the sense that they were being overwhelmed by smells, vermin, fleas and other bugs, workers literally embodied these changing meanings.

The practical implication of this was that as practitioners went about their work, the smell of practice became central to their experience of children and families. Another way of putting this is that practice was mediated *through* the body. In the course of developing time consciousness and speed over space the construction of danger to children invariably became focused on marginal, 'dirty' families such that in their pursuit of them it was dirt and smell that first hit practitioners in the face and caught their nostrils. This sensory experience is as constitutive of practice as other influences such as the law or what is in the mind of the worker. In their fleeting encounters with people's lives practitioners assessed the well-being of children through their *own*, as well as the children's bodies. The (dis)comfort of their body was a crucial guide to how practitioners literally felt about children and families. In this the smell of practice was crucial as this was not simply a visual and aural practice. For Simmel, who pioneered a sociology of space and the senses, the sense of smell, unlike seeing and hearing which themselves form or seek out an object, 'remains trapped as it were in the human subject' (Simmel, in Frisby, 1984, p. 129). Such ostensibly trivial and ephemeral engagements were regarded by Simmel as just as significant a factor in constituting everyday perceptions as any large scale social processes. For him, the sense of smell is a particularly 'dissociating' sense which transmitted more repulsions than attractions, inspiring 'invincible disgust' (Guerer, 1993, p. 34; Frisby and Featherstone, 1997, p. 72; Urry, 2000, p. 98). The paradox of the politics of smell for social work in this formative historical phase was that it both distanced practitioners from their ('dirty') clients, yet brought them closer together into complex, meaningful engagements and relationships because of how smell evoked danger to children and the wider society. Effective child protection meant confronting the smell head-on.

This argument has two main consequences. First, I am arguing that a subtle shift occurred in the hierarchy of the senses. Visuality, literally 'supervising' and setting eyes on children and families, remained central to the ideals, the 'vision', of child protection. But in addition to the gaze, in practice smell and touch took on increased significance in the sensuous hierarchy in ways that were more important even than what professionals were prepared to hear from parents and children about their experiences. Smell in some respects organized sight. But in many respects they complemented one another. Second, smell can be taken as a useful metaphor for the contingent and unpredictable nature of child protection as a modern practice. Whatever the premeditated intention of intervention, because of how practice is experienced through the body and relationships, there can be no guaranteeing what will happen once actions are literally taken.

As Urry (2000, p. 96) suggests, 'Olfaction seems to provide a more direct and less premeditated encounter with the environment; and one that cannot be turned on and off. It provokes an unmediated sense of the surrounding environment, of proximate objects, townscapes and landscapes.' Smell, then, literally embodies the immediacy of the unknown and the uncontrollable in social intervention. It speaks to the centrality of what in the Chapter 4 I shall call, after Giddens (1991), 'fateful moments' in child protection work. In that sense, 'smell reveals the artificiality of modernity. ... The modern project to create a pure, rational order of things is undermined by the sweet smell of decomposition that continuously escapes control and regulation' (Bauman, 1993; Urry, 2000, p. 99).

The dynamics of this are exemplified by the child protection worker's experience in the Green case cited above, where he was driven out of the house by the smell, but only after having taken a considerable time to persuade the highly resistant client to let him into the home in the first place. Consequently, social practices within the context of modernity need to be understood as deeply subjective modes of lived experience:

> The essence of modernity as such is psychologism, the experiencing and interpretation of the world in terms of the reactions of our inner life and indeed our inner world, the dissolution of fixed contents in the fluid element of the soul, from which all that is substantive is filtered and whose forms are merely forms of motion. (Simmel, quoted in Frisby, 1985, p. 46)

In how they turned the laws and agency rules they embodied into practice, child protection workers were bureaucratic modernists who in their ceaseless movement had to grapple at all times with the impact of how the often disgusting, yet invariably exciting and dynamic smell of practice touched their inner life and blew hot and cold through them.

The body and the new order of child protection

A remarkable feature of such accounts is the apparent absence of direct concern for the children in the sense of what today we would regard as life-threatening injuries or conditions. Descriptions of children often suggested very poor and unpleasant living conditions and real discomfort to their bodies. Comments such as 'The children were fairly healthy but dirty and verminous' now abounded on files where children were taken into care. But judgements that this was despite an apparent absence of direct concern for the children miss the point. In their own times and spaces, such conceptions of child welfare could not have been more powerful and meaningful and while it would be easy to condemn these practices for missing what seem to us obvious links between poverty, lifestyle and child welfare, it is the underlying meanings of these social practices that need to be made explicit.

The dirt on children's bodies and in their homes symbolized the threat of germs and pollution to their well-being. Yet the underlying concern was not simply for the children's welfare per se but for the community and deep seated contamination fears that these families would infest all those with whom they had contact and bring down the moral worth of the nation itself. The removal of such children from home can be understood as a need to exclude them through what Douglas (1966) calls 'purity and pollution rituals'. Its corollary was an optimism, so prevalent from this time, about the impact of practice on families which was structured symbolically in terms of the 'de-contaminating touch' (Stallybrass and White, 1986) of social work.

The entire discourse, therefore, is not really about dirt at all, but *order*. The lives of these families represented dirt in Mary Douglas's sense of 'matter out of place'. As Douglas (1966) famously argued, shoes are dirty when they are on the table, because placing them there transgresses the boundary classification of purity and danger. As a result of consensus classifications, the associated boundaries of cultural practices come to be regarded as reflecting, as opposed to constructing, the natural order. Transgressions of that order then threaten the foundations of the 'real' world (Nettleton, 1988, p. 161). It wasn't simply that these houses and children were literally materially smelly and deviant, but that where age, ethnic and gender roles weren't played out according to social norms this rendered them (morally) dirty. When Mrs Green told the Inspector who was clearly horrified and disgusted with the home conditions that 'she could see nothing wrong at all', she added that because her husband refused to give her money for housekeeping, 'she was not going to work when she got no money'. The social worker's response was to write that 'The woman seemed to me to be a bit daft.' In 1910, such proto-feminism was simply not how 'good' mothers thought or behaved.

The broad terms on which 'good' parenting were negotiated were that men were expected to go out to work and be good providers, while women were the primary subjects of casework which was oriented to enforcing maternal responsibility. But it would be mistaken to overlook the impact that these disciplinary practices had on men and the construction of cultural meanings of competent fatherhood and masculinities. Social commentators of the time observed how industrialism had bred a type of man for whom 'the main object of his life is to be at work: that is the one absolute necessity' (Bell, 1985, p. 3). The industrial character of a particular era can stamp its identity upon the notion of masculinity and femininity (Mills, 1989, p. 37). Labouring men predominated in casework and the utilitarian ideology of child protection was such that the 'absolute necessity' was to get men to work. These discourses articulated aspects of what Bourdieu calls 'the practical philosophy of the male body as a sort of power, big and strong, with enormous, imperative, brutal needs, which is asserted in every male posture' (Bourdieu, 1986, p. 192). There was a kind of celebration of the brute power of men, which was connected to their potential labour power. To check whether or not they were squandering the family wage, information was routinely gathered from local employers on men's earnings – for which special forms were even printed – and men were helped to get jobs. In 1911, when faced with a father who had just served a prison sentence for cruelty, an Inspector 'promised him every help to get him work so far as lay in my power and do what I can for him' [CR 19113468; CR 19113652]. This included helping men without partners by providing housekeepers to care for children while they were at work [e.g. CR 19103262].

Mothers expected fathers to provide, just as men expected mothers to mother. As a mother typified it in 1912 in a case that had been known to the NSPCC for at least seven years due to the father's failure to provide and his tyrannical behaviour: 'I had Inspector _____ to him and I shielded him as he promised me to do different. But if he won't after this then I hope you will have him before the Magistrates' [CR 19123832]. Patriarchal power (quite literally) returned to visit men here in the form of the enforcing of modern ideals of respectable fatherhood. Professional men were seeking to remake male agency clients in the image of upright, good provider, masculinity they saw themselves as embodying, and female agency clients in the image of maternal domesticity that characterized working definitions of a 'good' wife and mother. Such class-gendered assumptions were the basis of the 'hope' that now lay behind the reformative ideology of child protection. As the narrative of a 1910 case typified it, 'the man is working and the case improves' [CR 19103301]. Meanwhile, mothers were expected to be good enough housekeepers, even in conditions of dire housing and poverty. As an Inspector warned a mother in 1909, 'I told the woman she was getting enough money to keep ordinary clean' [CR 19093262]. 'Keeping ordinary clean' can be taken as a defining metaphor for the notions of respectability and order that were now at the heart of definitions of child abuse and what child protection was all about.

The tragedy of modernity: the failure to protect sexually abused children in time

I have been arguing that in the first decades of the twentieth century child protection was constituted as a quintessential experience of modernity. It became a form of bureaucratic modernism in how the administrative powers it embodied developed on a transformed social and cultural space where it became a mobile, embodied experience of space and time. Thus child protection's modern character came to be constituted by the aesthetic (movement, creativity) and expressive (the psyche, emotional life and symbolic) realms, as well as by administrative powers. I have tried to show how the body and senses act both to enhance the capacities of professionals to protect children and to subvert those aims. A particular smell and/or (contamination) fear can create a distance from children and families, or bring professionals closer to the task of protection. What gets 'seen' is influenced by smell, sound, taste. Contrary to the dominant image of the static gaze located within the kinds of disciplinary institutions of incarceration described by Foucault (1977) and theoretical work influenced by him, child protection became an experience of mobility. And because its primary site of practice became the family home, its experience of space and time was and remains ephemeral, fleeting and contingent. While later in the book I shall suggest that the embodied nature of child protection has to some extent been reconfigured in late-modernity, the continued significance of the processes I have outlined here are evident throughout contemporary practice, not least in tragic cases, for instance, where children have died due to the contamination fears of workers preventing them from doing home visits and engaging with children when they do (Laming, 2003).

The politics and poetics of space and new construction of child protection that emerged from this time had contradictory implications for children at risk, on the one hand making it possible for many more children to be reached and protected in time. Yet, on the other hand, its practices were bounded in ways which limited the range of options that were open to professionals in using their discretionary powers, especially with respect to sexual offences against children. I shall conclude the chapter by arguing that the failure to recognize child sexual abuse for most of the twentieth century was a consequence of the same social and political formations surrounding social class and the body that focused attention on highly gendered notions of 'order', marginalized families and a particular definition of danger to children.

A mixture of social and administrative influences led to the definition of what ways and to what parts of children's bodies practitioners looked for signs of abuse. What Nettleton (1988) calls 'vulnerable margins' of the body in medical and social work practice were encoded in modern child protection through this process. However, the abused child's body was encoded in a selective way at this time. The genitalia and surrounding areas were not apparently regarded as vulnerable, which was of vital importance to the cultural history of the recognition of child sexual abuse, or the *absence* of such a history. Difficulties in successfully taking sexual abuse cases through the courts was due to 'the often insuperable difficulties in the way of getting corroborative evidence' (NSPCC AR, 1914, p. 33), as so much hung on the testimony of the victim 'in what is likely to be one of the most trying times of her life' (NSPCC AR, 1913, p. 21). Only rarely were cases brought before the courts on incest or indecent assault charges, and even more rarely did such prosecutions succeed. Such were the difficulties involved that recognition of child sexual offences had virtually disappeared by the time of the First World War. More accurately, a form of cultural and professional accommodation was reached with the problem.

The dynamics of this can be seen from one of the rare cases of substantiated incest to survive in the child protection archives.[1] The 'Wilsons' were NSPCC clients from 1901 through to 1909. Mrs Wilson had died in 1900 leaving Mr Wilson, a casual labourer, with four children, of whom, in 1909, two lived at home: 11-year-old 'Emily', and her 17-year-old brother. Mr Wilson had long been viewed as a neglectful parent. He had been prosecuted for neglect in September 1901, when the case was adjourned for 'Better Behaviour'. He was 'warned' about his parenting in November 1901, in September 1903, and again in October 1906, on each occasion for 'neglect'. In 1909, following an investigatory visit into a fresh complaint of alleged 'child neglect and carnal knowledge' of Emily, the Inspector considered that 'Things seem to be worse than ever now.' The complaint of neglect was thought to be well founded: 'I examined her she was filthy with head and body vermin black with dirt. The clothing were old worn out rags. ... But the child though small, is well nourished and healthy looking.' The child was found alone in the house, with an absence of food.

The two-roomed house in which the family lived had the same appeal of 'neglect', reflecting the degree to which professional judgements were now heavily based on a concern about dirt and a new conception of domestic order. The worker observed that Emily and her father shared the same bed. This led him to take up the alleged incestuous relationship by interviewing Emily, who made a full disclosure:

> I asked the little girl if she went on all right. She said, yes, 'me dada takes me to the "Grand" and to the "pictures" and "Hipperdrome" but he will not buy me any more clothes and boots and I don't like sleeping with him because he hurts me in bed'. She said he lay on his back and then set her on top of him and pushed his thing against her thing.

She said, he used to do it to my sister but she went away and then he started to do it to me. He did it on Monday night and 3 times last week. It always makes him sick and bad next morning. She says it must be that so he is going to 'knock-off' now [sic]. It makes me feel bad too and gives me stomach ache. I do not cry much I am too much out of breathe and he says if I tell anyone he will hit me and not take me to the 'Grand'. I have only told my sister and she said she would tell you (the Inspector). Did she send you. I told her yes; and that she was a good girl to tell me about it. I asked her if her brother knew and she said no. I asked her if he heard her cry and she said, she did not cry a big row. I asked her if her brother ever slept with her and she said not for a long time now. I asked if anyone else hurt her. She said her brother hits her and then she tells her father and he hits her brother. She said, she would not let anyone else do to her what her father does in bed. She would kick them and tell her father.

The case provides immediate confirmation that sexual abuse of children is not a new phenomenon. Indeed, in terms of the frequency and pattern of the incest, the use of coercion and enticements and insistence by the abuser on secrecy, the case contains evidence of what is understood today as a standard pattern to this kind of abuse (Herman and Hirschman, 1981; Finklehor, 1984; Nelson, 1987; La Fontaine, 1990; Corby, 2002). What was historically unique was the form of professional response to that victimization. In the course of the interview, Mr Wilson arrived home 'bringing a small sandwich for the girl's dinner'. The Inspector 'drew his attention to the state of the home and especially the way he and the child were sleeping'. The man 'said he could not help it and wanted to know if I could put the child into a home'. The worker responded by telling 'him it was high time she was removed from out of his control. I told him that I should report him and should see him again.'

The family had 'only been in the house two months' and the Inspector's local 'enquiries' met with resistance: 'the neighbours said they scarcely ever saw any of the family. I could find me no information, but it is a low class street, a slum.' The social class basis of child protection transcended all forms of child cruelty as attempts even to regulate incest were open to resistances and questions of social justice in the community, responses which played an important part in the disclosure and concealment of cases. It was also noted that 'the house this man lives in now is known as "murder house", a man killed his wife there some time ago'. The sense of mystery and aura that surrounded cases was now unmistakable, confirming the dominant representation of such households as outsiders who lived on the margins and beyond the boundaries of sociability and normality.

It would be mistaken to characterize child protection in its relationship to these working class communities as only about resistance. Often these marginal households disgusted their neighbours as much as they did welfare professionals, which meant that child protection often worked within consensus norms within communities. Yet patterns of resistance and reciprocity were themselves highly contingent as social workers could never be sure what kind of reaction they would get on a case-by-case basis.

At the Inspector's request, Emily was then medically examined at home by a General Practitioner, who wrote in his report:

> I found a slight soreness of the external genitals and that the hymen was absent but otherwise there were no marks of violence. There were no lacerations at the entry to the vagina nor was the passage dilated as one would have expected if complete connection had taken place. I am therefore unable from my examination to confirm the child's story.

The doctor was far more certain about the neglect charge for which he wrote a separate certificate and concluded: 'The condition described is such as to cause the child unnecessary suffering and if continued will undoubtedly cause a permanent injury to her health.' Emily was removed to a Place of Safety and Wilson was convicted of neglect under the 1908 Children Act. His case was separately considered for charges under the provisions of the Punishment of Incest Act 1908, but the Director of Public Prosecutions to whom it was necessary procedurally to submit all such cases for consideration advised that they should not press the incest charge (on the background to this clause and the Act, see Bailey and Blackburn, 1979; Bell, 1993).

If convicted of incest, Wilson could have been sentenced to between three and seven years in prison. As it was, he was convicted of neglect and sentenced to two months imprisonment with Hard Labour. This was the outcome despite the fact that the practitioners appeared to believe the child's story. 'It looks as though we shall not be able to charge the man with "criminal assault"', the Inspector wrote, 'but it is mine and the doctor's belief that the man is doing to her all she says he is'. This should not be taken as evidence that all children who disclosed sexual abuse to professionals were believed. But as Linda Gordon (1989) has argued, despite the fact that the sexual abuse of children has barely been recognized historically, a straightforward 'denial' model underplays the subtlety and complexity at work in how such cases were regulated. American social workers in Gordon's study did not so much disbelieve children, as re-categorize their disclosures of incest. Sexually abused children, she argues, were labelled as sex delinquents and this was partly due to workers' perceptions of the morally contaminating effects of the sexual victimization itself:

> Sexuality in children was an aspect of ruin, a sign that they had been assaulted. Insistence on the sexual innocence of children was parallel to an overall view of children as pure, passive, and malleable. False accusations were not assumed to be fantasies, but deliberate lies of girls made promiscuous and 'hardened' through ill use. (Gordon, 1989, p. 217)

Similarly, I would argue that the 'denial' of incest must be explored at the level of the formation of administrative powers to protect children and their constitution as cultural practices. The workers' pessimism in the Wilson case probably had much to do with a lack of faith in the administrative system through which the state now processed incest cases. In relation to no other form of cruelty offence was it necessary to defer to the DPP's office for a decision on case-management. The NSPCC had complete control over its actions in all other types of cases. This meant that child protection workers could exercise less influence in incest cases because they were filtered through another level of administration, a factor which played a key part in professional accommodation to child sexual abuse.

The administration of the problem of incest was, however, only part of the issue, as procedures were themselves constituted in a climate of ambivalence and denial that men sexually abused children. A reluctance to name the problem was apparent within public discourse. Newspaper representations of Wilson's trial are instructive here. Under the banner headline 'HIS MOTHERLESS CHILD', the local press reported that, 'The little girl was starved, ragged, and in a bad state of neglect, and begged the [NSPCC] officer to take her away from her father against whom she made serious allegations, which were being investigated.' While the neglect conditions, to which Wilson pleaded guilty, became common public knowledge, the incest was mentioned in only the most oblique terms, and not named at all. As the NSPCC rightly recognized: 'Publicity given to facts' in sexual abuse cases had 'another advantage. There is less danger that offences of this nature will be hushed up' (NSPCC AR, 1914, p. 32).

At the level of practice, the medical signs of sexual abuse were not deemed sufficient to bring the case within the law. Legal and medical definitions of incest limited the scope of recognition of abuse to penetrative sexual intercourse, thus organizing out of official classifications a wide range of non-penetrative behaviours which contemporary studies suggest are the most common forms of sexual victimization (Finkelhor, 1984; La Fontaine, 1990; McGee *et al.*, 2002). The suspicion, or knowledge, of incest played a part in framing the decision to protect Emily ultimately from neglect. Although I have no way of knowing the extent to which sex offending may have been a hidden reality in casework, in accommodating to it professionals may well have resolved to protect some such children through neglect charges in the knowledge that these cases were relatively easy to get through the courts. In any event, a combination of legal and administrative processes, the logic of medical and social work practice, cultural attitudes and constructions of the body conjoined to restrict sexually abused children's apparent sexual victimization being categorized and acted upon *as sexual victimization.*

Emily never returned home as the NSPCC applied to the courts and parental rights were ceased. Parental custody was terminated only after welfare workers went to great lengths over the years to try and keep the household together. Children's Homes records show that the Wilson children experienced two previous admissions to the Cottage Homes. They spent 17 days in care in 1903, and another period of 17 days in 1904, both while their father was in prison for non-child care related offences. On both occasions he took the children out of the Homes on his release from prison. It wasn't just that the state did not want custody of these children, but that they had different strategies in mind with respect to (changing) their carers. There was something in the very solid class-gendered character of social regulation which now mitigated against sexual offences against children being 'seen' in practice. Because child protection so optimistically sought the moral reformation of parents, it seemed to induce in practitioners and in popular culture an incapacity to regard the sexual violation of children by men as possible. Practitioners were too busy looking for signs of irresponsible fatherhood in men's fulfilment of their public duties to look for the more private signs of evidence of sexual victimization of children.

The meanings of sexual offences against children and their regulation were not constant. Just, as Chapter 2 showed, social regulation helped to change the very character of the public domain through the demise of 'cruelties of the street', so too did the meaning of 'immorality' cases change. The problem was domesticated as a result of the transformation in co-existence and the formation of the home as a sacred family space that occurred across this period. Ordinary citizens acquired a practical sense for what it was possible and desirable to report and be reported for in child protection. Crucially, children were now entrapped within a hierarchical model of relations with parents and other adults which denied them the kinds of authentic rights to be heard and believed which are essential to true child protection. Cultural norms and perceptions of family life and privacy were shaped in a way that made the concealment of sexual offences all the more possible. While the domestication of child cruelty and construction of a mobile, embodied child protection led to so many neglected and, to a lesser extent, physically abused children being protected, it is a tragic irony of this history that at the same time that the power to protect children in time was constituted as a cultural practice, the sexually abused child virtually disappeared as a subject to whom that power was applied.

4
From Day-to-Day Quietly and Without Fuss: Child Protection, Simple Modernity and the Repression of Knowledge of Child Death, 1914–70

By 1914, the foundations were laid of the very notion that through forms of social intervention children could and should be protected in time. Here, it is argued, are the cultural roots of modern child protection and of an ideal and practice which carries so much in Western culture. In this chapter I will focus on the continuities in the 'modern' forms of child protection after 1914 and how critical issues like child deaths were managed up to the upheavals that began in the 1970s. Once again, I shall use actual developments in the nature of and responses to child abuse as the basis for developing conceptual thinking and theorizing protection practices. If relatively little has been written about child maltreatment and child protection in the period up to 1914, virtually nothing is known of these cultural practices in the inter-war years and up to the 1970s. In an afterword to his *Child Abuse and Moral Reform in England 1870–1908*, Behlmer wrote that 'there remains to be explained the curious decline in public interest in child abuse between 1914 and the early 1960s' (1982, p. 225). Wolff argues that 'If child abuse came out' in the late nineteenth century, 'it was soon buried and forgotten again'. For Wolff, the true and lasting 'discovery' of child abuse was made by Henry Kempe in the 1960s with the recognition of 'the Battered Child Syndrome' (Wolff, 1988, pp. 61–5).

Developments since the 1960s have indeed had a very significant impact on child protection policy and practice. It is necessary, however, to situate and rethink these post-1960s developments in the context of a broader historical and sociological framework, which this book is attempting to do through linking child protection to the concept and consequences of modernity. Within this, we need to think of two 'modernities' (Beck, 1992): the period of 'simple modernity' which ran from around 1914–70, on which I shall focus in this chapter, and our current phase of 'reflexive modernity', which came after. What commentators have taken for the 'disappearance' of public interest in child maltreatment was really the symptom of more complex sociological processes. Far from constituting a break with the past, the more hidden character of child protection after 1914 was a direct *effect* of the forms of social organization that characterized welfare practices in conditions of simple modernity. It reflected the impact of the process of 'sequestration' (Giddens, 1991), which refers to the structured concealment of potentially troublesome information which threatens the trustworthiness of expert systems, especially with regard to welfare practices which have at their core a concern with child life and death.

While now having a fundamental scientific basis, such practices still carried deep symbolic resonances. In fact, far from being in any simple sense displaced by the rationality of science, I want to suggest that the influence of the aesthetic and expressive dimensions of child protection actually *increased* during the era of simple modernity. Science and symbolism, reason and emotion, coexisted in what must be understood as a multilayered social practice. The most vivid expression of this was a hardening of the meaning given to smell, dirt and disorder in decisions about parental deviance and children's well-being, an order of meanings which could have cruelly disastrous implications for children and the legacy of which we continue to grapple with to this day.

The sequestration of child death and protection

By the inter-war years, the numbers of cases handled by child protection agencies was some 10–20 per cent lower than just before the First World War. In the United Kingdom and Ireland this still amounted to some 40–50 000 cases per annum. However, the marginally lower rates of *cases* should not be taken as a sign of a relative decline in public interest in child cruelty, as, in terms of case-*work*, child protection agencies were in fact much *busier* after 1914. This paradox can be accounted for by the changed nature of child protection practices. As Foucault (1977, p. 186) writes: 'The old form of inspection, irregular and rapid, was transformed into a regular observation that placed the patient in a situation of almost perpetual observation.' The routines of child protection demanded more time and effort in casework: 'Satisfaction in these cases is not always obtained quickly, and many visits of supervision are frequently necessary to secure permanence of the improvements effected' (STAR, 1938, p. 4). As well as intensive home-visiting, from the mid-1930s, a new category of 'misc. visits of enquiry' reflected the much higher levels of work that was demanded with respect to inter-agency coordination. The disciplines of medicine, social work, the police and the courts now made up the institutional framework for child protection, but the range of professionals soon expanded. In 1917, for example, a Police Surgeon entered child protection for the first time [CR 19174571]. Local inspectors were also doing increasing amounts of work for other Branches so as to patrol mobile families within national boundaries.

What had changed after 1914 was not 'public interest' in child maltreatment, but the *public visibility* of all the professional work that now constituted child protection. As I have shown, until the early 1900s there was an ease in child protector's representations of their work, which suggested that the objectives and practices of preventing cruelty to children were well understood and integrated into local communities. By the 1920s and 1930s this certainty that the public had such a well developed knowledgeability of the practice had gone and in its place was a problem of representation in making people aware of the routine practices of child protection which were 'going on from day-to-day so quietly and without fuss' (STAR, 1924, p. 2). As one branch remarked in 1935: 'The work of the Society is carried out with a minimum of publicity and in a report such as this it is impossible to explain exactly what this quiet, effective ministration has meant to the community' (HDAR, 1935, p. 3).

The consolidation of the pre-war trend of low prosecutions was a factor in this as press reports of court cases had always been an important source of public disclosure of child cruelty and protection work. But rather than being the cause of the reduced visibility of child protection, a low prosecution rate and system of home visiting is best seen as an effect of a new order of practices which rendered highly spectacular, punitive and visible forms of social regulation unworkable. The paradox was that, while the numbers of penal and welfare organizations now involved in the work of child protection were such that its penetration into the local community increased, its visibility decreased. This was, in part, a product of what Foucault has called 'an inversion of visibility' in modern penal-welfare practices:

> Disciplinary power ... is exercised through its invisibility; at the same time as it imposes on those whom it subjects a principle of compulsory

visibility. In discipline, it is the subjects who have to be seen. (Foucault, 1977, p. 189)

Giddens makes a number of important and in many ways more subtle observations than Foucault about the discrete nature of social regulation in modernity. This phenomena, which he refers to as 'sequestration', relates to 'forms of structured concealment which separate from view a range of persons who in some way deviate from the normal run of activities in day-to-day life' (Giddens, 1987, pp. 14–15). He argues that while the total institution is an extreme form of structured concealment, it is but one form of a more general process of sequestration which extends into the mundane routines of the management of an ontologically secure self in everyday life. Processes of sequestration have the effect of removing basic aspects of life experience, and especially moral crises connected with madness, criminality, sickness and death, sexuality and nature from the regularities of day-to-day life (Giddens, 1991, p. 156).

Some forms of sequestration are directly organizational, such as the medical hospital and the mental asylum. Others depend more on the *institutional repression* of potentially troublesome information connected with the management of existential dilemmas such as birth and death, which are hidden from the run of everyday life. The problems and tensions experienced by the child protectors in making their work public were a product of the logic of modern sequestration and a particular relationship that had developed between risk, trust, self-identity and expert systems. Here, I am arguing, lies something of an explanation for what the form of 'this quiet, effective ministration has meant to the community', and the so called 'curious decline in public interest' in child protection.

A defining example of the process of sequestration in child protection discourse was the institutional repression of information about the deaths of children in casework. Rates of children who died in NSPCC casework continued to be classified and presented annually for public consumption until the 1930s (see Table 4.1), although the rhetorical use of such child death statistics that typified the pre-1914 period continued only in a modified form thereafter. For example, in Dublin in 1921 it was revealed that 'sixteen children died while their cases were under enquiry' (Dublin and District NSPCC Annual Report, 1921, p. 9), while in Wexford in the South-East of Ireland, out of a total of 436 children involved in new cases in 1922, '10 children died whilst their cases were under enquiry' (Wexford and District NSPCC, 1922, p. 6). By the

Table 4.1 NSPCC cases ending in the death of children, 1915–36

Year	Total cases	No. of children affected	Cases ended in death
1915	49 046	143 025	951
1916	44 051	133 796	862
1917	42 835	129 089	806
1918	38 422	112 024	715
1919	34 397	96 854	832
1920	36 780	98 624	568
1921	38 174	101 085	533
1922	36 027	92 364	531
1923	38 027	95 627	494
1924	39 430	98 023	440
1925	38 559	95 512	442
1926	38 959	95 906	406
1927	38 005	92 949	349
1928	39 774	98 158	308
1929	40 541	100 958	400
1930	43 048	107 172	334
1931	42 601	105 873	347
1932	43 246	106 046	261
1933	43 521	106 382	327
1934	44 356	108 918	327
1935	44 886	109 471	264
1936	45 658	113 034	277
Totals	**900 343**	**2 340 890**	**10 774**

Source: NSPCC AR, 1936, pp. 34–5.

mid-1930s, the number of cases involving death had fallen to 0.25 per cent of all children involved in casework. Given the relative decline in the quantity of such cases, the deaths of children had a far more limited presence in actual casework compared to the pre-1914 period.

The mode of representation of practice had changed and the issue gradually went out of sight through the 1920s and 1930s. Underlying these developments a different trend emerges. As I have already shown, prior to 1914, in a context of extremely high infant mortality rates, child protection agencies came into contact with many children who were dying anyway. As the work developed and more cases were opened, ironically, the greater number of children were dying in child protection. By the 1920s and 1930s, however, the more involvement professionals had with reported cases, the *fewer* children died. This served to strengthen further the faith of expert systems in their ability to assess risk and in the transformative capacity of social intervention to protect children in time.

On the evidence of case files, it can, with certain reservations, be argued that the deaths of children might well have been greater but for interventions. In 1936, for example, an Inspector protected a six week old baby girl from parental neglect and almost certain death.[1] The police had referred the case as suspected ill-treatment of the other child in the family, a boy aged 16 months. But the Inspector found 'no evidence of this ... although the man admits he tapped him'. The Inspector's attention quickly turned to the baby girl, about whom he wrote:

> The baby is just six weeks old. She is in a wretched condition. Her little legs are no thicker than a mans finger. Her little arms are of the same thickness. Her little body when unclothed was merely skin and bone. The bones seemed as if coming through her skin. The inside of her legs was red and scaly. In appearance this child seemed to me to be wasting away.
>
> She weighed just five pounds with clothing this date. When born she was a normally healthy baby. It can thus be seen she is not making any reasonable progress. On the contrary she gradually seems to go back.

The Inspector immediately summoned a doctor to the house and he 'very willingly' made a joint home visit. The doctor was 'very much perturbed about the baby's condition'. His examination suggested that 'if something was not done for the baby it was [the doctor's] considered opinion she would die'. The doctor recommended the removal of the child, writing in his report that 'Unless the child is placed under skilled and proper care without delay she will certainly waste away in a very short time.' The Inspector 'acted on the doctor's advice' and immediately removed both children to a place of safety. He felt optimistic, having 'no doubt [that] the skilled care of the institution will bring a good change in the health of and condition generally of this baby'.

Within two weeks, on visiting the children in care, the Inspector felt that they 'looked very well. In fact it is difficult to believe they are the same two children as were removed.' The children continued to thrive during the four months they were in care, after which they were returned to their parents following a hearing in the Juvenile Court. The NSPCC's view was that the 'whole atmosphere of this case seems to point to the unsuitability of these parents to have the care of children'. The children's mother did not visit them once during their time in care.

Their father disowned all responsibility for them, and there was evidence that he was violent to his wife. But against all the better judgements of the Society, the police and medical practitioners, the Magistrates refused to give custody of the children to the authorities. This was largely due to the Courtroom view of an Official from the Poor Law Guardians Office that the children should not be at the charge of the ratepayers. There is no further record on the file of what became of the children after they were returned home [CR 19356669].

Although there was a discernible pattern to the basis of child removals as I shall show later, the ultimate decision of the court in this case demonstrates again the contingencies involved in whether or not children were removed from parental custody. The case also shows clearly the extent of professional faith in the transformative capacity of child protection interventions, in the expertise – 'skilled care' – that now existed to promote child survival. To at least some extent agencies handled fewer cases of child death by the inter-war years because they, in collaboration with other professionals, *were* effectively protecting (most) children in time. However, the 'success' of child protection interventions must be seen in the context of important demographic changes that were occurring around this time, such as the decline in infant mortality rates. Due to public health reforms and improved child care and living standards generally, child health improved significantly and fewer children were dying from *all* causes (Lewis, 1980; Crowther, 1988, p. 67). A similar pattern of decline is in evidence in infant mortality rates to the decline in rates of death in child abuse cases. In the first decade of this century, the risks to life were such that new born infants 'stepped into a minefield' (Urquhart and Heilmann, 1984). In 1907, an estimated one in seven infants died in the first year of life, as compared with one in 67 by 1977 (Giddens, 1991, p. 115).

Crucially, from the 1930s child protection work largely involved children who were *living anyway*. These trends suggest that, historically, child protection interventions have been most effective in preventing death the higher general standards of child health have been. At a fundamental level of policy formation, the ability of professionals to protect children is deeply connected to the quality of social provision which promotes healthy childhoods generally. Ultimately, however, professionals could not reasonably be expected to protect all children from dying, and case histories show just how fine the margins of doing so have always been. Yet the optimism and sheer faith of professionals in the instrumental value of 'skilled care' and expertise in helping children to survive now implied otherwise. Through social intervention, children not only could but, it was held, *should* be protected in time.

Four inter-related processes can be identified which shaped this professional outlook. First, it was a direct product of the increased scope of administrative powers, mobility and new mentalité and time-consciousness of child protection discussed in earlier chapters. The meanings of the new penetrative expectations surrounding child protection often found expression, paradoxically, in situations where supervising families was problematic, such as when professionals complained of 'losing sight' of households who had managed to escape their net, only to be discovered by social workers in other branches [CR 19133954]. That nomadic families could now be picked up by a nation-wide network of authorities was a mark both of their marginality, vulnerability to being spotted and of the sheer scope and power of child protection after 1914.

Second, and linked to this, is the internally referential character of systems of knowledge and power in conditions of modernity (Giddens, 1991). The child protection system had become an internally referential one in that externalities to do with nature were excluded from its discourses. The range of social factors which contributed to the promotion of healthier childhoods and reduction in the death rate became absorbed within the discourse of child protection and appropriated as a product of its effectiveness. This hardened further the professional belief in the technical capacity of face-to-face professional interventions to keep children alive. Hereafter, the practical management of life and death for abused children would be considered solely with reference to the internal codes of the child protection discourse itself and various 'system principles' (Giddens, 1991). Externalities related to wider social conditions – such as poverty and other forms of social exclusion – were now routinely bracketed out – even though, as I have suggested, those conditions impacted greatly on the ability of professionals to help children survive. Effective child protection became associated with such things as the timing of referral information, communication between professionals and various issues of skill at risk assessment, confronting parents and so on.

Third, the importance of professionals being seen to effectively protect children both contributed to and drew sustenance from changes in the ideology of childhood and social value of children. The enormous loss of life sustained in the First World War had a profound effect on social policy and on the meaning of life in post-war culture (Cannadine, 1981). After the First World War, the NSPCC broadened its conception of the issue of child survival by explicitly connecting it with discourse on the general social problem of infant mortality and the 'waste of child life'. In 1919, the society produced a pamphlet entitled 'How much is a Baby's Life Worth?' in which it linked the objective of the prevention of cruelty to children to the re-evaluation of human life and desire in the wake of the Great War to preserve infant life (Parr, 1919).

An answer to this question concerning the 'value' of children can be found in the work of Zelizer (1985) who describes the profound transformation that occurred in the social value of children across the twentieth century. This arose from the introduction of child labour laws and compulsory schooling which transformed the wage-earning 'non-child' of the nineteenth century labouring poor into the category of the economically worthless child scholar. By the 1930s children had gained a new sentimental value – while they were now economically 'useless', they were emotionally 'priceless'. The defining characteristics of 'the child' today – parental dependence, economic and sexual inactivity, and absence of legal and political rights were largely born here (Cooter, 1992). Professionals contributed to, and drew from, the 'sacrilization' of childhood, which changed thresholds of tolerance of child death in society generally. In the process, 'the death of all children – rich and poor – emerged as an intolerable social loss' and was 'transformed into a public campaign for the preservation of child life' (Zelizer, 1985, p. 27). Avoidable child death became publicly unacceptable and helped constitute the ideology that children should be prevented from dying through child protection interventions.

Fourth, and closely linked, were changes in the meaning and management of death in society generally. The relationship between death, culture and welfare practice is a complex and fascinating one (Gorer, 1965; Whaley, 1981; Richardson, 1988; Walter, 1991; Searle, 1998). Aries (1974) has shown that by the middle of the twentieth century Western attitudes toward death had reached the culmination of a dramatic process of historical transformation. From being a relatively open and well accepted part of life from the middle ages up to the first half of the twentieth century, 'Death, so omnipresent in the past that it was familiar, would be defaced, would disappear. It would become shameful and forbidden' (Aries, 1974, p. 85; see also, Elias, 1985). In the acceleration of this process, particular importance has been placed on the medicalization of death and the physical phenomenon of the displacement of the site of death which occurred between 1930 and 1950. 'One no longer died in the bosom of one's family, but in the hospital, alone' (Aries, pp. 87–8). The process of protecting children helped to accelerate this shift. By the First World War in cases of a life and death nature, children were removed to hospitals which were now formally designated as places of safety (NSPCC *Inspector's Directory*, 1904, 1910, 1914). They lived or died in those institutions. No longer, as a rule, did they die at home. In this respect again, the medicalization of child life and death played an important role in the construction of meanings in child protection in the decades *before* Kempe's work in the 1960s (Kempe *et al.*, 1962). Indeed, it is here in the first half of the 20th century that we find the cultural conditions of possibility which made Kempe's work and subsequent disclosures about child deaths so powerful, exerting an influence on cultural practices surrounding child life and death which – as the Climbié and all other scandal cases show – remains significant to this day.

Public visibility and use of knowledge about the deaths of children in child protection cases changed at the time when the site of practice with the problem shifted. At around the same time as the professional ideology of child protection was consolidated, the deaths of children in cases became hidden and disappeared from public view. Through the 1920s and into the 1930s the problem gradually went out of sight. The 1936 NSPCC Annual Report was the last year in which a category of 'cases ended in death' was given in annual breakdowns of the Society's work and the subject ceased to be mentioned in any form by the Society. Its disappearance corresponds to the changing management of death and relative historical demise of the public visibility and acceptability of death in general, and the deaths of children in particular.

One administrative factor was that in 1936 the NSPCC changed the way in which it tabulated its annual figures for past and present. From a system in which figures were given on every year of practice since the Society began, a more summary format was adopted. There were perhaps now too many years' work to list consecutively on tables. Yet in subsequent reports no other categories were omitted beside 'cases ended in death'. One possible explanation for this lies in the fact that the numbers of children who died in cases could have become so limited an aspect of practice that it lost its significance. It might even be argued that information on the deaths of children in child protection cases disappeared from view because the problem had been 'solved' – that such children had simply ceased to die. However, any claim to this effect was conspicuously absent from NSPCC discourse. Had children ceased to die in child protection we can reasonably expect that child welfare organizations would have made a great deal of the fact in rhetorical claims for the benefits of their practice. The way in which casework practice with the death of children went out of sight reflected changes in the management of information concerning child protection and child death, rather than the fact that children no longer died. In the context of changing cultural meanings surrounding child death this relative statistical decline had the effect of *increasing* the symbolic significance of the deaths of children in casework and accentuating the process of sequestration of child protection.

This pattern is characteristic of the way existentially troublesome information is managed by welfare organizations in modernity (Mellor and Shilling, 1993). Knowledge about the deaths of children in child abuse cases was sequestered in a directly organizational way as those children who died became hidden within the walls of the medical hospital. Such knowledge was also institutionally repressed in that the NSPCC ceased to make data or statements about the subject available in the public domain. The combination of the four processes outlined above hardened expert belief in the technical effectiveness of child protection resulting in the structured concealment and institutional repression of knowledge about the deaths of children in cases. By the late 1930s knowledge concerning 'failures' to protect the emotionally 'priceless' child were no longer made public, in a context in which a new sensitivity had entered the field of welfare practice in the management of death generally. The NSPCC stopped making claims about the effectiveness of its work in terms of a discourse around child death. The faith in technical expertise that held that it was possible to protect children in time now expressed itself in every way other than references to death which, while still having a presence in practice, had become shameful and hidden in professional discourses.

Knowledge of such deaths now threatened people's sense of what Giddens (1984, 1991), after Laing, calls 'ontological security': their routine sense of 'being' emotionally in a secure, manageable world. Death went out of sight in order to promote public trust and feelings of security in child protection and to repress people's worst social fears about families and violence. From here on in welfare organizations such as social work performed a vital function as 'containers' for social anxiety. Understanding such organizations would hereafter depend to some extent on the psycho-dynamics of how they defended themselves against such anxiety (Menzies, 1958; Hinshelwood and Skogstad, 2000) in carrying the increasingly heavy 'symbolic load' (Douglas, 1970) of child protection.

Child protection and fateful moments

By now, the slippery, uncertain nature of child protection was such that it was constituted in terms of what, after Giddens, I will call 'fateful moments': 'Fateful moments are times when events come together in such a way that an individual stands, as it were, at a crossroads in his [sic] existence; or where an individual learns of information with fateful consequences' (Giddens, 1991, p. 113). Such moments include the decision to get married, to separate and part, taking examinations, giving up one job in favour of another, hearing the result of a medical test, winning the lottery, or losing a big sum of money on a bet. Child protection interventions potentially have fateful consequences which extend to children being taken into care or the death of children. Thus the very act of becoming a subject of intervention itself is a fateful moment, as is the act of intervening. This is exemplified by how the little girl in the above case example whose life was saved was not even the initial subject of the referral, the worker only finding her in this neglected state after he had checked out the well-being of her older sibling. She could easily have been missed, especially as she was not even the named subject of concern in the case.

Such fateful moments capture the contingent, fortuitous and fleeting dimension to these practices that were now at the heart of modern child protection work. Despite all the powers, optimism, scientific knowledge and technology at their disposal, effective child protection ultimately depended on fateful encounters on client's doorsteps, in their homes, reactions to smells, sights, sounds; on the dynamics of encounters between parents, children and agency workers. Fateful moments cut both ways. What we always hear about today are those children who, despite being the known subjects of concern, are fatefully missed in the sense of not being fully seen, engaged with or seen at all, and end up dying or suffering for much longer than might have been the case. But many children about whom there was no particular expression of concern are discovered by professionals in fateful ways.

The contingency of these practices is such that the entire enterprise of child protection needs to be understood in terms of fateful moments. This is important because it gets us away from the kind of objectified, 'solid' thinking which characterizes the rationalist approach to understanding child protection and which vastly oversimplifies the entire endeavour. While inter-agency procedures and organizational issues are central to child protection, ultimately it is the dynamics of interactions between parents, children and workers – the smell of practice and how it is managed – that is crucial. The notion of fateful moments allows for child protection as a phenomenological enterprise to be understood and theorized, especially in terms of how all those solid laws and procedures and professional belief systems are prone to melt into air, with ambiguous and frequently unanticipated consequences.

Child protection, trust and ontological security

With the creation of the welfare state after 1945, child protection was now part of an expert system which was concerned generally with child welfare. The pervasiveness of modern institutions was now such that no one could escape their impact or the power of expertise in the management of day-to-day life. Child protection now operated in tandem with an evolving child welfare system of provisions that transformed parental capacities to keep children alive; child health provision which further helped to institutionalize cultural expectations of child survival. From its origins to the present, the welfare state has been concerned with the management of risk, as efforts at risk management is a basic part of what 'government' in general has become. The welfare state implicitly acknowledged that childhood adversity was no longer simply an event in nature, something that just 'happened'. 'The rise of the concept of social insurance reflected not so much novel perceptions of social injustice as the ascendancy of the idea that social and economic life can be *humanly controlled*' (Giddens, 1994a, p. 137, original emphasis).

Because of the deep, but generalized nature of the affective involvement of lay people in everyday modern life and their structured dependence on expert systems, the sequestration of child protection became essential to the sustaining of manageable routines and the maintenance of optimum levels of trust in expertise and feelings of ontological security. The child protectors were highly successful in promoting a trustworthy form of practice. The true sign of this and of 'public interest' in child maltreatment was referral practices. From the 1930s the general public reporting rate rose to 72 per cent, and the 'continued confidence of the public' was celebrated in terms of their 'readiness to report complaints' (MDAR, 1926). A measure of the popular respect that now existed for the technical specialism of child protection was recognized from the 1920s in a new category of 'Advice Sought' cases, which could 'scarcely be classed with ordinary "offences" ' and involved general child welfare issues.

The meanings that child protection had in local communities continued to be mixed, however. At the *face-to-face* level of practice any amount of 'fuss' was still going on, day-in and day-out. Patterns of ambivalence, resistance and reciprocity were now at the core of these cultural practices. Ambivalence was now a part of how all interventions in child protection were constituted, which had its roots in the universal forms of scepticism and fear that accompanied the foreclosure of options that came with the institutional requirement that citizens have trust in the expert system of child welfare and protection and must use for children's benefit (Bauman, 1990, p. 199). Nonetheless, as referral patterns show, lay persons in working class districts continued to take initiatives on behalf of children by calling in child protection workers to protect them. Not only did neighbours still report cases, some women and children who were victimized members of households were prepared to request help from child protection workers and draw the latter into their survival strategies. In the majority of cases that came through the general public referral route – especially those emanating from family members themselves – child removal was not on the agenda. The pattern was for mothers who invited social work intervention in support of their care and protection of children to be invested with considerable dignity by workers, their referrals being seen as a sign of their commitment to parental responsibility and self-defined child care standards.

This pattern is exemplified by a 1934 case where a 31-year-old man was convicted of the ill-treatment of his three year old step-son. The child's mother had reported the case and welcomed the punishment of her husband. The Magistrates, however, resolved not to imprison the man 'in order to save his employment', and bound him over for two years:

> there seemed some indignation amongst some men after the hearing because the man was not sent to prison. There was a visible groan of apparently disgust when the man in defending himself said the occurrence was an accident. The Mayor in sentencing this man gave a very grave warning to him. I believe he would have been sent to prison were it not for the fact he would lose his work. The Justices were in no way sympathetic towards him. [CR 19346438]

The class-gendered nature of modern child protection is clearly illustrated. The contradictory effects of regulating men according to normative criteria of hegemonic definitions of masculinity and good fatherhood were apparent in the (unmet) desire for punishment and the utilitarian consideration that he keep his job and a means to provide for the household [see also CR 19346391]. The reaction of 'disgust' also shows that child protection interventions were now symbolically deep events and matters of real seriousness which involved not just the state, but the community in matters of ultimate common concern (cf. Garland, 1990a, p. 10). As a cultural practice child protection now supported a complex pattern of regulatory and expressive effects and had a profound cultural resonance.

Within this complex pattern of expressive effects, the particular meanings attached to child protection meant that, as well as reciprocity, a whole culture of resistance had become established, a refusal to accept the definition of oneself as a client of child protection. Resistance went well beyond the fact that invariably poor parents resented such intrusion or feared the potential for loss of their children at the hands of social workers. An important source of resistance lay in continued connections between child protection and the hated Poor Law. The classic choice that parents were given up until the abolition of the Poor Law in the 1940s and 1950s was to enter the workhouse or have your children permanently removed from you. However, these stigmatizing meanings have continued to exist even with the creation of universal benefits within the welfare state. These kinds of cases strongly correlated with reports from professional sources and agency clients contested case definitions and interventions because the flow of initiative came from state experts. If anything, struggles in these kinds of cases intensified as the years passed. In the process, to be a subject of child protection came to be identified as a profoundly shameful thing, especially when it occasioned uninvited visits from social workers.

Disgust, the grotesque body and exclusionary dynamic of child protection

> But the basic pattern remains the same, dirt, disorder and a smell which defies the imagination. (Allen and Morton, 1961, p. 64)

Nowhere was the power of the cultural resonance of child protection greater than in the arena of what were defined as serious child neglect cases, usually occasioning the removal of children from parental care. Both prior to and after the creation of the post-war welfare state, refusals by parents to accept child protection constituted the main grounds for the removal of children from parental care. This invariably occurred in 'neglect' cases which were based mainly on assessments of parents' moral characters as child survival and near death situations such as those profiled above and earlier in the book were by now exceptional.

With the creation of the post-Second World War welfare state, far from abating and creating more tolerance and compassion towards marginal 'problem families', the obsessive, highly driven concern with dirt and order and exclusionary impulse of child protection actually *intensified*. It is impossible to exaggerate the symbolic power that these families had in the social order. While they were socially marginal they were symbolically central to the entire meanings of social work and child protection (on this formulation, cf. Stallybrass and White, 1986; Babcock, 1978).

The following quote from a 1951 case-file exemplifies how up to the 1970s levels of disgust were expressed more intensely than ever:

> 10/12/51. I visited at 3.55 pm. Mother did not immediately open the door, I saw her through the letter box rush upstairs apparently to see to bedroom. She kept me waiting about five minutes, then when she answered the door said she had been out the back when I first knocked. Children were dirty, [names of 2 children] are both poorly according to mother, told her to take them to the doctor. Pram was filthy. Bedroom as usual was in a disgusting state, the mattress is now urinated right through. The room littered with filth and about twenty matchsticks. The smell was overpowering.
>
> I severely WARNED [sic] mother again, in front of p/g [paternal-grand] mother, that I would give her one more chance to pull herself together, there is nothing wrong with her, just too lazy to even wash herself. I told mother that it is no wonder that the children are always poorly, and that they continue to be so while they have to sleep in such a filthy and disgusting room and bed.
>
> I told mother that she now has her last chance, if conditions are the same next time I visit I shall bring along the M.O.H. [Medical Officer of Health] and remove all the children.[2]

And this is precisely what the social worker did. The children never returned home and their mother was convicted of child neglect and sentenced to six months imprisonment. The sheer weight of judgement and sexism evident here is typical of the period and shows the extreme degree to which notions of child neglect and abuse were tied to visions of order based on social class, gender and nation. Here, the dominance of the body and 'flesh' was such that judgements as to what constituted child abuse were heavily dictated by the degree to which practitioner's stomachs turned.

An obsession with dirt and smell was not only part of the 'private' discourse of practice in case-files and agency reports, but pervaded the *public* discourse of post-war child protection. In their standard history of child abuse and protection in the United Kingdom and Ireland, *This is Your Child* (1961), Allen and Morton quote an estimate that between 6 and 7 per cent of children 'are at some time during their childhood so neglected or ill-treated' as to require protective intervention. Of these children they write:

> It is almost impossible to describe the conditions of acute neglect, filth, degradation and stench in which many of those children exist.

No descriptive writing can bring to mind the air of total disorder, the lack of warmth or comfort, or the smell of the saturated beds, unwashed people, absence of feminine hygiene, and putrefying food that add up to the truly neglected household.

Six years earlier, in 1955, in his book *The Prevention of Cruelty to Children* Leslie Housden also recognized the struggle involved in adequately representing the smell of practice, but attempted just such a description when talking about the 'hopeless home':

From such matters as these, it is easy to pass to the next criteria of the Hopeless Home. The Smell. Easy to pass to it but much more difficult to convey its character in writing. It is a curious mixture of dirt, ill-ventilation, bugs and body excretions. No one can accurately describe it. It is very slightly sweet, yet almost acrid, and invariably revolting. I cannot get used to it, yet on only one occasion have I found it quite unbearable. (Housden, 1955, pp. 172–3)

The chapter of Housden's book from which the above quotation is taken was written by Dr Robert W.L. Ward, a Medical Officer of Health, who had extensive experience of visiting such homes on the invitation of NSPCC officers. Ward lists nine 'disgusting features' of the 'Hopeless Home', although 'It would perhaps be better to say that there are nine features which impinge on one's senses. They hardly need searching for' (p. 168). The first 'is the status of the mother', who is described as either a prostitute or women with illegitimate children who are 'surrounded by the products of their faulty technique'. Next is the pantry, the actual situation of which varies: 'Sometimes food is stored in a drawer of a dresser, or a cupboard by the side of the fireplace, or, more simply is left on the table, day and night. ... If food is kept in a drawer for many months, crumbs, dried jam, crumpled margarine wrappings and mice excreta make an unsavoury mixture.' He goes on to comment on the amount of food and 'household requisites', there being 'a certain minimum below which I feel no home should go. ... There is generally *one* pan. In this is cooked everything. That is not much. In this is washed everything; nor does this add up to much. There is one dish-cloth.' And so it goes on, ranging over the lack of furniture, the beds, and 'the question of lavatories', which, it is emphasized with horror, are allegedly rarely used at all by children or parents in Hopeless Homes.

This evidence supports the argument I made in Chapter 3 in how this entire discourse is not really about dirt, but *order*. This is directly related to power relations in how the entire discourse of child protection was riddled with class (as well as gender) divisions. In relation to 'the cultural side of these Hopeless Homes. The use of that word seems a little farfetched. ... the children rarely hear sounds other than mother shouting "Clara come here or I'll knock yer bloody 'ead off' ". Their senses are rarely assailed by [anything] but the unpleasant yells, screams, clouts, stinks, fleas and filth.' Many vivid descriptions are offered of the kinds of things that are absent from such homes:

> Flowers have no place in these homes. There are no pictures except, maybe, a dusty, glass-less one of General Gordon, or of a couple of effete young creatures sitting in a most unreal garden and labelled 'Love's Young Dream'. There are no curtains, chintzes, lamp shades or carpets. There is no polish, no shine, no brass-ware, no glint of copper, no gloss of walnut, no dark satisfying surface of oak. The lidless kettle stands black and sooty on a copy of the 'green 'un' or 'pink 'un' or some other racing paper, on the cindery hearth. (Housden, 1955, pp. 182–3)

Child protection here is not just about untidiness, dirt and odour but, following Bourdieu (1986), *taste*. The orientation of such professional work constitutes a 'habitus' (Bourdieu, 1977), an embodied way of being in the world which is pervasively related to class relations and lifestyle distinctions. These service user households disgusted professionals because by the bourgeois standards of the 'respectable' classes they were uncivilized, common – judgements that are based on the minutiae of their intimate lives and routines, from the utensils they use, to how they eat, speak, sleep and use the toilet; the hobbies they follow, and so on. Such parents and children are, above all, *moral* dirt.

The discourse is utterly constituted in terms of representations of 'high' and 'low' culture, which gives a central significance to Bakhtin's (1968) contrast between notions of the 'classical body' and the 'grotesque body'. For Bakhtin, the 'classical body' denotes the inherent form of the high official culture and speaks in 'high' languages which attempt to legitimate their authority. In terms of the classical statue for instance, it was always represented on a plinth, which meant that it was elevated, static and monumental. Having been 'put on a pedestal', the viewer ('the low') is forced to gaze up at the figure and wonder. The classical statue has no openings or orifices whereas, Bakhtin observed, grotesque costume and masks emphasize the gaping mouth, the protuberant belly and buttocks, the feet and genitals. The discursive norms of the grotesque body include impurity, protuberant extension, disproportion, a focus upon gaps, orifices, symbolic filth, physical needs and pleasures of the 'lower bodily stratum' and parody. While the classical body 'rises above' and keeps its distance, the grotesque body emphasizes a subject of pleasure, a mobile, split, multiple self which is never closed off from its social context (Bakhtin, 1968).

Baktin's work has been developed to brilliant effect by Peter Stallybrass and Allon White in *The Politics and Poetics of Transgression* where, by examining the psycho-symbolic meanings of the slum, the domestic servant and the carnival in early modern and modern Europe, they map 'domains of transgression where place, body, group identity and subjectivity interconnect' (1986, p. 25). 'The "grotesque" here designates the marginal, the low and the outside from the perspective of the classical body situated as high, inside and central by virtue of its exclusions. ... [T]ransgressions of gender, territorial boundaries, sexual preference, family and group norms are transcoded into the "grotesque body" terms of excrement, pigs and arses' (Stallybrass and White, 1986, pp. 23–6). These are precisely the kinds of psycho-symbolic dynamics through which child protection clients were represented as (and through) the lowest of the 'low'. As I have already shown in this book, late-nineteenth and early twentieth century social workers and reformers routinely referred to the 'low' districts and the slum areas in which they did most of their work. Protocols of the classical body gradually came to mark out the identity of progressive rationalism itself and this explains, first, the very exclusions which created the grotesque body of child protection clients as I have traced them in this book and, second, the persistent, obsessive attacks on these marginalized people that occurred over the twentieth century. Thus we can see in the above typical descriptions of the 'hopeless home' how 'the grotesque physical body is invoked both defensively and offensively because it is not simply a powerful image but fundamentally constitutive of the categorical sets through which we live and make sense of the world' (p. 23).

There is, as Stallybrass and White argue (p. 25), 'a secular magic to these displacements, and its law is the law of exclusion'. A psychic internalization of the excluded Other occurs, who becomes part of the collective unconscious as a symbol of fear, depravity and disgust that all respectable citizens must avoid be(com)ing at all costs. 'Others' represent what is excluded to create identity as such. This shows the ambivalent nature of such exclusion insofar as it coexists with desire and fantasy. While disgusted by hopeless homes, bourgeois commentators are fascinated by them and take perverse pleasure in accounting for their every 'low' detail. Thus, while excluded, the grotesque body of child protection cases were still relentlessly focused upon – but, for most, at a safe distance of the texts of agency reports and, increasingly as the twentieth century develops, through photographs which illustrate just how disgusting such homes and families are seen – and smelled – to be (see, for instance, Allen and Morton, 1961). This all helps to explain how outsiders like child protection clients come to be invested with such powerful social meanings in that 'what is socially peripheral is often symbolically central' (Babcock, 1978, p. 32).

An intriguing feature of the habitus of child protection and these discourses around (dis)order and dirt is a certain playfulness. In describing their horror and disgust at the sheer lack of standards of these families middle-class professionals and bourgeois commentators cannot resist a kind of jokiness and game-playing with or about the families. There are remnants here of what Baktin calls the 'carnivalesque', as Bourgeois commentators mock client's apparent fondness for gambling, wrestling, bingo. But the families too are capable of active resistance. Although we must rely historically on what others such as social workers wrote about them, even this conveys a huge resistance to being told to change by a bourgeois state. Lack of 'respectable' standards did not simply reflect a lack of discipline and domestic skills but an awareness of a marginalized class position. Corbin perceptively observes how the derision directed by the poor at hygiene consciousness and the streams of abuse might be interpreted as acceptance of an allotted role in society.

> The masses, aware of the difference in thresholds of tolerance to smell, assumed the existence of this division and set out to align themselves openly against the deodourization practices. Throwing filth or its verbal equivalent became an acknowledgement of a position as much as a rejection of discipline. By throwing his excrement, the 'little man' was doing nothing more than throwing a challenge to the people who avoided contact with him, in the same way that they avoided contact with excrement; he strengthened his own excremental status by his actions and words. (Corbin, 1988, pp. 214–15)

As I shall show later in the book, this kind of 'carnivalesque' dynamic continues to infuse twenty-first-century child protection as service users continue through such struggles to demonstrate their awareness of their marginal position and to turn it onto their 'oppressors'. Dirt – throwing filth or its verbal equivalent 'in the faces' of professionals – becomes a medium for resistance, a defiant rejection of the state and all that it is insisting people do.

The implications of this for children were generally dire. Far from leading to a compassionate response, children who were removed from 'Hopeless Homes' and placed in care were systematically excluded from their communities, sent to the colonies or foreboding institutions in their own country, where they were invariably treated harshly and at its most tragic systematically abused in care. A belief in the transformative power of social intervention in individual cases was linked to a desire to purify the entire community and child protection was a key practical strategy towards this end. The essential dynamic and hope of child protection was the 'de-contaminating touch', that is moral reformation and re-inclusion of recalcitrant families into the social order and good citizenship. When this failed, intervention shifted into an exclusionary dynamic whereby children were removed from parental custody, a form of response which itself must be seen in terms of what Douglas (1966) calls 'purity and pollution rituals'. In its deep connections to class and notions of nationhood, in its own way this was a persecutory form of 'ethnic cleansing'.

Developing the discussion of constructions of childhood from Chapter 2, the children of such parents were viewed as being in moral danger because of how child welfare continued to be framed within a romaniticized (Victorian) middle-class notion of childhood 'innocence'. The child was viewed as being born innocent and it was the environment which led to corruption, which involved the child being prematurely exposed to adult knowledge. Abuse or neglect had 'polluted' and contaminated the child with 'impure' adult knowledge. But this was viewed differently for girls and boys. 'In boys, corruption began as petty thieving and led into a downward spiral of criminal activity. For girls it took the form of immorality or sexual precocity (Jackson, 2000, p. 6). Unless worked with such children would be a huge threat to future social order. Treatment was framed in terms of moral reclamation and a return to the lost state of childhood innocence. Thus the moral status of abused children was seen as dubious. Children were not worked with in terms of what they were – such as victims of adversity and/or abuse and neglect – but *what they were going to be*. They were seen as future threats to social order as much as victims. The child in danger would in time become the dangerous child. The challenge then was to catch these children early and channel them into an appropriate regime of moral rehabilitation (Mahood and Littlewood, 1994, p. 555).

No type of child at risk or abuse victim was immune from this kind of treatment. Indeed, those children who we might expect to be most in need of a different kind of response – such as sexual abuse victims – were viewed as the most 'contaminated'. As Louise Jackson has shown, while the act of sexual abuse was regarded as the most heinous crime, it was viewed as having corrupted the girl and effected her 'fall' from innocence. Within a Christian moral economy the child sexual abuse victim was given a special status as a 'fallen' girl/woman and seen as a threat as well as victim. 'The associations between delinquency, corruption and sexual knowledge had a significant impact on the treatment of the girl victim of sexual abuse' (Jackson, 2000, p. 6; see also, Mahood and Littlewood, 1994, pp. 568–9). Yet what Jackson fails to notice is that, while sexual abuse survivors did indeed have special needs, stigmatization and exclusion were the lot of all abused and neglected children, whatever form it took. Thus, the neglected child was also treated as a polluting presence. This also helps to explain why boys and girls were kept in separate spheres within institutions, or separate homes were created for them, and why they were kept apart from 'normal' children in schools. Such children were seen as a polluting presence, and a particular danger to other children, and in need of retraining and reforming. These children were the 'moral dirt' of society and other children needed to be protected from their 'contaminating' influences.

This view of childhood and the corrupting influences of family and environment also helps to explain further why child care institutions treated children in the ways that they did. Intervention approaches in institutions were based on children 'forgetting' their past abuse. This was exemplified in a 1958 physical abuse case in Ireland where the ISPCC had placed the seven year old victim in a convent institution and wrote that, 'it is to be hoped she may forget the past, under the care of the nuns' (ISPCC *Annual Report*, 1958). This seems odd to us today with so much emphasis on psychology and the importance of remembering past abuses. But for most of the twentieth century the effects of abuse on children was seen as moral damage rather than psychological trauma. Treatment was therefore seen in terms of religious conversion rather than psychotherapy (Cox, 1996).

Research suggests that within this kind of belief system helping children to 'forget' their past abuses may have actually helped some of them, but that this depended entirely on the amount of love and compassion that children were shown by individual child care workers (Jackson, 2000). In some regimes, however, such as the Irish industrial school system, 'forgetting' the past extended into systematic abuses which involved the annihilation of identity itself, such as only being known by a number, and being sent as far away as possible from one's family and community of origin (Raftery and O'Sullivan, 1999). As religious conversion was seen to be central to saving the souls of these 'impure' children, they were systematically regarded as second-class citizens, as undeserving of the kinds of love and care afforded to 'uncontaminated' non-abused children. Re-moralizing children meant returning them to 'innocence' by knocking the devil out of them. Thus what children were supposed to be helped to forget provided the context for their systematic abuse. This had disastrous implications for all abused children whose experience of being sexually as well as physically abused within such institutions was never responded to and remained hidden behind a veil of secrecy, repression and social fear. Moreover, such institutional abuse was able to go on because of the ambivalence of ordinary citizens towards the children and the powerful blame culture that surrounded such 'grotesque' families, sharing aspects of the belief that the children were undeserving and that the community as much as the children needed 'protection'.

Child protection and the legacy of simple modernity

The evidence presented in this chapter emphasizes again the importance of connecting child protection to broad social and historical processes and indulging, in the present context, in 'a tactical onslaught upon historical ignorance of the cultural history of death' (Richardson, 1989, p. xiv). The chapter has shown how under simple modernity state intervention was applied to a 'given' world of nature, people and society. A strong demarcation was fostered between experts and lay people, who nonetheless demonstrated a critical awareness of welfare practices and the state. This was evident, as I have shown, in considerable levels of ambivalence and resistance to child protection interventions. However, such reflection was part of a context in which expertise and belief in a 'science' of child protection remained largely un-interrogated at a public level. Lifestyles and intimate relationships had a similar 'solidity' as through to the 1970s, intimate relations were fixed around a clear sexual division of labour where men/fathers were providers, and women/ mothers homemakers and child protection interventions both shaped and rigorously policed these boundaries. [Hetero]sexuality was treated as fate (Giddens, 1992), with a resulting absence of a concept of intimacy as a negotiable entity or of self-identity as something that could be reflexively made by the individual.

The sequestration of child protection could also go on in a context where, relative to the reflexive social conditions of today, no one worried too much about what went on behind the scenes in terms of how they were governed. Not only could all sorts of patronage and even corruption survive, but this sometimes became the accepted way of doing things by political leaders and others in positions of authority (cf Giddens, 1994a, pp. 84, 114). Nothing exemplified this more dramatically than the (largely hidden) decisions that were routinely made to separate children from parents permanently and send them to institutions to 're-socialize' them and the lack of accountability for children once institutionalized (Bean and Melville, 1989; Raftery and O'Sullivan, 1999).

Because knowledge of such matters and of the considerable numbers of children who died in child protection cases was hidden from the public in a context where powerful scientific claims to knowledge and enlightenment were made by agencies, child protection discourse was spared the application of scientific scepticism to itself (cf. Beck, 1992, p. 155). Science remained a 'tradition' as expertise was approached as though it were akin to 'traditional authority' (Giddens, 1994b, p. 128). This enabled experts to fudge over knowledge about agency failures and any scepticism they had about the real limits to protecting children in time, while at the same time advancing the application of their results to the lay public in a highly optimistic, authoritarian fashion. Thus it was not that error did not occur in child protection. Rather, the lack of public attention to such issues such as child death was a reflection of how the treatment of mistakes and risks was socially organized in that phase (Beck, 1992, p. 159).

The plausibility of experts was, at worst, only superficially under-mined by accidents (Beck, 1995, p. 67). On the rare occasions when 'fail-ures' were publicly disclosed prior to the 1970s, errors served in fact to expand the power bloc of child care experts within the welfare state. This was evidenced in the United Kingdom, for instance, by the tragic case of Denis O'Neill, who was placed in care by the NSPCC and whose death in 1945 at the hands of his foster parents led to an inquiry which had a profound impact on the development of post-war legislation and the establishment of statutory child care social work departments (Monckton, 1945; Packman, 1981). Social work and child care experts could face a public sphere whose doubts they could sweep aside by claims of their success and promises of further liberation from the con-straints not yet understood (cf. Beck, 1992, pp. 154–5).

The process of sequestration extended into all areas of the conceal-ment and disclosure of issues related to child protection. But while the institutional repression of potentially troublesome information served to bolster the trust that lay persons had in the expert system of child protection, it also hid from view some of the deepest assumptions and tensions that lay at the heart of the entire project of protecting children in time. Even with the creation of the post-war welfare state, matters did not change much for sexually abused children as the trend of a very low incidence of incest and indecent assault cases never changed, such cases staying at well under 1 per cent of casework. The sequestration of child protection, with its attendant secrecy and careful concealment of information, played into the very dynamics which kept the problem of sexual offences hidden, compounding the entrapment of victims, both in their silence and literally in the domestic domain, and the public and professionals accommodated to the problem (Summit, 1988).

Changes in the law and shifting administrative responsibilities which came with the creation of the welfare state after 1945 meant that the Poor Law was eradicated and the duties of local authorities to provide preventative services for children 'at risk' were transformed. In the wake of these institutional developments, voluntary organizations simply could not keep pace with providing for the increasingly sophisticated technology of child welfare and protection. Consequently, the post-war years saw the relative demise of the SPCCs as agencies of child protection practice. The positioning of statutory agencies as the dominant providers of child welfare services was accelerated further by the professionalization of social work in the late-1960s and 1970s, while the further encroachment of medicine following the absorption of the work of Henry Kempe in the 1960s further expanded the scope and significance of child protection by 1970.

Although the administrative reforms that occurred with the creation of the welfare state and up until the 1970s were obviously of significance, practitioners essentially reproduced the routine practices and system of symbolic meanings that were already in place. The boundaries to practice continued to be encoded in law as well as various agency rules which centred on the body and pollution beliefs. Agency guidelines relating to the 'cleansing of hands' remained in force until the 1960s (NSPCC, *Inspectors Directory*, 1960). What has prevented us from realizing the continuities from 1914 is the ways in which socio-historical commentators have mistaken the changing *form* that the social regulation of child abuse has taken for the disappearance of the social problem. They have charted the late-nineteenth and early twentieth century beginnings and some of the transformations that constituted child protection, but have failed to register its displacements into other forms of modernist discourses and practices. Adopting a simplistic empirical approach they have asserted the elimination of all but consensual responses to child protection and the disappearance of 'public interest' in child abuse in a manner which belies the complexity of the social changes that were actually taking place. Historical commentators have treated the impact on the lifestyle of the poor of the practices of social work and welfare organizations as a process of more or less complete destruction of the ability of ordinary citizens for autonomous action. Yet this book suggests an alternative interpretation is necessary. The scale and intensity of home-visiting certainly rendered problematic the survival of an autonomous working-class culture of communal support free from shame and stigma. Nonetheless, attention to the aesthetic and expressive dimensions of these modern practices enables us to see how the powerful cultural and professional ideal that children can and should be protected in time became deeply embedded. In the process, intense resistance to intervention, as well as reciprocity, remained at the heart of child protection. Against this background, the scene is now set to engage in a detailed analysis of events and processes since the 1970s that would see the re-emergence of child death as a social issue and the (re)discovery of child sexual abuse as a social problem and lead to the protection of children in somewhat newer times.

5
Child Physical Abuse and the Return of Death Since the 1970s: Child Protection, Risk and Reflexive Modernization

While I shall now begin to show that significant changes have occurred in child protection since the 1970s, I am also arguing that the core theoretical arguments already made in this book stand the test of (late-modern) time. I have characterized child protection as a form of bureaucratic modernism in terms of how it is constituted through administrative powers deriving from the law and agency procedures, which are enacted through movement in time and space, most significantly in terms of encounters with client's homes and lives, which gives to it its ephemeral, fleeting, contingent nature. Linked to this is the centrality of fateful moments in the unfolding contingency of child protection as a practical experience. Thus the *form* that child protection takes today remains broadly the same as when constituted early in the twentieth century, in the sense of the aesthetics of its modernist routines and everyday practices: referral taking, investigation, home-visiting. The *experience* of modernity in child protection, meanwhile, continues to be one of deep engagement with psychodynamic and symbolic processes filtered through the human body, senses, the inner-life and the emotions.

Practitioners remain bureaucratic modernists, but it is a 'late-modernism' that is enacted today in an order of 'reflexive modernity'. In 'late' or 'reflexive' modernity a number of things happen which I shall document in the remainder of this book. These include transformations in the nature of 'child abuse' as child protection systems come to routinely engage with forms of childhood adversity, cruelty and suffering beyond anything that was recognized in simple modernity. The source and experience of risk also changes, in the context of transformations in the relationship between expertise and lay people. Late-modernity is a 'risk society' (Beck, 1992) in which levels of anxiety appear to have increased, both for individuals and institutions (Wilkinson, 2001).

A key paradox is that while risk anxiety and the sense of contingency in doing child protection – the 'riskiness of risk' (Giddens, 1994a) – has increased dramatically, this is not because the endeavour is in itself any riskier than it was before. On the contrary, in general terms, it has never been less risky in the sense that child protection systems are probably dealing with fewer dying children today than ever before. A key dynamic in suggesting otherwise has been the high-profile 'scandals' and inquiries into system failures to protect children from death, into overzealous intervention into child sexual abuse, and into the abuse of children in care. The result has been a radicalization of doubt about the ability of professionals to protect children in time, while at the same time opening up new opportunities for children to be protected from traditionally repressed forms of violence. In this (and the next) chapter I will also suggest that these new opportunities link to how child abuse and protection now have a distinct relationship to processes of 'individualization' (Beck and Beck-Gernshiem, 2002) and the (changing) nature of self-identity in advanced modern societies. At its best, survivors of abuse are not only helped by social work and other intervention practices to gain protection, but also to achieve healing and to plan new kinds of lives for themselves.

In this chapter I shall focus primarily on the consequences of modernity for contemporary child protection in relation to administrative power, instrumental rationality and changing concepts of risk, and shall deal with physical child abuse and death. In subsequent chapters I shall explore the (changing) parameters of child protection in terms of the two other strands of the consequences of modernity, the aesthetic and the expressive, psychosocial dimensions, with particular emphasis on child sexual abuse, emotional abuse and neglect. In practice, these different strands of child protection's modernity interrelate, as so often do different forms of child abuse. Presenting them in this way involves largely analytical distinctions which are intended to bring maximum coherence to the discussion. Making this argument requires both empirically demonstrating the shift in question and theorizing it. The aim of Chapters 5, 6, 7 and 8 is to do this conceptual work by drawing, in part, on empirical data from a study of child protection practices in Ireland. While the empirical data is drawn from that particular place, my contention is that the practices and processes it reveals are typical of Western welfare states in general in the period of late-modernity and I use it to illustrate matters of general relevance to the protection of children in new times.

The '(re-)discovery' of child abuse

With the establishment of the post-war welfare state, in key respects how the new generation of child care professionals went about their work was little different to what had gone before. What became different from the 1960s was the social context within which child protection work went on, which significantly reconstituted that work and its focus. Central to the changes under discussion was the 'discovery' of the 'battered child syndrome' in the 1960s, which increased still further expectations that professionals should protect children in time from death and avoidable suffering. The work of the American paediatrician Henry Kempe and his medical colleagues and their construction of the 'battered child syndrome' (Kempe *et al.*, 1962) is often referred to as the 'discovery' of child abuse, a characterization that is misleading as it belittles the child protection work that preceded it (Behlmer, 1982, pp. 224–5; Ferguson, 1990). There is no doubt, however, that Kempe's work helped to reorient conceptions of child abuse in social policy, practice and in popular consciousness throughout the Western world (Nelson, 1984).

Kempe and his associates had been researching the problem with the support of the American Humane Association since the late 1950s. In 1962 they coined the phrase 'the battered child syndrome' to describe their findings and they published an article of that name in the prestigious medical journal *The Journal of the American Medical Association*. The article argued that the 'syndrome' characterized a clinical condition in young children, usually under three years of age, who had received serious physical abuse, usually from a parent, and that it was a significant form of childhood disability and could lead to death. It argued that the syndrome was often misdiagnosed and that it should be considered in any child showing evidence of possible trauma or neglect, or where there was a marked discrepancy between the clinical findings and the story presented by the parents. The use of X-rays to aid diagnosis was stressed and it was argued that the prime concern of the physician was to make the correct diagnosis and to ensure that a similar event did not occur again. The article recommended that doctors report all incidents to law enforcement or child protective agencies (Nelson, 1984, pp. 12–13; Parton, 1985, p. 51; Zigler and Hall, 1989).

Kempe's paper stimulated a new awareness of the problem of the 'battered child' in the professional and lay media in the United States of America. The emotive title 'battered child syndrome' was deliberately used to provoke public interest in the problem. In a matter of a few years mandatory reporting laws had been passed in most US states whereby when abuse was suspected by professionals they were legally required to report it to designated child protection agencies. Kempe's work soon found its way round the globe. Notions of the 'battered child syndrome' reached Australia by 1965 (Thorpe, 1994, p. 14). In Britain, sections of the medical profession were central to taking up the issue in the late-1960s, the impetus coming from forensic pathologists and paediatricians. Also significant was the NSPCC Battered Child Research Unit, established in 1968, and named 'Denver House' in deference to Kempe's work and its origins in Denver Colorado. Kempe himself visited the Republic of Ireland in 1976 and addressed a conference on Non-Accidental Injury (Kempe, 1976), where by the mid-1970s, 'medicalization' was a key factor in early attempts to develop more systematic forms of case coordination in response to what was now being called 'non-accidental injury to children' (ISPCC, 1976), reflecting the first impact of these conceptualizations as requiring a multidisciplinary approach. At the same time, the women's movement made domestic and sexual violence a public issue, calling the criminal justice system and social service agencies to account (Driver and Droisen, 1989). By the 1980s, child sexual abuse, domestic violence and emotional abuse had begun to be recognized and worked with in systematic ways as child abuse in all forms and the expert systems that regulate it gained a much higher visibility (Corby, 2000).

While there are some differences in how particular nation-states and cultures handle the issue, one common outcome is that child protection is commonly constructed in terms of what, in Chapter 1, I referred to as 'scandal politics' (Lull and Hinerman, 1997): a process of investigating child protection case 'failures' in the light of new demands for state accountability in the midst of aggressive media reporting of tragic cases. While common to most places, scandal politics in child protection have proceeded at a different pace in different countries. In the United Kingdom public disclosure of deaths in child protection cases began in 1973 with the public inquiry into the Maria Colwell case (Colwell, 1974; Parton, 1985). In Ireland, while the 1980s saw some concern for child deaths, it was in 1993 that a major inquiry into system failure first took place, and this did not involve death but the failure of professionals to prevent the serious physical and sexual abuse of a child/woman which went on for 16 years, having started when she was ten (McGuinness, 1993). The 'Kilkenny Incest Case' initiated a major transformation of the Irish child protection system and in public awareness of child (sexual) abuse (Ferguson, 1994, 1996). As has been the pattern in most countries, many subsequent inquiries into system failures involving death and serious sexual and physical abuse have followed initial disclosures. With the invariably aggressive attentions of the media, public disclosures of child deaths and inquiries into system 'failures' have played a crucial symbolic role in opening out child abuse and protection services, as well as professional anxiety, to public view.

Organizationally, the common pattern across all countries has been a predominantly managerial response in an attempt to close off the gaps in practice which have contributed to system failures. The key factor came to be seen as the inter-professional *system*, due to the demonstrable need and difficulties of agencies and professionals working together and communicating effectively enough to protect children in time. This has led to the creation of new legislation and bureaucratic structures and procedures to guide the investigation and management of child abuse, including child abuse or 'At Risk' registers, case conferences, interagency management committees and key workers. These have been and continue to be administered through a series of child protection guidelines which have tended to be issued in response to the various lessons and recommendations of inquiries as they unfolded over the years.

At one and the same time, professionals and organizations were confronted with new knowledge of risks to children and with shocking public disclosures which showed that child protection systems were failing to protect children from serious abuse and death. These were shocking in their own right because of the sheer extent of trauma and violence perpetrated against children, as each scandal revealed a similar pattern of starved, neglected, physically and sometimes sexually violated children who had suffered multiple injuries to their bodies from the abuse inflicted on them. They were also shocking in the sense that they appeared to be completely new and to reflect a real decline in professional standards. This misguided sense of newness had its roots in the sequestration of child death that I have showed occurred from the 1930s, after which experts hid any knowledge about agency failures to protect children in time, while advancing their claimed successes to the lay public in a hugely optimistic, authoritarian fashion.

Through the 1940s, 1950s and 1960s, even within the professional community itself there was no acknowledgement or discussion of death which meant that professionals had secrets that they had kept even from themselves. Thus, once child deaths became a public issue (again) from the 1970s, this meant that professionals had no historical perspective or sense of a baseline against which to assess the effectiveness of their interventions and the consequences of modernity for their work. Consequently, the very notion that (all) children can and *should* be protected in time was by now taken for granted. This is not to say that the nature of child abuse was just the same as before. While there were continuities, acknowledgement that serious harm is perpetrated against vulnerable children by 'dangerous' parents and other carers involved a distinct shift in recognition compared to the order of meanings of simple modernity. Indeed, the very term 'child abuse' as a generic term to cover physical, sexual, emotional abuse and neglect, entered the vernacular of child protection at this time in the 1970s and 1980s.

Processes of changing recognition of child abuse and the development of child protection systems have taken a remarkably similar form across the Western world, with dramatic increases in the numbers of reported cases of all forms of abuse (on Australia, see Parton *et al.*, 1997; on UK, Corby, 2002; on Ireland, Ferguson, 2000; on the USA, Besharov, 1990; Lindsay, 1994). Social workers and other child protection professionals now routinely work with the deepest existential dilemmas surrounding the meaning of life, death, human cruelty, love and sexuality as these find expression in their cases. While child protection professionals have always done this, today it has reached new depths of intimacy and they have to do it in the full glare of public attention, in the sense of knowing their work can be opened out to critical analysis in public should something go seriously wrong.

This is clearly borne out by the research on which the empirical dimension of this and subsequent chapters is based, which studied 319 referrals that were reported to three statutory social work teams in the Republic of Ireland between April 1996 and July 1996 and then tracked them for 12 months into mid-1997. The research used quantitative methods to produce a 100 per cent sample of all child care and protection referrals made to the teams over the three months which were surveyed again a year later and provided for an analysis of how the system processed cases, from the referral point to long-term outcomes. Qualitative methods were also used to develop a series of case studies in order to establish the deeper meanings of practice from the perspectives of the range of professionals and service users. A sample of 32 cases were chosen for in-depth analysis, which were representative of the typical concerns illuminated by analysis of all the referrals/cases involved. Eighty-two interviews were conducted with professionals – including 18 social workers, whose narratives I draw on particularly extensively in this chapter – 14 with parents (ten mothers and four fathers) and 12 with children. An earlier publication (Ferguson and O'Reilly, 2001) was based on a research report from the project and set out the essential findings from the study. The present analysis includes data not included there and generally uses the data in a much more theoretical and analytical way in order to help meet the (different) objectives of this book. My focus here is much less on profiling the nature of child protection in Ireland as such than on how the data illustrates themes of general relevance to theorizing the nature of Western late-modern child protection.[1]

The choice of Ireland as a research site was influenced by the intensity of disclosures of system failures in the 1990s which brought every conceivable aspect of the system into question (Ferguson, 1996). This enabled the research to capture the child protection system at a point of 'reflex' awareness of the impact of major system failures in child protection which Beck (1992, 1994; Beck *et al.*, 2003) argues is central to processes of reflexive modernization. In addition, as with legislative changes in other countries – such as the 1989 Children Act in the United Kingdom, for instance – the Irish 1991 Child Care Act placed new duties on health boards to promote the welfare of children in their area, as well as clarifying child protection powers and introducing administrative reforms like further child protection guidelines for professionals to follow. Such developments have opened up important debates as to how well nation-states balance responding to children 'at risk' and meet their statutory obligations to promote the welfare of children 'in need' more generally.

What is coming to light today is significantly a product of the development of ever more elaborate expert systems and shifts in social perception which has brought long repressed crimes like serious deliberate physical harm and child sexual abuse into view, rendering them classifiable in social practice. In my Irish study, in 13 per cent of all referrals child sexual abuse was classified by social workers as the main presenting problem. In some 8 per cent of referrals it was physical abuse, with 4 per cent emotional abuse, and 7 per cent domestic violence. Neglect, meanwhile, was the biggest 'abuse' category, accounting for 21 per cent of referrals. Information relating to a broad range of child care 'problems' concerning children who are suspected of being at risk of not receiving adequate care and protection flows into the health boards who carry statutory responsibility for child care. Thus, child behaviour/control problems also accounted for 21 per cent of referrals and another 16 per cent were primarily concerned with parental difficulties. The latter classifications refer to what social workers classified as the main presenting problem (for an extended discussion, see Ferguson and O'Reilly, 2001, Chapter 2). Typically, referrals contain a mixture of at risk/'abuse' and welfare/'in need' problems which make the boundaries between 'protection' and 'family support' cases extremely hard to draw. Similar patterns are evident elsewhere. In the United Kingdom, for instance, in 1978 less than 1 per cent of cases (just 89 cases) involved children being placed on child abuse registers as victims of child sexual abuse. By 1991, the proportion was 11 per cent, which in absolute terms represented a 58-fold increase, and by 1999 sexual abuse cases constituted 19 per cent (Corby, 2000, p. 89).

Against this background, a typical case study from the research will help to bring transformations in risk and the shift from simple to reflexive modernity that I am arguing has occurred into clearer focus.[2] Two year old Shane Smith was admitted to hospital with a serious arm injury. According to the hospital the child presented as 'unwell, irritable, depressed, cranky'. He was referred to various consultants and x-rayed on numerous occasions due to 'a high suspicion' of non-accidental injury. Shane's sister – here called Rachel – was three years old and although not a subject of concern regarding non-accidental injury (NAI), was known, like Shane, to the system due to child care problems and neglect. Their mother, Anne, lived apart from their father and Shane was in the custody of his father at the time of the injury, although his whereabouts were unknown to social workers and health workers. Anne was considered a borderline 'neglectful' parent.

The case was initially referred when Shane was ten months and Rachel two years old and both had been left in the care of the babysitter who their mother had approached on the street and was unknown to her. Shane became ill that night and the babysitter took him to the GP who had him admitted to hospital. The hospital contacted the police who located the mother the next day, and also referred the case to social workers. Anne was initially spoken to at the hospital and 'challenged' by a social worker to explain her whereabouts on the night that Shane was admitted. According to the social worker a 'tougher investigation' was carried out in Anne's home – by which time Shane had been returned home – when she was interviewed ten days after the referral. Several abortive home visits had been attempted.

At the time of the referral, both children were resident with their mother – a lone-parent – in local authority housing, living on state benefits. On this first visit Anne disclosed to the social worker that she was a survivor of childhood sexual abuse, had spent time in care as a child, and that she had experienced domestic violence by an ex-cohabitee. She also confessed to having a drinking problem. Attendance at a group in a women's refuge was offered to her and alcohol counselling was recommended 'which she agreed to attend' (social worker). Anne assured the social worker that she now made adequate child care arrangements when she went out. The social worker also offered support regarding child access struggles with her ex-partner. The assessment of the hospital staff concluded that the 'general care of the child was poor' and neglect was also substantiated for Rachel. The level of risk to the children was assessed as low. According to the social worker, although Anne's behaviour was considered 'neglectful', it was not deemed 'abusive' and the intervention was framed in 'welfare' terms around her apparent vulnerability and need for support.

The case was re-referred seven times over the next year, mainly for instances involving Anne allegedly being drunk in charge of the children or leaving them with inappropriate babysitters. The children attended a crèche and there were several incidents of Anne arriving to collect them while intoxicated. Anne had also arrived at the crèche with obvious physical injuries, bruising to the face and lips bleeding, alleging Shane's father had done it. The public health nurse was especially alarmed about this and the case was 'notified' to the official child protection system, which involved a multidisciplinary group of senior managers that processed and advised on all cases with abuse concerns. Shane's precise whereabouts were often unclear from information provided by various professionals in research interviews. It appears that he was residing with both his mother and father on a sporadic basis. Prior to the serious injury, attempts had been made to link Anne into virtually every service going, including addiction counsellors and a community-based family centre. In every instance Anne failed to engage despite always expressing a willingness to do so. This ambivalent relationship to professionals was mirrored by the research team's own failed attempts to engage with Anne who agreed on two occasions to meet for an interview, but, without explanation, just never showed.

Prior to the suspected NAI, different professionals had different knowledge and thresholds of risk with respect to the children. The hospital had concerns about frequent hospital admissions and failure to thrive, and made referrals to social services to this effect, while they and the public health nurse were concerned about Anne's inability to cope. Yet the communication of these concerns to social workers – both in the sense of how they were conveyed and heard – was not effective. The Family Support Worker was enlisted to help Anne with her drink problem and became an important ally for her. 'Basically I have tried as woman to woman to listen to her concerns ... and her concerns are many and deep ... and one of the things I gradually came around to was getting [Anne] to name her issues.' These included the child sexual abuse by her father and her drinking. 'I would feel that it was important to believe in her, I continued visiting her and hoping ... because I have worked a good bit with people with addiction and I think there comes a day when ... I wondered would she decide to eventually get help.'

Frontline social work, meanwhile, regarded it as a low-risk case barely worthy of ongoing intervention. The social worker regarded Anne as a 'genuine' person, and felt that 'the relationship with her is OK, she is not defensive, she is kind of open although she pays lip service to a degree, she agrees to things but she doesn't do them, she plans to do it, she's just not ready'. Social work maintained a nominal, case-management role – as 'more in the background, more like arranging services' – while the support and therapeutic work was attempted by other professionals.

For the consultant, the numerous x-rays of Shane's injury and second opinion arose from the difficulty that there was no accident or injury or an event that could explain the injury, yet the difficulty with confirming NAI was that a congenital disorder may have been the cause. The consultant met with the father and found him to be straightforward and concerned. The doctor did not however discuss the background to the injury with him. He saw his role purely in clinical terms as trying to establish medial facts and to offer an opinion on whether the injury was non-accidental. Several case conferences took place and in the research interview the consultant said he felt there was a strong desire from other professionals for him to support a 'traumatic diagnosis', but he felt that on the given evidence a conclusion that there 'was a high suspicion' of NAI was as far as he could go. A full care order was applied for but was not granted, largely because of the lack of medical evidence to prove NAI and the court accepted the explanation that Shane must have injured himself accidentally. In court Anne made very positive statements about the father which represented a complete reversal of how she had consistently expressed fears to social workers about his care of the child. The police attended case conferences and were kept informed throughout. Due to the lack of medical evidence, by the end of the study period it was thought unlikely they would investigate further or issue charges. The children returned home.

From risk consciousness to risk anxiety: child protection in the risk society

The nature and management of this case reflects important general patterns in the nature of child protection in late-modernity. It exemplifies the new focus on deliberate harm and non-accidental injury by parents and carers and the central role of managerialism, procedures and coordinated inter-professional work in assessment and case-management. Medical staff have a pivotal role in identifying and diagnosing such problems, but now doctors are no longer brought to client's homes to make clinical judgements, although this goes on in the hospital. This leaves social workers with an increasingly important role in engaging with parents through home visits and the gathering of 'social' evidence. They play an important role not simply in delivering services themselves, but as case managers of all the services that typically go into such cases. Although I deal with it in detail in the Chapter 6, it is also worth noting here how the relatively compassionate 'welfare' response to the mother in this case reflects the pattern for service users – or women at least – to now be recognized as having 'biographies' where the influence of their past life experiences on their capacities to parenting are taken seriously. While this does not always occur in all cases, and applies least to men and service-user fathers, it does suggest wider changes in therapeutic processes and identity (re)construction in child welfare work which relate to processes of 'individualization' and 'life-planning' (Beck and Beck-Gernshiem, 2002).

The upshot of these changes is a greatly increased sense of risk and danger in child protection, although the actual numbers or proportion of cases involving life-threatening situations for children is small. While exposure to violence and suffering are regular features of child protection workers lives, the most common cases that professionals deal with do not involve immediately life-threatening incidents of violence, but the grinding problems of neglect, emotional abuse, domestic violence, substance abuse and so on. Subjectively speaking, however, it does not *feel* like that, because of the future-oriented nature of the experience of modernity. Every case could be *that* case where serious harm or death occurs. This is exemplified in the Shane Smith case where, despite criticisms of the social work practice from some professionals, in the day-to-day lived reality of the unfolding of the case, no one surely could have predicted the fateful moment of the dramatic new direction that the case took in terms of suspected NAI, as it happened in such an apparently unpredictable way. Such uncertainty strikes at the core of what child protection is today.

The interviews I conducted with 18 of the social workers in my study show the dramatic extent to which child protection workers' consciousness today is infused with an awareness of risk. In one sense there is nothing new about that, as I have shown how the modern mentalité of risk awareness was constituted early in the twentieth century. Yet late-modern child protection is constituted by new parameters of risk which I shall characterize as a shift from risk *consciousness* to risk *anxiety*. Up to the 1970s under simple modernity professionals had an inherent belief in the capacity of their expertise to enable them to protect children in time. Even if in practice they sometimes failed to do this, the sequestration of child death both expressed and bolstered their faith in the science of child protection. The dominant belief among social workers today is that no matter how effectively the child protection system operates it cannot guarantee safety for children.

> I suppose it is constantly at the back of your mind, god, will I not assess this right? You know, am I going to miss something, are you going to miss a contact with somebody that may have very relevant, you know, relevant information. Yes, yes, honestly yeah, I would have that fear you know, I'd have the on-going fear that I would you know maybe miss something like or whatever.

Practitioners' language illustrates that underlying the anxiety is the 'explosive' nature of the work. Every referral is a 'potential minefield', cases 'blow up', 'explode', workers 'burn out'. All those solid laws and procedures that they embody keep threatening (along with the workers themselves) to melt into air. This is not simply a workplace experience, but one that is carried into every area of the professional's life. There is no escape even in sleep. A constant refrain of all social workers is that 'missing' cases is 'always a possibility' and having to live with those 'fears that there's something going on that you're not being told'. Every referral is a potential danger as well as opportunity to protect:

> because of the nature of the job, every one of them is a potential minefield, you know like if you sit down for five minutes you'll always have like 'I wonder have they done it again since', it's always a worry I find, you carry it with you in your head, you carry your work with you in your head at night.

For all the totality that the rational knowledge base and procedures suggest constitute what should be known about risk and children's lives, social workers' wisdom tells them that in practice they only see fragments of families' lives, passing truths. The experience of child protection continues to be that of the fleeting, the ephemeral and the contingent, but here the new parameters of risk anxiety in late-modernity mean that the solidity that surrounded it in simple modernity has gone and it has become 'liquified'. The 'social' glue which held it together under simple modernity has melted into air. The irony of this is that it occurs in the midst of developments which have attempted to 'solidify' it through changes in the law and bureaucratic procedures.

If under simple modernity expertise was spared the application of scientific scepticism to itself, in reflexive modernity, the sciences are confronted with their own products, defects and secondary problems (Beck, 1992, p. 154). Since the 1970s, the 'latency phase of risk threats' (Beck, 1992, p. 55) has come to an end. The world of late-modernity is a risk society, at the heart of which are processes of 'reflexive modernization' (Beck *et al.*, 1994). Problems of risk management in child protection come to concern hazards brought about by the development of the expert system itself. They are what Beck calls 'modernization risks' and Giddens (1994a) 'manufactured risk'. This occurs in how expert systems – social workers, doctors, health visitors, the police, courts and so on – routinely socially construct the universe of events surrounding 'cases' within a historically specific ideology of 'child protection'.

Modernization risks surrounding the deaths of children in child protection cases can be understood as 'side-effects' produced by modernity itself. This is implicit in how the difficulties revealed are invariably conceptualized as *system* failures and defined in terms not of an under-supply of practice, but of the multitude of (uncoordinated) work that went into the cases (Reder *et al.*, 1993). Controversies surrounding situations like the 'Cleveland affair' in the United Kingdom, where between January and June 1987, 121 children were taken into care as suspected victims of child sexual abuse, is a dramatic instance of over-intervention and child protection being confronted with hazards and insecurities induced and introduced by modernization itself. For the first time in its modern history, professionals were being told that effective child protection required them to slow down; to take time to consider coordinated intervention plans through 'strategy meetings' and case conferences (Bulter-Sloss, 1988; DHSS, 1988a). Responding to child sexual abuse had to mean protecting children in new times.

These processes have dramatic implications not just for institutions but also for individuals and the nature of *self*-identity. In late-modernity, identity is no longer something that is shaped by tradition, external controls (such as religion, the family and the community) and the class and gender roles ascribed at birth, but by individuals through reflexive engagements with expert systems and knowledge. The self becomes 'a reflexive project' (Giddens, 1991). This process of 'individualization' is now endemic to the Western world and means that the onus is on individuals to live what Beck and Beck-Gernsheim (2002) refer to as 'a life of one's own'. In reflexive modernity we largely govern ourselves, from within. I shall have a lot more to say about individualization and child protection in the Chapter 6, but what can be emphasized at this point is how people have to constantly use available knowledge to reflexively shape their own lives and, by extension, deaths, with all the existential angst this involves.

'Reflexivity' means something more than 'reflection' and the capacity to 'reflect', which people have always had a capacity for. This was demonstrated earlier in the book through the patterns of resistance and reciprocity that lay people have always shown towards child protection. An important dimension of reflexivity is about 'reflex' – a response to the side effects, the dangers produced by modernity itself. Unlike reflection, reflexivity is not just individualistic, conscious or intentional, but occurs on an institutional level as well. Reflexive modernization is in important respects about the reflex response of institutions to disclosures of the side effects produced by an earlier 'simple' modernity (cf. Lash, 1994, p. 200). Modernization can thus be said to becoming reflexive when it becomes its own theme (Beck, 1992, p. 19). The reflex response of institutions in turn produces new contexts for reflection by individuals, whose responses in turn reflexively shape the institutional practices they are reacting to. The concept of risk society provides a term for this relationship between reflex and reflection (Beck, 1994).

It is precisely this kind of reflexivity that the professional narratives on which I am drawing here demonstrate. It is both personal *and* institutionally and culturally driven. The child protection system is a classic form of advanced modern institutionalized risk system which has at its core the kind of reflexive monitoring of risk that is intrinsic to modernity; the 'risk profiling' that is based on analysis of what, in the current state of knowledge and current conditions, is the distribution of risks in acting on behalf of children in a myriad of possible ways (Giddens, 1991, p. 119). Fundamentally, risk concerns future happenings as related to present knowledge and practices. While the future has always been intrinsically unknowable, in late-modernity the future becomes a new terrain lending itself to colonial invasion through risk calculation. Risk is about 'colonization of the future' (Giddens, 1991, p. 111). The central importance that 'risk assessment' has taken on in child protection today concerns attempts to bring the future under control and render it safer for children identified as 'at risk' of future harm.

The roots of anxiety: blaming systems and fear of children's suffering

The reflex response of institutions to public disclosure of mistakes in child protection has resulted in the decision-making party concealed in such errors becoming visible (cf. Beck, 1992, p. 173). In circumstances of reflexive modernity expertise is demystified and loses its traditional authority. Expertise is targeted not only as a source of solutions to problems, but also as *a cause of problems*. Authority is pervasively questioned; every decision is risk-laden and potentially open to public scrutiny. As one social worker articulated it:

> I think social workers are much more aware that every decision you take can now be judged, so obviously you're conscious of that in your work and it does naturally bring a level of anxiety and pressure to the job.

At the core of risk anxiety in late-modern child protection are two primal fears: of being blamed with and by the organization and society for failing to protect; and of being responsible for prolonging children's suffering.

> my main fear would be if something seriously happened to a child and it was my case and I hadn't followed it up fully. ... I suppose the initial reaction is, have I covered my butt basically, and I think after that would be, 'is it my fault that this is happening to the child?' because I haven't, well the real concern to my mind is that I haven't followed up on it. It's like no matter what you do, it's not enough, with our up and down cases you know, you're finding about cases that there is something else known, do you know.

Child protection work, especially in terms of inquiries into system failures, now contains genuine dangers and fears for professionals. As Beck (1992, p. 75) observes, 'risk society contains an inherent tendency to become a *scapegoat society*; suddenly it is not the hazards, but those who point them out that provoke general uneasiness.' A 'blaming-system' emerges (Parton, 1996) where stirred up public fears and insecurities come to surround new perceptions of risks and danger and these are diverted onto those social workers and other professionals involved in 'scandal' cases who become 'receptacles for public anger' (Ruddick, 1991). The work of Mary Douglas on risk is also instructive here. For her, risk is seen as having largely replaced older ideas about the cause of misfortune, concepts such as sin. These are now discredited and have been replaced by the 'modern sanitized discourse of risk' (Lupton, 1999, p. 46). Douglas sees risk as acting mainly as a locus of blame, in which 'risky' groups or individuals are singled out as dangerous (Lupton, 1999, p. 3). A 'risky' Other may pose a threat to the integrity of one's own body or the community in which one lives, to symbolic order. What is striking today is the way in which this sense of threat to the community extends beyond the paedophile or parent who neglects or kills their child and has become focused on expert systems, especially social work. Risk acts as a 'forensic resource' in providing explanations for things that have gone wrong. Large institutions are singled out as responsible and 'to blame' for risks. Every death, every accident and every misfortune is 'chargeable to someone's account' – someone must be found to be blamed. As Douglas (1992, p. 16) writes:

> Whose fault? is the first question. Then, what action? Which means, what damages? What compensation? What restitution? And the preventive action is to improve the coding of risk in the domain which has turned out to be inadequately covered. Under the banner of risk reduction, a new blaming system has replaced the former combination of moralistic condemning the victim's incompetence.

The outcome has been precise attempts to 'improve the coding of risk' through proceduralization, greater accountability – or 'butt covering'. This has to be seen as a direct consequence of the 'heavy symbolic load' that I have shown child protection professionals, and especially social workers, have carried since early in the twentieth century when clear boundaries were placed around its practices. Because of its closeness to and structurally ambiguous relationship with those dirty, dangerous Others who abuse children, social work itself represents a threat to ontological security and becomes a focus of the blaming system. Now it is not only 'abusing' families but social workers too who are subjected to purity and pollution rituals by the community.

Risk anxiety also arises from deep existential fears of being – or feeling – personally responsible for children's deaths and avoidable suffering from child sexual abuse and other maltreatment. Feelings among the social workers that they had let children down were common, the consequences of which weigh heavily:

> I let this child down, that comes into it, there's a huge amount of things come into it really, well like if a child is being abused. In a case

where I was involved with a teenager ... after two and a half years she disclosed about CSA [child sexual abuse], and I felt I should have known this. I was involved you know, but it never came out, I didn't do enough, I should have picked up more, I should have, I suppose you are constantly questioning yourself.

This 'constant questioning' of the self is at the core of social worker's experiences of late-modernity and child protection and arises from the reflexive social conditions of our time (Dodds, 1999, p. 189). The paradox is that social worker's fears and anxieties have multiplied at a time when the actual phenomenon of child death in child protection is such an extremely rare experience that only a tiny fraction of professionals will ever encounter it. The monitoring that is endemic to reflexive modernity had begun to go on anyway prior to public disclosures of deaths, inquiry processes and so on, in that with the 'rediscovery' of child abuse in the 1960s and 1970s workers began to feel intensified anxieties for the lives and sufferings of children. The child death and sexual abuse scandals have intensified further awareness of the costs of those risks to children and added another layer of bureaucratic blame culture to what was going on existentially anyway.

Risk anxiety is heightened still further by the fact that not only the personal safety of the children but also that of professionals is a huge issue. As one summed it up: 'everybody I think within the team has been exposed to some level of violence either by threats or being physically assaulted'. Several social workers recounted incidents where their personal safety was threatened, such as 'an abuser turned up on my door and I live on my own, and I was very frightened, I was really scared'. Another had a client who discovered his home address and 'this guy was walking up and down outside my home. He said he knows I have a son.' One parent threatened to use a shotgun, 'he said he would shoot my fucking head off'. As a consequence, social workers often feel

extremely unsafe at times, extremely unsafe. You feel physically unsafe a lot of the time and you really have to come to terms with that and deal with that. I think at times you can feel very much out on a limb and very much unsupported by the [agency] and management at times in some situations.

If the agency lets frontline workers down by failing to understand and respond to the gravity of the dangers and their personal consequences, they are left to develop their own coping and survival strategies just to try and manage anxiety and get safely through the day (see also, Balloch *et al.*, 1998).

Protecting children in late-modern times

The issue of control – or the lack of it – is central to risk anxiety in child protection: 'the last thought I have nearly every night before I go to sleep is what I must do tomorrow that I didn't do today.' As another social worker exemplified it, 'basically you are chasing your tail all the time, just to try and keep up'. While doing child protection today fits well with Giddens' (1990) description of the experience of late-modernity as being like 'riding a juggernaut', whatever lay people typically experience in this regard can be multiplied many times over for professionals who work in child protection as the speed with which the juggernaut travels feels so much greater because the costs of its crashing – almost certainly bringing serious injury and/or death – are so highly consequential.

The speed of movement has a material basis to it: Practitioners *do* move more quickly than ever across space, having effectively conquered it. The mobility of welfare practices is a reflection of how everyday life has speeded up to an extraordinary degree (Urry, 2003). This is true at least in the sense of the speed at which social workers can get to the doorsteps of children's homes, while what goes on within private space *inside* the house has most certainly not been mastered. In my study, 92 per cent of all the 319 referrals were directly investigated. Some 40 per cent of the investigated referrals were seen within one working day of receipt of the information, while 74 per cent were investigated within five working days. The referral that took 80 days to respond to was a clear exception. Responding to children in time does not always mean quickly. A more 'timely' response in some situations involves 'taking' time to plan and strategize intervention by gathering further information about the child and family – either through a case conference, strategy meeting, or informal communication – thereby slowing down the actual process of making direct contact with suspected victims and abusers.

Ironically, what slows down responses to cases in a manner which is problematic and often dangerous are unplanned for delays caused by the imposition of the bureaucratic system itself, as, classically, social workers wait to gather more information from other professionals, to hold a meeting and so on. In fact, those cases that are *not* channelled through the official child protection system, on balance, get a quicker response than those that are (Ferguson and O'Reilly, 2001, pp. 73–5).

While social workers and managers (despite protests to the contrary) generally do have control now over the timing of interventions and seek to manage the rhythms of protecting children in time according to what is viewed as in the child's best interests, it is not the capacity to physically reach children in time but belief systems and organizational cultures and routines which cause most problems.

The key pattern in my study in relation to such difficulties and how they can lead to failures to respond to the actual risk to children is where a fetish is made of procedures as a kind of organizational response to managing risk anxiety. A typical example occurred in a case which was referred by a school teacher, concerned about possible physical abuse of a five year old boy, who said in class 'that his father tried to smother him'. However, the referral was made a whole four months after the child made this disclosure. Three days after the referral, the social worker met with the teacher who regarded herself as discussing her concerns rather than making a 'formal referral'. The social worker discussed it with her manager and brought it to a team meeting and the decision was to await clarification from the school before taking any action. It never came and the 'case' was closed three weeks after the referral – or *non*-referral? – was made. In her research interview the teacher claimed that she had tried to make the referral sooner by telephoning the social work department on five or six occasions, but 'there was nobody available'. She was fearful of the implications for herself of reporting it, such as a parental backlash and was exposed by the lack of a school policy on how to manage such concern.

Ten months after the initial (non)referral another teacher expressed concern regarding the child, who

> said that his daddy beat him with a pencil, initially the teacher made little of it saying that pencils were small, so [child] said no, that this was a big wooden pencil like you'd buy in the pound shop, so he became very tearful and upset that his daddy takes down his pants and shorts and hits him with this big pencil and keeps him until he calls water. [child] then asked [teacher] if she remembered his face being scratched some time previously and at the time he telling her he had fallen, he said in fact what had happened was that Dad had hit him with his pencil, but had threatened to kill him if he told anyone. (case file)

There were also concerns about possible alcohol and drug taking at home and that the child was left to watch television in his bedroom until late and was often tired. This second teacher was as concerned as the first about the parent's reaction to knowing she had reported it. Once again social services placed their emphasis on contact with the teacher to try to clarify the status of the referral information. However, four months after the second referral and despite being directed by the official multidisciplinary child protection committee to check back with the teacher and 'do a home visit', no investigation or any other kind of action took place. The social worker explained this as being due to the school holidays and the fact that they could not contact the teacher to clarify her concerns 'first hand', but conceded that 'I suppose a home visit perhaps should have taken place all right...because we had sufficient information.' The risk to the child – especially with respect to the quite alarming second referral – had got lost amidst organizational routines, role confusion, procedural delays and concerns about the formality of referrals, and a failure to take a solid child protection role. Thus it is never the content of information about children in itself which determines the timing and direction of professional responses, but how it is given meaning and processed by individuals and organizations.

The more that space has been conquered, the more time has become the locus of control. This is now such that practitioners feel under constant pressure to move cases on through the system: 'the more child protection stuff, the more pressure is on you to deal with a case, get it sorted and move on'. There is a reflex flow to the work which typifies the nature of social practices within reflexive modernity (Lash, 2002), which means that it needs to be done more and more quickly. So, having conquered space and developed their capacities to reach children physically, protecting children in time increasingly comes to be measured organizationally in terms of performance management targets aimed at pushing cases quickly through the system. A new form of temporality is emerging here which Urry defines as 'instantaneous time' which may in some spheres already be taking the place of the ubiquitous clock time (Urry, 2000, p. 123–30, see also Bauman, 2000). Instantaneous time arises from a number of factors, including: how, with computers and the internet, information and ideas can now be transmitted and simultaneously accessed across the globe; and a heightened 'temporariness' of jobs, products, careers, personal relationships. Because of problems in colonizing it and bringing it under control in managing risk to children, the future has become deeply problematic for child protection. This has resulted both culturally and organizationally in greatly intensified demands for instantaneous responses to children and, superficially, the conditions appear to be there to achieve it.

As Urry (2000, p. 128) observes, 'as a result of the need for instantaneous responses, particularly because of the speed implied by the telephone, telex, fax, electronic signals and so on, the future increasingly appears to dissolve into an extended present'. But what requires re-emphasizing is that instantaneous time and even clock time reflect organizational cultures and 'timescapes' (Adam, 1995, 1996) of the public domain. Meanwhile, how time is experienced by service users appears to still be predominantly as 'lived time', as organized around the private domain and routines of child care and family life. Here, gender and age differences in experiences of time are crucial. The time of a carer is open-ended, outside commodified clock-time which is much more men's time (Davies, 1990; Urry, 2000, p. 159). Because women continue to be the primary carers they live 'in time' and also have to give time (Adam, 1990, p. 99). We also need to think of 'children's time' as having a rhythm to it which is quite different to adult and clock times (James *et al.*, 1990, 1997).

An implicit awareness of the tensions in this clash of public and private, clock/instantaneous time and lived time creates in workers an awareness that they are not allowed the time to get to know the child and family in terms of the day-to-day rhythms of their lives. For workers, prevention is being sidelined and families 'don't really see it as an ally or as a support', as the work becomes dominated by 'crisis management' and just 'skimming' the surface of much wider and deeper problems and 'what we're doing is fire brigade work'. This is further compounded by how social workers have become case-managers and are increasingly losing the discretion and time to do actual therapeutic work directly themselves.

As the Shane Smith case exemplified, a complex division of labour now exists in the provision of post-investigative services, with social work having a core coordinating function. In my study, over the 12 month follow-up period, social workers had no active case work role at all or played solely a case-management role in 40 per cent of substantiated cases, while the primary therapeutic and support work was done by other professionals. And even in the 60 per cent of cases where it was felt that social workers did provide meaningful protection and welfare services, it was invariably under great time pressure and in combination with other services. This is not to say that under such conditions it cannot be effective. I shall give examples of how it can. The problem lies with the emergence of a dominant style and ideology of risk management based on control of worker's performance and time-use which interprets the speed of processing 'cases' through the organization as the measure of what protection in time means, as opposed to a deep appreciation of the degree to which the safety and welfare needs of children, carers and families are being met.

Body projects: living as well as working with child protection and risk

At the core of 'risk society', then, is an awareness of risk *as* risk. As social workers and other professionals now intuitively know, this involves knowing that 'knowledge gaps' exist which cannot now be converted into 'certainties' by religious or magical knowledge, or even scientific evidence (Giddens, 1990, p. 125). Hand-in-hand with this goes an awareness of the limitations of expertise: knowledge that 'no expert system can be wholly expert in terms of the consequences of the adoption of expert principles' (Giddens, 1990, p. 125). As Giddens (1990, p. 111) elaborates, 'Where risk is *known* to be risk, it is experienced very differently from circumstances in which notions of *fortuna* prevail. To recognize the existence of a risk or a set of risks is to accept not just the possibility that things might go wrong, but that this possibility cannot be eliminated.' This strikes at the core of child protection as a form of manufactured uncertainty. Modes of generating confidence in hazardous actions are by definition unavailable. High-risk enterprises undertaken in traditional cultures, on the other hand, were carried out under the auspices of religion or magic which very often provided a way of sealing over the uncertainties entailed in risky endeavours, translating the feelings of risk into relative security (Giddens, 1990, pp. 129–30).

This was apparent, for instance, in the transitional role that the Children's Shelters played in the symbolic system of protecting children in late-Victorian times, discussed in Chapter 2. With the development of highly rational, secular societies, today professionals have to find ways of trying to transmute risk into providential *fortuna*. Sensitized to these issues by Giddens' work, I explored with social workers their coping strategies for managing risk anxiety and found that reliance on superstition or other trinkets of providential fortuna have little place in late-modern child protection. One social worker wore a particular shirt to court appearances as 'it gives me, it's odd, but it does, I feel competent, but I don't carry trinkets around with me'. Another was given 'a couple of crystals' by her friend and would bring them to court. She also noted that 'there is a higher person out there and you have to depend on it'. One social worker mentioned that praying at night helps her to cope. Such practices and thoughts, however, were so far from the minds of most that they thought questions about superstition slightly bizarre and that I needed help!

In the workplace most adopt more rational approaches, as exemplified by one social worker who, when asked whether he was superstitious replied, 'well no, I wouldn't, I don't believe in that myself, but what I do believe in is practical measures you know like registering your car through the local hospital or the local health centre so that your home address can't be found by the potential client', thereby reducing the risk of being traced through his car registration and attacked by a client. Help sought within the agency revolved around getting advice and support for tricky cases. The presence of close, supportive peer relationships between colleagues was seen as crucial to survival, as was good supervision – which dealt with feelings and personal development as well as administrative and clinical issues – and effective workload management.

A powerful strategy for living with risk anxiety was what, after Shilling (1993), can be called 'body projects'. Social workers spoke of getting massages to help them relax, of the importance of 'spiritual' things, transcendental meditation, and going swimming, to aerobics and doing various other sports to help them cope with stress and bring balance into their lives. Exercise, as one put it, is 'very therapeutic', while for another, it 'gets the old aggression out'. Interestingly, in the interviews social workers were not led in any direction, such as being asked about the effects on their personal or home life. It was they who made the links with their own bodies and life outside of work. Effectively, then, for child care professionals working with risk anxiety is a lifestyle issue. Managing it (well) is incorporated within individualized life planning and strategies for living a life of one's own.

> I try to forget about it, I try to have a balance in my life, to you know to not isolate myself, to communicate with people and to develop my spiritual well being. I think it would be dangerous for my own well being if I was to come home and don't do anything don't get involved, well sometimes you come home you are tired and you might be over worried about things, I think it is important to just let go and do other stuff because like I say it is not my life, people have to live their own life and I am there maybe to sow some seeds that might grow in a few years time and I might never see that you know.

The demands of protecting the lives of others ironically left social workers feeling like they were losing their own.

Sequestration and death in late-modern child protection

I now want to show how the kinds of institutional reflexivity, body projects and individual reflection that are so central to contemporary risk anxiety in child protection were constituted in the context of changing meanings and experiences of death in modernity. The phenomenological angst that is at the core of late-modern risk anxiety in child protection is rooted in personal and professional engagement with existentially troublesome information concerning death, around which it has become increasingly apparent that knowledge gaps and manufactured uncertainties exist. Death, as Giddens observes (1991, p. 50), is associated in human consciousness 'with anxieties of an utterly fundamentally sort'. As I showed in Chapter 4, in order that citizens could maintain an ontologically secure sense of self, death in modernity has been sequestered. Thus it is not possible to present statistics for the post-1970 period on child protection 'cases ending in death' as I have done for the 1884–1936 period, because of how that information has been institutionally repressed by child welfare agencies. What we know about deaths in child protection work since the 1970s is represented in the scandal cases, inquiries and other administrative procedures, such as the Part 8 reviews under the UK 1989 Children Act, or research and government sponsored reviews of child deaths in the United States of America and Australia (Stanley and Goddard, 2002).

Such mechanisms as child abuse inquiries and texts constitute a new way of managing information about the deaths of children in child abuse cases within an overall sequestration of experience. They not only represent a partial overcoming of sequestration, but also a furthering of its processes. As Giddens points out, it would be wrong to understand the sequestration of experience as all-enveloping and homogenous, which it is not. It is internally complicated, throws up contradictions, and also generates possibilities for modern citizens to re-appropriate repressed knowledge. Nor is sequestration a once-and-for-all phenomenon which represents a set of frictionless boundaries. 'The frontiers of sequestered experience are fault-lines full of tensions and poorly mastered forces' (Giddens, 1991, p. 168). The inquiries have arisen in a cultural context of advanced modernity in which some changes are evident in discourses around death and there has been a resurgence of literature concerned with making the phenomenon of death a subject for wider public debate. The development of the hospice movement and debates around euthanasia are examples of this, as is the profound implication of the emergence of AIDS (Walter, 1994). The increased visibility of death in child protection discourse has occurred in the general context of healthy attempts to make death a subject for wider public debate; as part of a partial 'return of the repressed' (Giddens, 1991, p. 202).

On the other hand, I want to argue that death has become a subject of child protection discourse because the tendency that I identified in Chapter 4 for death to be constructed within modernity as a particular problem has intensified (see also, Smith, 2002). Although never explicitly recognized or openly discussed in the, by now, huge literature on child abuse, much of the discourse around advanced modern child protection represents an increased discomfort with death and a furthering of processes of sequestration. Whether or not child abuse deaths get made public in the first place is a highly selective process. Far from resulting from a more open attitude within welfare organizations to disclosing the presence of death, those cases which do become public tend to 'leak out', usually through the media and politicians following up on disclosures made at criminal trials of abusing parents. Moreover, even in those cases that do get publicly disclosed, through the inquiry reports knowledge of child abuse deaths continues to be heavily managed. The comparison that is relevant here is with the (literal) handling of death and relatively unmediated discourse which I have shown characterized child protection before the turn of the twentieth century and even up to the 1920s.

Within a sequestered realm of experience it is not simply the death in some authentic unmediated sense which is the primary source of concern. Attention is focused through the inquiries on the technologies of practice and expert systems which seek to prevent child death and manage it, rather than primarily on the deaths themselves. The treatment of death reflects the fact that outside of religious discourse, discussion of death has become largely a preoccupation with sickness. What is disturbing about AIDS is not that the consequences of the illness kills, but that it does so among the relatively young and often in the context of sexual activity. 'Death is only a "problem" when it is premature death – when a person has not lived out whatever, given certain risks, a table of life expectancy might suggest' (Giddens, 1991, p. 204). In this sense, there are few more disturbing phenomena in advanced modern society than the archetypal premature deaths of highly socially valued children who were *known* to be at high risk of such a fate: the deaths of children in child abuse cases.

The impact of this needs to be fully understood not only in terms of organizational responses and institutional reflexivity, but also at the level of individualization processes and changes to *self*-identity. While as recently as 100 years ago the sight of the dead was relatively commonplace, the extension of the average lifespan across the twentieth century has made death far more remote today than it used to be from living people in general. People can now grow up, live a long life and even die without ever having seen a dead body (Elias, 1985, p. 85). Death is no longer part of normal life. Moreover, death is increasingly taboo in a modern consumerist culture which routinely glamorizes and celebrates youth. The slim body, the healthy body, the normal body is a youthful body (Shilling, 1993). All signs of the dying and the dead are still heavily sequestered, pushed further than ever out of sight of the living and behind the scenes, expunged from the home and placed in the domain of medical experts in hospitals, hospices and funeral parlours. Even ambulances have typically blacked out windows, concealing the potentially disturbing spectacle of injury or death from the onlooker (Giddens, 1987, p. 14). According to Elias (1985, p. 85), 'Never before have people died as noiselessly and hygienically as today ... and never in social conditions so much fostering solitude'.

In late-modernity, demographic and lifestyle changes have, if anything, meant that the social value of children (discussed in Chapter 4) is on the increase. The birth rate has been on the decline since the 1970s and marital breakdown/divorce have been on the increase. In this context, 'the importance of the child is *rising*' (Beck, 1992, p. 118). The child in late modernity has become the focal point of a re-enchantment of private relationships and intimacy: 'the final alternative to loneliness that can be built up against the vanishing possibilities of love' (Beck, 1992, p. 118). These processes of individualization have both created the social conditions that make it more possible for children to gain more protection and for public outcry when they do not.

It is the uniquely individualized child who lives or dies, who has acquired not only a right to life, but a right to a biography, a life of its own. In the faces of Victoria Climbié and others we glimpse the vulnerability of our own children and ourselves as carers. Individualization, living a 'life of one's own', has had the effect of imbuing life with a hunger for life, adventurousness and combination of ebullience and mortal distress. The specialness and precariousness of what can be made in a life thus renders dying and death unthinkable. As Beck and Beck-Gernsheim (2002, p. 154) observe, 'If I suddenly cease to be there, others are no longer able to keep the end of the end under control.' This is especially true of the deaths of children. What happens in the end is not that they die but that child welfare and protection stops working (cf. Beck and Beck-Gernsheim, 2002, p. 153).

The effect is that today public disclosures of avoidable child deaths and suffering have become more intolerable than ever, with far greater accountability demanded when protection does appear to fail. The paradox of child death inquiries is that although they undermine professional competence by bringing expert failure into the open, they have been framed in such a way that they represent a continuation of the basic faith that exists in professional expertise. Underlying the inquiry process is an attempt to sanitize the death by endeavouring to learn enough to further the hope that such deaths can be avoided. While on one level they have created radical doubts in professional capacities to protect children, on another level they further the fantasy of total transparency of society and family life which I have shown has been a defining dynamic of the internally referential character of child protection discourse since early in the twentieth century. The administrative power and instrumental rationality which structure official narratives mean that their vision remains as solid as ever, while the tragedies they document show how in practice the ideal of protecting all children in time continues to melt into air.

In reality, by the 1970s the actual experience of dealing with child death among practitioners was rare and to this day the vast majority of professionals never encounter dead children in their work. The return of the repressed has meant that it is the *discussion* of death which occupies a form of public space, while actual bodily evidence of direct experience of death remains largely sequestered away from public gaze (Mellor and Shilling, 1993). Nevertheless the fear of confronting death remains no less real for all that. The kind of risk anxiety this all helps to create manifests itself in complex ways and not in any simple terms as a professional obsession with death. It translates rather into an inherent concern with the riskiness of promoting child life and preventing child suffering in the context of futures which are known to be uncertain.

Knowledge of risk as risk and its inevitability has to be lived with and strategies adopted to deal with it. Despite – and because of – the fact that they are so centrally involved in attempting to prevent it, social workers and other child professionals are no less likely to deny and defer death than anyone else. There are no 'others' with respect to the balance of security and danger which modernity introduces into our lives. All of us must ride the juggernaut, no one can be completely outside (Giddens, 1990, p. 149). As we have seen, as members of the 'new middle classes' social workers occupy a social space which has a central concern with 'lifestyle' and 'body projects', including healthy eating regimes and walking holidays (Bourdieu, 1986). The greater visibility of death and the reflexivity of late-modernity confronts people with the prospect of dying in a manner which can radically disrupt their lifestyle and body regimes. 'The more investment we make in body projects, the more difficult and disturbing it will be to come to their end' (Shilling, 1993, p. 187). Bauman (1992) argues that strategies of 'self-care' surrounding issues of health and the body now fill the gap left vacant by the relative absence of survival strategies derived from religion. The return of the repressed in child protection has therefore meant that social workers have had to confront an existential crisis not just with respect to the implications of 'professional' risks of serious abuse and death to their child clients, but also the meaning that such engagement holds in relation to their *own* lives and deaths. As Shilling (1993, pp. 189–90) argues, 'Unable to confront the reality of the demise and death of their own bodies, the self-identities of individuals are often made insecure by the presence of death in other people's bodies.' The very nature of self-identity in social work and child protection has changed as we confront the challenges of knowing risk as risk within the new existential parameters involved in protecting children in risk society.

Containing risk anxiety: rethinking bureaucracy in late-modern child protection

Against this background, the process of control and bureaucratization of social work and child protection on which critics have so relentlessly focused must be (re)framed as a dynamic and dialectical one. It has been part of an attempt to colonize the future and bring the promotion of safer lives for children under greater, if not total, control. 'Covering yourself' is the embodied metaphor for accountability and blame culture, basically meaning more bureaucracy and management with less individual discretion. Its demands restrict face-to-face work: 'you find yourself filling out forms, you know just writing things and you get very little time to go out and actually see anybody.' Workers perceive the focus of child protection to have become more legalistic, bureaucratic, authoritative and concerned with high risk cases, which some regard as deskilling:

> your time is limited, I see some of my colleagues who've spent all their time dotting the I's and crossing the T's and I think they're losing, they're being deskilled. I think that's not what we're about, I think what we're about is our relationship with families. I think we're getting more and more deskilled and more and more directed.

The standard representation of the managerial development of child protection in academic work has been a negative view of risk which relates it exclusively to blame. Social workers do certainly regard their child protection work as having 'narrowed to child protection now, [it] is very much child protection, investigation and assessment of risk', with less time for 'therapy'. Yet this intensified child protection role and bureaucratization is not experienced by social workers as all bad. For a start, riding the juggernaut is exciting: 'you get on a high from it, you get a buzz from all the activity and going out and you know it was yes. Yeah, there is a buzz about it, about being busy and on the go.' The adventure involved in doing child protection is a curiously under-recognized, but vital dimension of the professional culture and renders the work still further a quintessential experience of modernity. Some find the work fun and enjoyable: 'Like you are building up relationships with your clients you are having, you can have good fun with them, it's not all dreary work you know, there are some characters and you fit in with them and work it out.' For another: 'yeah I do, I really enjoy, I love my work. ... I do find that it can be very rewarding. I love working with kids.'

In addition, procedures and more managerial support are perceived as supportive and enabling, precisely because of the perception of more high risk work:

> it's very much structured now, there's more procedures in place, in many ways it's easier in that sense, that there's very clear procedures to be followed, you know with the team leader system, there's more seniors. It seems sometimes that cases that are referred are more serious, whereas before we dealt with everything, whereas now we're just focusing on the serious ones.

What these workers are experiencing are the personal and group effects of working in organizations which act socially as 'containers' for anxiety (Hinshelwood and Skogstad, 2000). Organizations defend against anxiety, just as individuals do. They have emotional lives and can come to embody the same kinds of patterns of splitting and projection as are evident in individuals and other groups like families (Froggett, 2002). The sense that they are 'skimming' the surface of what are in practice much deeper child and family problems reflects the real struggles that organizations who deal with child abuse today have in managing their own anxiety and more generally the emotional impact of the work on what they do.

This is why managerialism and procedures have brought indispensable existential gains for professionals in helping to manage anxiety and create areas of relative security for the containment of professional life in preventing child suffering in the context of such open, uncertain futures. On the other hand, bureaucratization has now developed to a problematic stage where it imposes clock time and instantaneous time to serve the anxiety management of the organization to the extent that the lived time and authentic needs of children and families, and indeed workers, are subordinated. Creativity and more intuitive, soulful forms of work are being suppressed. What is required are forms and styles of organizational life which 'contain' or 'hold' workers (Ward, 1995) in ways which promote their ontological security and capacities to develop meaningful relationships with children and families while understanding the psychodynamic and symbolic dimensions of the work and accepting the risks inherent to child protection. Finding this balance will not stop workers from feeling ambivalent about bureaucratization, but it can allow them to embrace child protection procedures and reflexively use such structures and information to reskill themselves, manage risk better and protect more children in new times.

6
Child Sexual Abuse and the Reflexive Project of the Self: Child Protection, Individualization and Life Politics

This chapter shifts the analysis from organizational life to focus in more detail on the kinds of relationships and work that goes on in late-modern child protection as administrative powers are turned into practices – on what has become of the aesthetic and expressive dimensions of child protection. Scholars have tended to characterize the nature of child protection and risk in one-dimensional ways: as about blame and regulation, hierarchical power and social control (Garret, 2003; Scourfield and Welsh, 2003). The wider aspects of children's and carer's needs are said not to form part of the assessments of the increasingly bureaucratic child protection systems (Parton *et al.*, 1997). While I have shown that this is a legitimate concern, it is not the full story. Not all professionals and users of services accept the official (instrumentally rational) version of 'cases' and struggle to create meaningful pieces of work. This shows how in the bureaucratic late-modernism of child protection the law, procedures and managerial guidance can provide the context and framework out of which professionals work creatively with and within structures to carve out actions which make a (positive) difference to service user's lives. Central to this is how the aesthetic sensibility in social work and child protection – its essential creativity – has developed to contain a significant emancipatory dimension which promotes democratic relations within families.

The empirical evidence I present here supports the argument for a new paradigm for theorizing welfare which moves beyond the traditional construction of a passive 'client' and professional to focus on the capacities that human agents have to act critically and reflexively in the world. Given that most users of welfare services are poor, a key emphasis in the new paradigm is on exploring the internal and external resources which poor people bring to the stresses in their lives and their interactions with welfare services; and on the resourcefulness of the 'creative, reflexive, welfare subject' (Titterton, 1992; Williams *et al.*, 1999). Much more fluid ways of understanding child protection are needed to reflect its fluid, multilayered character. In this chapter, I show how, alongside the major changes in how risk is experienced and manufactured by institutions that were set out in the last chapter, in late-modernity intimate relations too lose their solidity. The emergence of 'liquid love' (Bauman, 2003) is a key dimension of what gives to child protection its liquid character in how families and intimate relationships lose their traditional basis in (lifelong) marriage and the fixed gender and age roles which characterized the era of solid or heavy modernity. In late-modernity the family is being 'democratized' (Beck, 1992; Giddens, 1998). This reflects deep-seated changes in the nature of governance as processes of individualization give rise to new meanings and patterns of relationships through practices of help-seeking and life-planning within a new kind of 'life politics' (Giddens, 1991). New opportunities (as well as dangers) arise for people through child protection interventions to (re)shape those aspects of their lives connected with violence and trauma, which extend to even the most socially excluded members of society, although these possibilities remain incomplete. While this is relevant to all forms of maltreatment, I shall focus in particular in this chapter on child sexual abuse and domestic violence to illuminate the conceptual issues at hand.

Child protection, individualization and the reflexive citizen

The typical profile of children and families who come to the attention of child protection services is of non-traditional households experiencing poverty and other forms of social exclusion. My study typifies this in how some 41 per cent of the sample of 319 cases were lone-parent families, the vast majority headed by women, while 11 per cent were reconstituted families. Less than half of all cases that come to the attention of agencies contain a mother and father who are the same biological parents of all the children in the family. These patterns merely reflect broader social trends in lifestyle choices and changes in intimate relationships. In Britain, for instance, according to the Office of National Statistics, 'In the space of one generation, the numbers marrying have halved while the numbers divorcing have trebled and the proportion of children born outside marriage has quadrupled' (quoted in

Beck-Gernsheim, 2002, p. x). A profound expression of the broad acceptance of new lifestyle choices and politics – especially given the focus of
this book – was the decision in 2002 to legislate to change the UK adoption laws to allow gay and non-married heterosexual couples to adopt.
Although initially defeated in the House of Lords, such was the huge
wave of professional and lay opinion supporting the change that the
amendment was carried into law (The *Observer*, 20 October 2002). While
driven by pragmatic concerns to find more 'families' for children in
long-term care, this vividly illustrates the momentum towards the
democratization of families and personhood in which the very notion
of 'family' is being redefined.

The forms of child care policy that helped structure the welfare state
within simple modernity presumed a citizenry with more stable lifestyle
habits than are characteristic of late-modernity. As we have seen, prior
to the 1970s, child care professionals essentially sought to make women
better mothers/housewives and fathers better wage-labourers/providers.
More directive control of populations was possible then when people
had relatively stable lifestyle preferences and their level of reflexive
involvement with wider social processes was relatively low. The transformation to reflexive modernity has arisen from complex economic,
social and political processes, such as globalization, changes in the
nature and meaning of 'work' and the impact of new social movements,
especially feminism. The power of tradition, external controls (such as
religion) and ascribed class and gender roles has declined and the self
has become 'a reflexive project' (Giddens, 1991, 1992).

These processes of 'individualization' (Beck, 1992; Beck and Beck-
Gernsheim, 1995, 2002) mean that people are faced with new kinds of
choices about 'how to live' and 'who to be?' 'The tendency', writes Beck,
'is towards the emergence of individualised forms and conditions of
existence which compel people – for the sake of their own material survival – to make themselves the centre of their own life-planning and
conduct of life' (Beck, 1992, p. 88). People are now compelled to construct a biography, a 'life of one's own' (Beck and Beck-Gernshiem,
2002), as life becomes a 'planning-project' (Beck-Gernsheim, 2002).
While traditional 'authorities', faith related and others, may still have an
influence in some people's biographical projects, in reflexive modernity
the influence of experts, global media, books and so on significantly
increases as sources upon which people draw in reflexively making their
lives. Individualization processes do not mean that there is no longer a
structural basis to social relationships and identity formation. New
demands, controls and constraints are being imposed on individuals

which, through the welfare state, job market and a range of other institutions, tie people into a network of regulations, provisos and conditions (Beck and Beck-Gernsheim, 1996, p. 25). Individualization, then, opens up 'precarious freedoms' (Beck and Beck-Gernsheim, 1996, p. 25).

Expertise also takes on new meanings. The extraordinary growth in therapy, counselling and indeed social work services arises from the way in which lay people use such experts as 'sounding boards' for critical reflection on themselves and their relationships. What Giddens calls 'life politics' refers to the realm of experience where people are systematically faced with new choices as to 'how we should live in a world where everything that used to be natural (or traditional) now has in some sense to be chosen, or decided about' (Giddens, 1994a, pp. 90–1). Helping professionals such as psychotherapists are increasingly drawn upon to aid decision-making and provide 'methodologies of life-planning' (Giddens, 1992, p. 180; Elliott, 1996, p. 71). The same can be said for child protection which has prised open the 'traditional' family, rendering visible its darkest secrets – the 'battered child syndrome', emotional abuse, child sexual abuse and domestic violence – making the family accessible to new forms of intervention. In the face of public criticism for child protection failures, expertise becomes demystified and loses its traditional authority. People are exposed to new insights into how they are governed and are able to be 'cleverer' than in simple modernity (Giddens, 1994a, p. 94).

The reflexive citizen comes to possess a good deal of information that is available to professionals themselves, and this very reflexivity informs how people act and react in conducting their lives. This does not mean that they are intellectually superior and 'cleverer' in the academic sense, but that they have to be able to cope with so many more (multiple) choices and information, much of it contradictory (Beck and Beck-Gernshiem, 2002). This now includes significant amounts of information about child abuse and protection systems as, with the development of global mass media, most people live in the same 'discursive space' and child abuse – how to stop it, survive it – and risks to children are staples of media reporting and perhaps the most heavily discussed social issue of our time (Jackson and Scott, 1999).

The spiral of the reflexive construction of identities has taken hold *inside* the family. The roles of men and women are no longer structurally fixed in the traditional mode. Women in general now *have* a biography, the opportunity of a life to plan beyond motherhood and nurture, and have acquired rights to protection from abuse. This does not mean that all women get to fulfil such rights. They too often still have to be 'won' on a case-by-case basis, however, professionals can no longer deny them without justification. Men as fathers are increasingly challenged to become good at intimacy and caring as well as the traditional male role of providing, although generally, women continue to do more domestic work and child care (Burgess, 1997; McKeown *et al.*, 1998). The net effect is a new requirement for openness and negotiation in intimate relationships: who does what, who goes out to work, minds the children, does the dishes, and so on, all has to be decided by the couple. And as children grow older, it involves them too. Such negotiation requires men, women and children to know what they want, which demands self-knowledge and emotional literacy. Thus, for Giddens, the new 'intimacy' is now 'above all, a matter of emotional communication with others, and oneself, in a context of equal relationships' (Giddens, 1992, p. 139).

This is not to say that all relationships are now organized on such a negotiated basis (Jamieson, 1998). 'Marriage' cannot be said to be 'a meeting of equals' in many ethnic and cultural groupings in the United States or Britain, or amongst the travelling community in Ireland, for instance. Evidence of unequal relations of power between the genders is apparent in continued high rates of domestic violence. In 27 per cent of all the referrals in my 319 case sample domestic violence was a known problem either in the past or the present (94 per cent of which was men's abuse of women). But despite, and in some respects because of, such problems, the empirical evidence suggests that a structural transformation in intimacy has occurred which has radically altered the conditions within which self-identity and social intervention are constituted today.

The very role of welfare practitioners is shifting to provide protection, assist people with life-planning and promote the *democratization* of intimate relationships and families. And where this doesn't happen, it *should*. No social group has embraced and promoted these changes and the democratization of personhood with more enthusiasm than social work. In challenging accepted norms and conventional boundaries, since the 1970s it has been the 'expressive' profession *par excellence* (Martin, 1981). The definition of effective work in protecting children in time has come to include not merely survival and having a life, but promoting children's welfare and autonomy to live a life of their own.

Help-seeking, creative, reflexive agency and the complexities of child protection

The implications of this can be explored in terms of two key processes which emerge from the data in my study: help-seeking behaviours, and life-planning. The relationship between experts and lay people in terms of referral practices and what Giddens (1990) calls 'access points' provides a crucial analytical vantage point from which to assess the meanings of welfare. How the state gains access to vulnerable citizens, and vice versa, is a curiously under-analysed area of social policy and social work. The data demonstrates the positive use of (child) welfare services by creative reflexive citizens, especially women. By far the most significant referral source in my study was mothers, who raised initial concern – either directly themselves or through telling another professional who told social services – in 27 per cent of cases. In 11 per cent, children brought the concern to light either by directly reporting it or, much more often, by telling someone who then reported it. Some 61 per cent of these mothers had histories of social work involvement and were therefore re-referring themselves in a context of already having had received a social work service. The state also initiated intervention and the key professional referral agents were schools/teachers, police and public health nurses.

Referring oneself to child protection agencies is no guarantee of remaining in control of the process and not all who did this were to become satisfied consumers as some did not get the kind of service they wanted. I shall return to this point later, but for the moment want to focus on the constructive aspects of help-seeking. Many service users not only get the service they want but actively help to shape it. This has to be seen in the context of their very real struggles to cope with their lives and relationships. In other words, they recognize their own or their children's need for safety, and emotional as well as practical help and ask for it. Or, when reported by someone else, some accept their need for help and go on to fully engage and 'seek' it out. However, the complexity of this is evident in how even in those cases where one or more family members found the child protection intervention a positive experience, other members of the same household experienced it negatively. To speak of 'the service user' as if all family members shared the same needs and interests is deeply problematic. In individualized social conditions the desire to live a life of one's own causes and expresses as many differences and tensions in families as it does alliances.

A typical case study from my research will help to illustrate and draw out these issues further.[1] Sixteen-year-old 'Fiona Murphy' lived with her 12-year-old sister Paula and both their parents. Mr Murphy worked as an unskilled labourer and Mrs Murphy was a full time homemaker. The case was referred by a school because Fiona 'disclosed to teacher that her paternal uncle sexually abused her by inappropriate touching of a sexual nature and by exposing himself' (case file). Thus Fiona's disclosure, as conveyed through the school, provided the basis upon which intervention proceeded. On investigation, sexual abuse, domestic violence, parents experiencing mental health problems and housing problems were identified as known or suspected child care/protection problems. Sexual abuse was regarded as the main presenting problem by the investigating social worker. It appeared that Fiona had been fondled by her uncle, an alcoholic, who also flashed his penis at her. There was concern about domestic violence and the state of the home was judged to be very poor. It emerged that the family were well known to child protection services in America, where they used to live, particularly with respect to sexual abuse of Fiona by men in the community. An older child, now a young adult, was resident in America.

A decision was soon reached to accommodate the girls in voluntary care, which the parents agreed to on the basis that it was temporary. Fiona was then referred by the social worker to a specialist unit which carried out child sexual abuse assessments. These were established in the late-1980s, to ensure as accurate as possible a gathering of forensic evidence in suspected cases, to avoid 'secondary abuse' in the form of multiple interviews of children (Butler-Sloss, 1988), all of which must be seen in the context of controversies concerning how child sexual abuse was drawing middle-class families into its net (McGrath, 1996). Fiona went on to disclose over 20 instances of being sexually abused by men during her life and the assessment concluded that in all probability this did occur, including abuse by two relatives. The children also disclosed serious physical abuse by their mother, although Paula was less forthcoming on this. Their father noted, defensively, in the research interview that '[Paula] won't talk, she won't talk but the older girl, she's a different kettle of fish. She'll talk to everybody, she'll spill the beans.'

Having taken immediate protective action with the girls entering care, the social worker went on to complete a 'comprehensive assessment' of risk and the family. The voluntary reception into care which was supposed to be for four or five weeks was made permanent when social workers went for and got care orders. The parents' lack of protective behaviour was the main basis for securing care orders. The social worker's view was that the parents 'minimized' the alleged abuse, that 'on some levels they kind of acknowledged it, they were very difficult to, they were both unable to focus on the needs of the children, they were self engrossed'. The parents were allowing the uncle who was now a 'confirmed perpetrator' access to the children. For the social worker the concern was not that the father was sexually abusing his daughters but his 'lack of protection, it's like he puts them in a situation where they'll be abused'.

Mr Murphy played no real part in the comprehensive assessment as he withdrew co-operation due to his anger at the children being taken permanently into care. They were a mobile household, reflecting a key shift in late-modernity towards globalization in how the movement is now not (just) within national boundaries, but across international borders. Detailed knowledge of the children's history of being on an 'At Risk' register in America formed a crucial part of the Irish risk assessment and keeping hold of the children's passports became a child protection issue. The father expressed his anger and sadness because the children 'were not released' from care, as planned. He 'fought for my kids. I love those kids more than my own life, they were my whole life, but once they took them that was it, I had no trust in the [agency].' Because of fears of child abduction, access was supervised, but he 'wanted no part of supervisory discussion, we happen to be a very close family'. At the time of research interviews Mr and Mrs Murphy were separated. Although 'she was back and forth' and 'used to move to refuges' he was adamant that 'I never hit her', and claimed that she hit him. For him, 'this marriage is finished, I don't like getting hit and too much has happened'.

Mrs Murphy also expressed dissatisfaction that her children were still in care in view of the social worker's 'promise' that the children would be returned to her care after five or six weeks. Mrs Murphy presented herself as more of an ally of the girls and therefore took up a stance where she felt she gained something from statutory intervention. According to her she played a part in the abuse of the girls being disclosed and was more accepting of the fact that Fiona in particular was at risk: 'the environment that she [Fiona] was in, she didn't have nothing, she didn't have a proper home, she didn't have a proper family'.

However, she felt intimidated by social workers to co-operate or lose the children altogether but felt that ultimately the children had been protected: 'yeah, I suppose in a way, yeah the girls being abused you know, not much every day, every third day maybe if they were lucky. They didn't have a good environment for starters.' She was as much concerned about the conditions they were living in as the sexual abuse and the fact that the children 'were freezing to death, I wanted to put the heat on, you'd see ice on the windows, child in bed, but I got out and I told everything'. She felt that social workers were 'watching' her: 'they're like a fly, they'll follow you around'. They did not 'listen' to her, 'well they listen to your story but they're not listening that I want my girls back'. Mrs Murphy attended one case conference but 'didn't say anything, I just sat there'. It was at the case conference that 'it just hit me, the aspects of what really happened to my girls, you know what was very real, the abuse you know, the mental abuse, the physical abuse, it was going to their minds ... it took me a long time to realise what was happening'. Her long-term hope was to 'have my family back ... well have the girls back'.

In her research interview Fiona explained the problems and how they came to light.

> I was in school one day and I'd slit my wrists a few times, with a maths compass, and I went to school and I told the teacher that I'd slit it and she said why and I started telling her about my parents and everything, and then they told social workers and social workers got onto foster care and then we just came to foster care, because I'd told the people in school, I told them like that my parents were fighting a lot and always hitting each other and we never got to do our homework with all the noise and the neighbours always stare at us.

Then there was her uncle, 'the worst alcoholic you could ever meet in your life', who used to disturb them at three in the morning, who slept with his dog, was unkempt and whose 'house must be the messiest one in [place]'. Fiona also recalled incidents in the car: 'we'd be trying to sit down in the car peacefully like but he'd [uncle] be like putting his arms back touching our legs and everything'. Fiona felt comfortable approaching a teacher to discuss her problems, 'yeah it was alright, I'm more used to it like, I've told the whole entire world my problems, I've told teachers, I have a psychologist at the moment, I've told social workers, everybody'. She regarded foster care positively: 'it's been better for us because if I was still living back [home] I wouldn't be living there, I'd probably be dead, buried, six foot under'. This was because 'there was nothing to eat really' because of how her parents didn't cook or provide and 'probably losing all my blood from slitting my wrists. I wouldn't be alive'.

Fiona described her own and her sister's appearance before their move: 'our hair was Jesus, manky, long scraggly hair, very thin faces, not many friends at school'. The social worker also commented on the positive difference in the children's physical appearance since coming into care. Fiona felt that social work intervention had 'changed my life. I mean changing my life in a good way', although she sometimes regretted leaving her parents, 'not really my dad but my mum because I feel so sad for her sometimes because she's out in [place] by herself. She has nothing like, she's sitting there by herself. I'm not really angry with social workers, my dad is but I'm not one bit like him.' She currently sees her social worker on a fortnightly basis and a psychologist weekly. Talking to the psychologist 'helps her': it's 'grand, we talk about the past and mum and dad fighting'. She feels she is more 'confident' since she entered foster care, 'everything is going fine at the moment, school work and mum is grand'.

Paula's view of the reason for social work intervention was 'because my sister went in and told all of her problems and I had to go in'. At the time she was 'thinking there's nothing wrong with me'. Paula felt that social workers ask too many questions, some of which she finds 'hard' and resented being asked about personal details. Paula considered the social worker's role was 'to help people, that's all I think', and conceded that 'they helped us for a bit like'. In response to what her weekly sessions with a psychologist did for her she felt 'dunno, not much'. She felt that where the family were living prior to her entering care was 'too dirty and smelly and stuff out there, all farms and stuff' and that foster care had at least changed that. Paula felt 'sad' about moving into foster care, but said that she didn't 'really' talk to social workers about her feelings of sadness. 'I don't know, I can never, I can never talk to people, there's something wrong with me, I just can't.' In terms of her hopes for the future, Paula, similar to her sister, wished to return to America with her mother. Overall, Paula felt that social workers did not 'really' help her.

The case illustrates the intensified socio-legal and administrative structure and multidisciplinary network that globally surrounds child protection: the case conferences, 'At Risk' registers, the careful attention given to interviewing children in alleged sexual abuse cases in ways which extract legal evidence in forensic ways acceptable to the courts, and the comprehensive assessment used to gather knowledge on which to base risk assessments and long-term planning. It also reflects attempts to more actively include (non-abusing) parents in decision-making, such as at case conferences, and to take at least some account of children's wishes. It shows that not only is child sexual abuse now squarely on professional agendas, but the extent to which such harm to children is defined in broad ways to include non-penetrative sexual violation. Both parents disclosed incidents of serious sexual abuse in their own childhoods, neither of which were recognized or dealt with when they were children. The fact that they can now disclose this and that children/young people can make such disclosures of sexual abuse today and have a good chance of being believed illustrates the extent of the shift in question. Concerns about domestic violence and the impact of the parental relationship on the children, the poor living conditions and the general character of parent–child relationships illustrate the deepening emphasis today on emotional life and harm.

These comments should not be taken as an unqualified celebration of progress in child protection which can be generalized to all cases. The consequences of modernity for children at risk and their families are much more varied and complex than that. Major problems undoubtedly persist and too many children still are not effectively protected in time or even at all. Indeed, the Murphy case illustrates the complexity in that Paula was clearly unhappy about being in care and saw little value in social intervention, while her older sister experienced it as life saving and life affirming. Equally, the parents are (literally) divided in their perspectives on events in a context where the family is thoroughly individualized: mother left father, the marriage is over and each makes claim and counterclaim about domestic violence. The child sexual abuse exposed fractures within the family in terms of the lack of parental capacities to promote their children's welfare. Traditional notions of 'order' in terms of a strict sexual division of labour and gender roles are less prominent now than an ideology which holds that parents – and mothers in particular – need to be seen to do their best for their children. This now implies an *emotional* contribution to child welfare, as well as the traditional concern with physical care and management of children's bodies and (dirty) homes. Practice, however, is no less gendered (Scourfield, 2003). The mother remains the responsible, engaged parent involved with her children in care and ambivalently supports social worker's actions in taking custody of the children, while the father withdraws, hurt and angry.

On the positive side, such case work provides evidence of some change in definitions of the 'child' reflecting a move away from a construction of childhood as simply a period of dependency and powerlessness to seeing children as social actors (James and Prout, 1990, 1997). The social construction of the child today is more ambiguous than ever as, on the one hand, cultural obsessions with risk have become focused on childhood which has led to a diminishing of children's freedom to be autonomous actors by 'paranoid parents' who fear the abduction, sexual abuse and murder of their children (Furedi, 2001). On the other hand, within welfare discourses, children are now beginning to be understood as having the capacity for individual or collective action, as moral actors and given rights to be heard and influence decisions about their lives.

Since the 1980s this change has been written into legislation which prescribes that the child's wishes must be taken into account. It is also finding expression in the development of policies and practices of child and youth advocacy which attempt to provide structures, processes and supports which give 'voice' to children in decision-making about their lives (Dalrymple, 2003). Awareness of the abuse of children looked after in care has been especially influential in creating the dynamic for such changes (Corby *et al.*, 2001). On balance however, such change is uneven in terms of the practical application of children's rights on a case-by-case basis (Thomas, 2002).

Fundamentally, however, this case example shows how children/ young people and women who disclose abuse can be seen to be choosing to report abusers whose crimes remained hidden within the traditional family and community. Such individuals are engaged in historically new ways in reflexively constructing their own biographies and planning their life-projects. In the past, as earlier chapters have shown, women have always been active referral agents and users of such services (Gordon, 1989; Ferguson, 1992). But what is historically significant is that the nature of what gets reported today has broadened to include much wider definitions of such problems as child sexual abuse, and what service users expect in terms of rights to protection and Western child protection workers are challenged to provide in terms of longer-term life-planning work is significantly different. The same applies to those who disclose their own problems and need for help to become a 'good enough' parent.

The help-seeking behaviour of children and women in cases of intra-familial child sexual abuse, often responding to the initial disclosures by children of abuse by fathers or relatives, involves them making crucial life-political and life-planning decisions, having to make immediate choices about their relationship with the alleged abuser or others. The same is true of victims of domestic violence who seek safety by reporting their abusers to the police or seek help from refuges or social services. They are drawing social workers into a process of engagement around who they are and how they want to live, as mothers and women (Featherstone, 1999). The mothers in my study were invariably aware of the risks of engaging with child protection agencies for fear of losing their children or that the professionals may fail them in some way. As one put it: 'in this town social workers have an awful bad name. If you get involved with them at all they will take your kids, they will do this, they will do that, it is unbelievable what they think.' Yet the same woman formed a deep attachment to social workers and went on, by her own account, to be helped to make changes in her life. Like others, she took the risk of engaging because not to do so felt even riskier. Such is the 'cleverness' now required to deal with contradictory information and difficult choices and decisions.

The paradoxical outcome of the crisis in trust in child protection experts and greater social reflexivity is that it increases the knowledge-ability of the abused and excluded about their plight and welfare services and enables them to consider taking the risk of referring themselves for help. Such decisions to engage with professional help shows how reflex-ively organized life-planning involves consideration of risks as filtered through contact with expert knowledge and how such reflexive aware-ness is a central feature of the structuring of post-traditional self-identity (Giddens, 1991, p. 5). Individuals are engaged in seeking to colonize the future for themselves as an intrinsic part of their life-planning – a form of mastery or control which parallels the overall orientation of modern institutions towards colonizing the future (Giddens, 1991, p. 125).

In late-modernity 'risk' is not just a negative, dangerous phenome-non, but brings opportunities for protection from violence that was tra-ditionally repressed. While significant problems remain for too many abused children and non-abusing parents, not least, as I show later, in terms of the emergence of an absolutist forensic approach to child sex-ual abuse (Wattam and Parton, 1999), viewed historically and in general terms, we are talking here about extraordinary shifts in recognition which provide new and very positive opportunities for protection. The relevant comparison here is the experience of children like Emily Wilson from the 1909 case profiled in Chapter 3, whose sexual abuse was not formally acknowledged or worked with, despite being removed into care because of parental neglect.

A further significant pattern is that today children's well-being is no longer a matter of religious conversion but of psychological well-being. One casework pattern (although as I show elsewhere in the book, not the only one) is for children to have acquired an identity which is not just based on what they are going to be – the primal fear being criminals or rebels – and are entitled to responses as victims in their own right. If anything, psychological concepts have become so embedded in such work that this provides for forms of power over children and carers where if they don't disclose or express themselves emotionally it can become a source for pathologizing them. A Christian morality is replaced by a therapeutic morality. The power of this 'confessional imperative' (Foucault, 1979) is such that when not delivered, very vul-nerable people can be negatively judged by experts and even by *them-selves*. This was evident in Paula Murphy's remark that, 'I don't know, I can never, I can never talk to people, there's something wrong with me, I just can't.' Yet, the complexities of this are again apparent even in the same family, as her sister Fiona spoke positively of the outcome for her of how she had 'told the whole entire world my problems' and this help-seeking and life-planning work was enabling her to come to terms with the past and present.

Child protection interventions and life-planning

Some 74 per cent of the families in my study lived on social security benefits, illustrating the predominance of poverty and social exclusion to the lives of typical subjects of child protection. It gets worse in fact, as many of these women also had to cope with domestic violence, addiction problems and histories of abuse in their childhood and had to deal with child behaviour and control problems, as well as a violent partner either present or in the background. Sixty-seven per cent of the children who entered care were from these backgrounds. Given such disadvantage, a key research question surrounds just what real scope there is for those who are the subjects of welfare interventions to be 'reflexive' and influence their life narratives and chances? A common criticism of the theory of reflexive modernization is that its model of the self-reflexive individual relates primarily to people who are socially and economically privileged, those who have the cultural and material resources to pay to go to a psychotherapist and engage in self-inspection. As one review of the matter puts it, 'many people simply lack the resources and techniques with which to engage in the project of self-reflexivity' (Lupton, 1999, p. 114).

Critics tend to draw selectively from Giddens (1998) on such things as the need to provide counselling in some situations of disadvantage rather than benefits. This is seen as supporting a shift away from a redistributive model of social democratic politics towards a re-structuring of welfare which is really about disciplining the poor through work fare and other schemes where rights and responsibilities are perniciously connected to obligations (Levitas, 1998). Social work and child protection are then said to become focused on 'enforcement' and regulating the lives of the poor and marginalized whose lives are said to be so embedded in disadvantage that this leaves little scope for service users – and the professionals who work with them – to act to shape their lives or the nature of the service that is provided to secure positive outcomes (Jordan and Jordan, 2000). This has led critics to argue that the proper focus for social work and child protection is not life-politics but 'emancipatory politics', which places the emphasis on people's marginality and (lack of) life-chances (Garrett, 2003).

Even some commentators who are generally sympathetic to the paradigm of reflexive modernization have their doubts. Thus Lash argues that there are 'reflexivity winners' – those who have the resources and capital to engage in self-reflexivity – and 'reflexivity losers', the poor and socially excluded, who don't. He asks, 'Just how "reflexive" is it possible for a single mother in an urban ghetto to be? ... Just how much freedom from the "necessity" of "structure" and structural poverty does this ghetto mother have to self-construct her own "life narratives"?' (Lash, 1994, p. 120). However, posing such important questions in this manner misses some crucial dimensions of the scope for reflexive action by all citizens, even those who are socially excluded. The very idea of providing counselling to such a 'ghetto mother' instead of material resources to help her live a life of her own free from struggle seems oppressive and morally unjust when the issue is framed in this way. Yet, in circumstances of struggle involving not only poverty but such problems as abuse, addiction and trauma, my data suggests this is a crucial dimension of what many marginalized agency clients need and desire and social policy needs to respond accordingly.

The notion of life-politics captures the complexity of the interrelationship between structural processes and biographical experience. It contains an anti-oppressive, emancipatory dimension but is firmly grounded in attention to the strengths and vulnerabilities of the lived life (Ferguson, 2003c). This argument hinges on the introduction of greater clarity about the life circumstances of welfare clients/service users and how self-reflexivity connects with the changing relationship between expert systems and lay people. A central problem with Lash's and other's criticisms – and to an extent the work of Giddens and Beck itself – is the lack of specificity in relation to domains of action where the (re)constitution of selfhood is possible in late-modernity (see also, Taylor-Gooby, 1999).

A second pattern to emerge from the data with respect to creative, reflexive actions shows how today longer term intervention work is not just about 'protection' in terms of providing safety for children and women, but is also fundamentally concerned with 'life-planning'. This process means maximizing opportunities for clients 'to harmonise present concerns and future projects with a psychological inheritance from the past' (Giddens, 1992, p. 180). Most of the mothers in my study who had child abuse/care problems – and some fathers too – had experienced abuse in their own childhoods and were struggling to free themselves from a lifetime of toxic attachments and the psychological inheritance of that trauma in how they related to their partners and children. Intervention provided a 'methodology of life planning' which enabled women (and the far fewer men who engaged) to make crucial decisions about their lives, such as do I want to stay in this relationship? What kind of life do I want? It also involved promoting healing through exploring deeper questions to do with the psychological inheritance from the past and the constitution of the self, such as why am I in this kind of relationship to begin with?, and what do I need to do to ensure a happier future for myself and my children? As I have been suggesting, at its best child protection provides the same resources for life-planning for children and young people, where they are given real choices about where and how to live and opportunities to deal with the legacy of pain and any abuse they have experienced. In my study, life-planning transcended the manner in which the agency became involved and was also evident in cases not initiated by children or mothers, but by the state.

The case of 'Maureen', a single mother of two children aged seven years and 18 months at the time of referral, typifies these processes.[2] In an attempt to ward off poverty and have a life outside the home she got an evening job which meant working long hours into the night. However, she was reported to child protection social workers for 'neglect', having an under-age babysitter. The public health nurse, on visiting the home one afternoon, also found the children at home alone. The social work investigation found Maureen to be under great stress, both from poverty and the extreme domestic violence perpetrated over many years by her partner. Soon after, she and the children went into a women's refuge, but according to her, 'It kept me safe yet it did not mentally give me a break, you are pulled from your home. I hated having to leave my home.' That kind of 'mental' relief began to come when she finally managed to have her violent partner legally barred from the home and he was imprisoned for assaulting her. The social worker engaged in [some 10 months of] long-term work with her, on the basis that: 'If the mother could be in touch with her own stuff, she may be able to free herself from all the energy she was putting in to protect herself and she could protect her children.' Although very positive about the social work intervention, like many such women, Maureen was critical of the response she got. Fear was crucial to stopping her take action sooner against her partner and she needed help sooner to feel safe.

Maureen had never known any other kind of close intimate relationship that did not involve the victimization of other women, including her mother, and her own relationship with the children's father.

> It was sweet like for the first year like everything, and little things start up and they end up in violence in the end of it all. And you do not believe you are in it until you are actually, like you can get hit once and you can get hit twice and this is going, you can get over this

like, but it is unbelievable how fast it works into a relationship. Without you knowing it even though you are the person being hit, without you actually sitting up and realising this is what you are actually being, battered, this is what is going on like. It took me an awful long time. It took me a long time, it shouldn't have had really because I watched it at home for years me. I just did not want to think this was going to happen me like. Because my Dad was very very bad as well, a very very violent person.

Here we see the woman beginning to revisit her life narrative and question how she became a victim and the psychological inheritance from the past which contributed to her sense of self in the present and being placed at risk. Her self-esteem was very low – she was only beginning to stop blaming herself for the violence – and the social worker tried hard to get her to take better care of herself, enabling her to enter a refuge and getting the police to take the domestic violence more seriously and act upon it. Once safety is secured, the woman is freed to begin a therapeutic journey of healing (Herman, 1992).

I think I know it has been ten months and I know things have gone well for me, but I still haven't had time out for myself, there is an awful lot there that a good reach in myself will do me a world of good. Whether I stayed in the room and cried or did something different, you know, I feel myself there is a lot in there. There is often a night if I am not working and I could have been doing something in the kitchen and the tears will just roll.

Her healing journey had only begun: 'I'd say I am still going through it in the back of my head, it is all still there and all. Time will heal'. In the process she was now planning a new kind of present and future through reviewing her biography and changing her life narrative. Crucially, this does not only involve work which promotes reflection and insight through the mind – narratives of the self – but by working on the emotions. As Maureen put it, when she started to 'work with' the social worker she [Maureen] 'Just cried. The social worker told me that is exactly what she wanted me to do. To get it out no matter, whatever it was. And I got to trust her then and that's how I started to work out of it.' The social worker's wonderfully skilled response was such that Maureen felt understood, comforted and safe talking about her life and the violence. As Maureen herself notes, 'I'd do the talking and they'd [social workers] do the listening, It's good to talk.' This shows how life-planning work is about promoting people's 'mastery' over their day-to-day lives in order to assist people to be able to control their life circumstances, control the future with some degree of success and 'allow the social and natural framework of things seem a secure grounding for life activities' (Giddens, 1992, p. 202).

Another crucial feature of this in terms of creative reflexive practice is that the referral had been 'notified' to and processed by the official child protection system which recommended 'monitoring of situation, ensure adequate baby sitting arrangements if mother is to continue working'. Here we see the woman being positioned by the official discourse in purely utilitarian terms, as a mother. The wider aspects of her humanity and needs do not form part of the discursive reasoning of the bureaucratic child protection system. Crucially, however, neither the social worker nor the mother herself accepted the official (instrumentally rational) version of the 'case' and combined to co-construct a highly meaningful piece of work together. Here we see just how much the reflexive action taken by professionals and users can and does shape intervention. As the social worker observes, 'I suppose the mother kept the heat on us because she was not getting protected and that was really why we had more involvement.'

This kind of creative, reflexive response is all the more impressive given that it went on in the environment of risk anxiety and increased proceduralization and managerialism that I outlined in the last chapter. This vividly illustrates the constructive parameters of child protection as a form of 'bureaucratic late-modernism' in how the law, procedures and managerial guidance should merely provide the context and framework out of which health and social care professionals can work creatively with and within structures to carve out actions which make a (positive) difference to service user's lives (Ferguson, 2003b).

There were still, however, deficits in the intervention. Despite concern about significant harm to the children from 'neglect' and witnessing domestic violence, no direct work was done with them, which this book shows fitted an established historical pattern. This was a symptom both of a social worker being overworked and an ideology which regards mothers as central to casework: 'The children never even came into my way of thinking, being really honest, I don't know when I could do it.' The casework largely failed to go beyond the tendency for children and mothers to be treated synonymously, which is contrary to constructing children as individuals in casework (Wise, 1995). In effect, the intervention did not individualize the family members enough and relate to their lives of their own. Indeed, the mother herself was critical of this aspect of the response, feeling that her capacity to parent well was so diminished that her children should have been temporarily taken out of the violent situation. However, practical support could only come from the social worker because Maureen refused to work with a family support worker. And, ironically, having been critical of a lack of child-centredness, the mother would not allow her seven-year old to be interviewed for the research for fear that it would distress him.

On the other hand, what was achieved through the mother affirms Featherstone's (1999) argument that it is in the interests of good *child* protection for professionals to help women to develop their own sense of self outside of the life of their child(ren). Individualization processes remain fundamental to how the lone-parent and her children need to be worked with in terms of each family member having – or being helped to have – a life of their own, by dealing with the background to and legacy of separation and practical and emotional needs. The social worker's decision not to directly confront the violent father but leave this to the police and criminal justice system to engage him through sanctions is commendable in terms of the necessity for justice-making and a first step to him possibly taking responsibility for his problem with violence (Hearn, 1998) and doing some life-planning work on himself.

Awareness of such deficits again highlights the importance of historical context to evaluations of (best) practice. For instance, the very recent development in the United Kingdom of a systematic framework for assessing children in need changes the definition of best practice considerably (Horwath, 2000), as has the report into the tragic death of Victoria Climbié (Laming, 2003), such that it would now be impossible to exclude real expectations of such child-centred work. Yet, such case studies also demonstrate the journey that still has to be travelled, from government policy and guidance to changing practice.

Men, individualization and child protection

An important pattern to these interventions is the neglect of men and the tendency to place sole responsibility for children's well-being on women. This was even so in many cases where the men were the suspected offenders of woman and/or child abuse, yet were not engaged with by the system. Hoggett suggests that women's lives are so embedded in the endless demands from caring responsibilities that 'we need to give some thought to whether the notion of the "reflexive self" is not itself gendered, expressing an essentially masculine experience of autonomy in contrast to a "relational self" in which the self cannot be understood except in its relation to other' (Hoggett, 2001, p. 45). On the evidence of my child protection study, and a subsequent one which strategically identified work that *does* go on with fathers (Ferguson and Hogan, 2004), the assumption of a clear association between autonomy and a reflexive self is questionable.

The subject of intervention remakes her or himself through being deeply embedded in the intimacy of a relational world, not separate from it. I would argue that it is the very relational skills that women acquire that provide the basis for reflexive encounters with welfare professionals. The gendered expectation that women are and should be relationally responsible, for themselves and their children, while men should not, means that professionals and women actively engage one another, while men generally exclude themselves and are excluded. Fathers were the referral agents in just four of the 319 cases in this sample, and most of these involved non-resident fathers reporting concern for their children who were resident with the mothers and their new partners. The risks for women of 'mother blame' are considerable (Scourfield, 2001), yet the potential gains in terms of opportunities to engage in life-planning and the reflexive creation of a protected, healed self are equally significant.

The benefits for men are that they evade responsibility and sanctions, but the costs are huge in terms of the lack of reflexive engagement with a life narrative in any intimate sense. This helps to keep men stuck in a traditional model of non-reflective masculinity. But when men do actively engage they are just as able as women to be creative reflexive welfare subjects and benefit from life-planning and healing work. This is typified by a serious emotional abuse case in which the professionals visited in the evening when the man came in from work, something he very much appreciated:

> Most of the time it's nine to five and if you're not in, good luck! But the social worker and family support worker had never kind of done that you know. If you needed a later time, they'd arrange it. There is very few people who have done that.

There was a worthy attempt here to develop a father-centred practice which included a recognition of the man's positive capacities to care for his children and partner, an inclusive approach he – like other men – can greatly appreciate (Hawkins *et al.*, 1995; Dienhart and Dollahite, 1997; Ferguson and Hogan, 2004). Interventions need to focus on what men have to offer as well as any risks they represent (McKeown *et al.*,

1998; Daniel and Taylor, 1999) and on how men should or could assume greater responsibility for child care (Milner, 1993, 1996; Edwards, 1998). Gaining 'mastery' requires working with the inner life and feelings and is an emotional as much as a practical achievement. The closer men become to their children, the more they are able to open up to themselves and their partners, the closer they become to knowing themselves. It is through a deeper connection with their emotional lives and a move away from traditional masculine autonomy that men are facilitated by social professionals to become reflexive and gain true mastery over their lives.

Individualization becomes public: child protection and intimate citizenship

What we have witnessed in recent decades is a genuine transformation of the public domain in which child abuse and protection have played central parts. Scandal politics such as those surrounding the child death inquiries and the failure of the Churches worldwide to bring known clerical offenders to justice have weakened the hold of science and traditional 'authority' over lay people. A crucial outcome of this has been to transform public space in a way which creates more opportunities for disclosures. A good example of the dynamics of this was the response to the Cleveland affair in 1987 where comparatively high numbers of children (121) were removed into care as suspected victims of sexual abuse. Two local doctors took it upon themselves to proactively look for signs of child sexual abuse in troubled children who came through their hospital surgeries. In the immediate aftermath of the massive 'Cleveland' discourse – in modern times 'only the Falklands war attracted more publicity' (Community Care, 12 December, 1988, p. 13; Franklin, 1989) – the numbers of sexual abuse cases reported to the NSPCC increased by 21 per cent (NSPCC Annual Report, 1988). As a report in the *Times* put it, 'A big increase in the reported number of sexually abused children has dispelled fears that the Cleveland child sexual abuse controversy would deter the public from reporting such cases and doctors from treating them.'

While the sudden rise in sexual abuse referrals was thought to be happening *despite* the Cleveland affair, in a context of high reflexivity and critically knowledgeable citizens, it is more accurate to say that increased reporting of the problem was *because* of the re-constitution of child protection that Cleveland brought about. Similar types of high profile scandals and subsequent increases in child sexual abuse referrals have occurred in other countries (on Ireland, for instance, see McGuinness, 1993; Ferguson, 1994). The effect has been to create a new global consciousness and discursive space surrounding child sexual abuse as part of a new social context which Plummer (1995) characterizes as 'intimate citizenship'. A new confessional intimacy is now a defining feature of the public domain as abuse survivors tell their stories on radio and television talk shows and through print media. Professional consciousness has been radicalized and victims/survivors have responded by making decisions to report their abuse and bringing more and more cases forward, which is crucial to the process where service users are now reflexively constructing their own biographies.

The circularity of knowledge from media coverage, court cases and local knowledge, feed back into people's reflexive awareness of their lives and decisions and more victims feel empowered to come forward to seek help, providing a quality of belonging to a wider community of survivors. This typifies late-modern social relations in that it amounts to a permeable membership of a community and fluid identity which reflects the fragmented fashion in which we now shape our world. Such critical awareness helps to provide a momentum to clear away the toxic bonds and structures which held simple modernity together. Individualization, then, does not remain private, but becomes public and political in new ways.

This typifies what Beck (1997) calls 'sub-politics': how individuals from outside the political system appear on the 'stage of social design', as do collectivities such as 'citizen initiative groups' and self-help groups to shape and 're-invent' politics, challenging powerful groups and transforming structures. This is apparent in the initiatives taken by courageous women and men to tell their stories of abuse in public, take court action against abusers, form self-help and survivor groups, and publicly challenge the state for failing to protect them (McKay, 1998). The reinvention of politics arises from the flow of information generated from the agent upwards by the process of reflexive monitoring (Giddens, 1994a, p. 15; Dodd, 1999, p. 199). The new public discourse of rights, justice-making and recovery has not only transformed individual lives but helped to rewrite cultural scripts of power, sexuality and the gender order.

The ambiguous politics of child abuse and barriers to effective child protection

Yet, there are limits and real struggles involved in all of this. The mostly positive developments that I have been focusing on are far from the full story. Three other patterns are in evidence. First, it is clear from prevalence studies that significant numbers of abused children do not even make it into child protection systems in the first place. The numbers of adult survivors and children disclosing abuse in research studies considerably outnumber the rates of children coming to the attention of protection services (Cawson *et al.*, 2000; McGee *et al.*, 2002). One of the biggest challenges facing child protection is how to develop forms of 'active trust' (Giddens, 1994a) in services which will lead to disclosures, reports and protection for all of the abused children who need it.

Second, it remains quite typical for some children who *are* reported not to be engaged with *at all* in child protection interventions, as the case materials used in this chapter have also shown, and for therapeutic and support services not to be provided in substantiated cases where it is known there is risk and need. In my study, 26 per cent of the substantiated cases did not receive a meaningful post-investigative service (Ferguson and O'Reilly, 2001). The two main reasons for this were that the services were not available and even more commonly, that some parents, carers and children did not want a service. I deal at length with this profoundly significant pattern of resistance to using child protection services in Chapter 7. Third, and relatedly, despite intentions to do good, interventions into some children's lives are experienced by them as an abuse of power – as illustrated, for example, by Paula Murphy's response. The use of power to protect abused children is inevitable, it is the manner in which it is used, and especially the degree to which young people feel included in shaping these profoundly consequential decisions about what happens to them that matters.

An important element in sustaining these negative practices and outcomes is the persistence of institutional practices which have not kept pace with social change and have become what Beck (1992) calls 'zombie institutions'. Once again, the emergence of child sexual abuse as a social problem can be taken as an exemplar of this situation (Hooper, 1992; Farmer and Owen, 1995). During periods when disciplinary practices like child protection are in the process of being reconstituted and, in this instance, in the shift from simple to reflexive modernity and recognition of new forms of abuse, the redrawing of traditional boundaries to cultural practices involves the disruption of the conventional *fields of interaction* through which practices go on (Bordieu, 1977, 1986). A classic example of the dynamics of this is the Cleveland affair in the United Kingdom in 1987. Following the initiatives of the Cleveland doctors to proactively look for signs of child sexual abuse in troubled children who came through their hospital surgeries (Wyatt and Higgs, 1991a) and so many children being taken into care on court orders, the trust inherent to the expert system of child welfare was breached. A central aspect of the massive 'Cleveland' discourse was the voicing of fears by parents as to how safe it was for them to bring their children to hospitals for examinations about routine child health problems. This illustrates just how strongly attitudes of trust, or lack of trust, towards specific expert systems are liable to be influenced by experiences at 'access points', and updates of knowledge about them via the media and other sources (cf. Giddens, 1990, pp. 90–1).

In simple modernity the field of interaction in child protection almost exclusively surrounded working-class and marginal families. The disruption of this had the effect of drawing in social groups who are not conventionally a part of the field of interaction. In eschewing the traditional referral routes in child abuse cases (that is third party sources), the Cleveland doctors' initiatives on behalf of suspected abused children bypassed the traditional reliance on 'social evidence' in making child protection assessments. In so doing it cut through the established fields of interaction focused around marginal families to include a relatively large proportion of middle-class households. The Cleveland doctors themselves became aware of the fact that the children on whose behalf professionals take such initiatives 'may come from a wider range of social groups, including professionals and higher social classes' (Wyatt and Higgs, 1991b, p. 60).

In transgressing conventional boundaries, Cleveland professionals turned the world upside down. In the midst of the huge (negative) media attention and demonizing of the female doctor in particular, Dr Higgs, the discourse surrounding the professionals' actions was saturated with pollution fears of middle-class families (Nava, 1988) underpinned by disbelief that anyone other than the lower, working-class, dangerous, dirty client group could abuse children and have anything to do with such inherently stigmatizing services (see Bell, 1988). This demonstrates the significance of what I am calling the expressive dimension and cultural power of that which is marginal; how what is socially peripheral is symbolically central (Stallybrass and White, 1986). In this instance professionals who had routine contact with 'dirty', 'problem families' were perceived as polluting the 'clean' and respectable. The 'habitus' (Bourdieu, 1977, 1986) of modern child protection clients, which in earlier chapters I showed was resolutely lower working-class, began to be reconstituted so as to include the middle classes, a transition which remains partial and problematic to this day.

The Cleveland doctors placed particular emphasis on the use of a diagnostic tool which was largely new to child protection, the Reflex Anal Dilatation Test and the nature of clinical evidence in child sexual abuse and the examining practices of the medical professionals became the subject of heated debate and criticism (Butler-Sloss, 1988; Campbell, 1988). Due to its detailed attention to the genital and anal area, the Cleveland crisis was fundamental to constituting a new 'vulnerable margin' (Nettleton, 1988) of children's bodies and legitimate boundaries to protecting children from sexual abuse. The 'social' body was torn apart, disrupting an order which I have shown was set in place some 70 years earlier that had enabled child sexual abuse to be accommodated and hidden. The outcome has been a structural transformation in trust relations to enable more sexually abused children to be legitimately recognized and risks taken on their behalf. But hand in hand with this has gone the routinization of much greater caution and legal control of professionals in dealing with child sexual abuse.

In my study, social workers, other childcare professionals, as well as non-abusing parents, felt hugely constrained by the operation of the legal system as it operated in response to child sexual abuse. A significant minority of parents or carers who reported cases were very dissatisfied, especially some who brought to light child sexual abuse. Major efforts are expended gathering evidence that is 'forensically' sound with often minimal beneficial outcomes for children and families (Wattam and Parton, 1999). Intervention even makes matters *worse* in some child sexual abuse cases as the children and (non-abusing) parents are left (alone) to carry the burden of cases that take an extremely long time to process through the criminal justice system and rarely end in prosecutions (see also, Wattam, 1997; Soothill and Francis, 2002). Parents are, rightly, perplexed at the extreme caution with which the social and legal system approach suspected abusers and a perception that little seems to be done to protect the children with whom they continue to have contact.

Social workers fear being perceived as having interfered with correct 'forensic' investigative procedures by saying the wrong thing to or 'leading' a child and 'contaminating' evidence by rendering the child's statement inadmissible in court. Consequently, they do not really engage with such children or support their parents. Some social workers who specialize in child sexual abuse assessments are so concerned about how to conduct interviews in a legally acceptable way, they even feel restricted in offering comfort to suspected abused children (Ferguson and O'Reilly, 2001). The net result is that not only is justice not served, but also many sex offenders remain free and untouchable in the community, which has huge implications for child protection since this is a compulsive form of behaviour which offenders don't give up voluntarily (Finkelhor, 1984; Morrison *et al.*, 1994). Sanctions and 'treatment' programmes offer the only real chance to stop such abusers and protect future victims.

In this respect, child protection is as resolutely 'solid' as ever, the problem being that the law has failed to keep pace with the individualization of families and social relationships. The essential problem then becomes one of trust (Smith, 2001). Just as I have argued the disclosure of survivor's stories of abuse and information about the operation of the system can encourage people to take positive decisions to report their own or other's abuse, negative imagery and stories, especially regarding the operations of the legal system, can lead to a fear of child (sexual) abuse being brought forward by or on behalf of victims. This shows how some of the most oppressive, undemocratic practices that go on involve simply doing nothing for suspected victims, or doing them too late to create confidence that the system can protect children in time.

More positively, this chapter has shown how a new cultural space has opened up which enables the most vulnerable members of society to seek to become reflexive citizens by engaging with child protection in ways which enable them to find safety, engage in life-planning and longer term healing. Not all agency clients use that space in a creative reflexive way, however. Some, as I shall show further in the next chapter, refuse to be clients of child care agencies at all. I have shown how the self-reflexivity of contemporary Western welfare subjects connects with the changing relationship between expert systems and lay people and have argued that advances in theorizing child protection and reflexivity require greater specificity in relation to domains of action where the (re)constitution of selfhood is possible in late-modernity.

Many of the welfare subjects featured in this book clearly embody what Hoggett (2001, p. 45) refers to as 'that sense of agency which will enable them to "make out" or "get by" or turn a constraint into an opportunity. And because of their marginal position in the social order welfare subjects always tend to start out from a position of being objects of circumstance rather than shapers of their own lives.' On one level, the kind of reflexive action identified here means returning troubled people to normative functioning, assisting the vulnerable to be able to control their life circumstances and the future with some degree of success (Giddens, 1992, p. 202). Thus these same people continue for the most part to live in poverty, and it is vital that welfare regimes urgently address the structural changes needed to promote equality. But such individuals have still had an opportunity to live a safer life within the structural constraints governing their lives and to develop themselves in a manner which has enduring effects for their lives. Reflexive life-planning is categorically not simply something that is open only to those who have the material resources to do it. In the domain of life-politics and welfare intervention a 'life of one's own' refers not to absolute freedom, but principally to gaining 'mastery' over one's life to the extent of enabling people to develop the practical and emotional skills needed to achieve ordinary functioning and an 'actualization' of the self within the structural conditions in which life goes on. While there are limits to the degree to which individuals and especially the poor, can rewrite their life scripts, there remain personal and collective transformative possibilities in these social practices.

Individualization, then, has created a mixture of opportunities and dangers for children and their carers. The blatant sexism and 'ethnic cleansing' of child protection in simple modernity has gone and been replaced by the *democratizing impulse* of social intervention. The essential paradigm for child protection in post-traditional society is the 'democratic family' (Giddens, 1998). This should be understood both in terms of what is currently going on and as an aspiration in relation to changing non-democratic interventions. In general, women are expected to carry too much responsibility for child care, while men are too often excluded and exclude themselves from engagement in welfare work. The child in particular remains disenfranchised, without a public voice in modern society. Yet when it does go on and child protection is structured through the democratizing impulse, at its best this involves practitioners trying to allow children to be heard as well as seen, women to have an identity not just based on motherhood and fathers to have emotional lives as well as mothers. The effect of this is that on a case-by-case basis intervention outcomes are highly variable and contingent. While there are discernible patterns to interventions, the future is always uncertain as to what the outcome will be in the unfolding of any particular case. The dramatic effect of this is that even within the same family/case, individual's experiences and perceptions of their interests and needs can be quite different. Thus use of generalizations which attempt to speak to or about the experience of family members or 'service users' in a singular voice claiming to represent them all are no longer valid. There are multiple 'truths' and narratives which reflect how today – in the individualized conditions of reflexive modernity – all family members now live 'lives of their own'.

7

Into Another World: Child Neglect, Multi-problem Families and the Psychosocial Dynamics of Late-modern Child Protection

In this chapter I want to continue the project of theorizing modern child protection as a deeply embodied practice, which flows through the body and inner life and is enacted through movement. I shall do this by developing further an understanding of the expressive dimension and exploring how it has evolved into the present within the transition to reflexive modernity. In many respects, earlier chapters – and especially the last two – have dealt with the rational features of contemporary child protection: how in reflexive modernity risk is known by social workers and other professionals as risk and the future always known to be uncertain; how lay people engage in life-planning by using incoming information to weigh up the increased choices they face and make decisions about their lives. The implication has been that these are *conscious* decisions and that at all times people basically know what they are doing and why. Yet, this is palpably not the case. A central element to child protection, like reflexive modernity itself, is about what is not and perhaps cannot be known in the unfolding of social practices. There is a fundamental dimension to child protection that is irrational, that swirls around the mind, body, organizations and social systems; that is inherently chaotic, uncontrollable. This is the aspect I call the 'expressive' domain, which encapsulates the psychodynamic and symbolic realms of embodied child protection practices.

I shall argue that in addition to external mobility – movement across space and time – there is an 'internal mobility' within the self, the body, the psyche. The inner world, emotion, energy is 'in movement' even

163

when the body is relatively static, such as when seated on a visit to a client's home. The home is a metaphor for intimacy. Houses are within us and we reside in houses (Bachelard, 1969; Urry, 2000, p. 117). Yet, despite the centrality of the home visit to protect children, the implications of these psychosocial processes and the 'poetics of space' have been completely ignored in child protection studies.

While, prior to the 1970s, practice was shaped by the law and agency procedures, in many respects practitioners constructed their own practice, albeit within tightly drawn cultural boundaries. In the 2000s, however, practice is chronically mediated by legal and administrative rules, regulations and procedures. The 'bureaucracy' in the bureaucratic modernism of child protection has, as we have seen, well and truly come into its own. Perhaps it is this compelling, almost obsessive instrumentally rational character to contemporary child protection which accounts for the almost complete absence in the literature of analysis of the other constituent features of its modernity. The increased presence of rules and regulations has led to a dominant paradigm which implicitly holds that there is no human agency, psychological and emotional experience or expressiveness (left) in it. Typically, the experience of doing the work is framed in terms of rational rule following and read off from what is prescribed in practice manuals. But despite (and perhaps even because of) the intensified rationality of welfare states in reflexive modernity, the psychodynamic, ritualistic and symbolic dimensions of child protection have evolved into intensely meaningful (and meaning giving) forms. Emotion as well as reason, ritual as well as science are everpresent and constantly interrelate. Even if child protection studies have effectively ignored psychosocial processes, psychodynamic and symbolic processes have not ignored child protection.

Violence and resistance in child protection work

While these 'expressive' processes permeate all forms of child abuse and child care problems, I shall draw them out by focusing in particular on child neglect. While in recent years child physical and sexual abuse have gained much greater recognition, child neglect continues to be the most common form of child maltreatment dealt with by child protection workers across the Western world (Swift, 1995; Ferguson and O'Reilly, 2001). Scourfield (2000) argues that neglect is gaining increased recognition and is undergoing a process of 'rediscovery' as a form of serious adversity to children after a period of being relatively neglected in policy and practice.

Of all the constants that exist over the entire modern history of child protection, two in particular stand out. First, the cultural positioning of child abusing families as beyond the margins of decency, as the dirty, disgusting, socially excluded 'Other' and, second, the pervasive resistance to agency intervention by such families. Resistance, outright hostility and often violence towards social workers and other professionals have been a constant feature of child protection cases, including most of those since the 1970s in which children are known to have died. However, the sheer scale of resistance and hostility that professionals have to bear in child protection, and its implications, has hitherto been inadequately accounted for (an exception is Ballock *et al.*, 1998). I was interested in my study to gain a broad sense of the nature of client–professional relationships in child care practice and found that in 34 per cent of all the cases the social workers worked with they defined the parents or carers as involuntary clients who did not want a service.

Lack of co-operation does not of course always mean no involvement. Where the level of concern is sufficiently high, social workers and other professionals seek to work with the children and family despite the lack of co-operation. A consistent finding of research over the past 30 years – my own included – is that there is a hard core of cases on social workers caseloads that demand huge amounts of time and energy that is disproportionate to their number (Mattinson and Sinclair, 1979; Thoburn *et al.*, 1995). Although a social worker will typically have cases where the families are glad to see them, it is these difficult kinds of cases that are crucial in setting the tone of the work and the office. This, then, is the other – darker – side to the more positive, optimistic view of child protection and creative reflexive actions of help-seeking and life-planning that I drew out in the last chapter.

In an important sense, child protection systems have been chronically enmeshed with certain kinds of high-risk children and families for as long as there has been a child protection movement. There is a discernable intergenerational transmission of child protection work where generation after generation of the same family (or types of families) and welfare systems are caught up in intense relationships. This is reflected in a core pattern of long-term, multi-problem, multi-referred child protection cases which keep coming (back) to professional attention and which are at the heart of high-risk work. In my study, 33 per cent of all referrals were re-referred at least once within a year. Some 70 per cent of substantiated child protection cases had histories of social work involvement. Professional systems are chronically enmeshed with certain types of cases and families who live in poverty, the parents often have addiction problems; there is an over-representation of lone-parents (overwhelmingly mothers), who, like women with partners, tend to suffer other adversities such as being survivors of childhood abuse and domestic violence from a current or former violent partner who may or may not be the father of the children. Yet, the full implications of this have not been fully recognized or theorized.

The 'underclass debate' typifies how at least some strands of welfare research, especially but not exclusively from the political right, have approached this issue in terms of dysfunctionality and pathology (Murray, 1996). Another strand of theorizing welfare, which comes mainly from the political left, tends to focus on what they see as the oppressive 'limited repertoire of services' of child protection now on offer which do not bring satisfaction to consumers who then withdraw goodwill (Thorpe, 1994; Parton *et al.*, 1997). The big problem with this critical perspective, however, is that it focuses in a one-dimensional way on the services that are on offer. The State is always at fault because interventions are allegedly not what service users want, so it is the services that need to change to be tailored to what is said to be genuinely needed. While strong on holding the system to account, this argument completely ignores what the client/service user, her or himself, brings to the equation. Moreover, the traditional construction of the welfare user in the critical theory of child welfare is not merely of a passive 'client', but an idealized one who apparently can do no wrong. As Williams and Popay (1999) argue, research paradigms need to transcend this unhelpful dualism of 'bad system/good client' to look at what both the system and welfare clients contribute to the meanings and outcomes of interventions.

The big gap in the sociology of child welfare undoubtedly concerns what the welfare client brings to these dynamic relationships and a more subtle analysis of the interface between clients and professional systems, between the social and psychological. In attempting to move beyond this, my argument in this book is framed within the terms of a (new) paradigm for welfare research and its focus is on the resourcefulness of the 'creative, reflexive, welfare subject' (Williams *et al.*, 1999), which I have set out in earlier chapters in terms of processes such as help-seeking practices, life-planning and the reflexive project of the self. But as Hoggett (2001) suggests, we need to go beyond simply an optimistic view of the positive possibilities of the reflexive agent to include an account which acknowledges not only creativity, but the limits to the abilities of people to reflect and know why they act as they do, and the refusal by some to be a user or client of welfare services in any meaningful sense. My research findings support Hoggett's contention that a robust theory of agency is required in social policy and social work to do justice to the complexity of human subjectivity; one which grasps our irrationalities, the impact of the unconscious and our capacity for sabotaging and destroying ourselves and others, as much as good intentions and our 'cleverness' in what we know about why we act as we do. The key task and challenge in theorizing the nature of human action in welfare practices is to develop a non-unitary concept of agency, one which acknowledges that we are multiple selves: some strong, some vulnerable; some creative, some destructive, and 'that it is both possible and necessary to explore such "negative capacities" whilst maintaining a critical and realist stance' (Hoggett, 2001, p. 38).

The complexities of human agency and the psychodynamics of child protection

The complexity of service users and the enmeshment of child protection in a range of biographical, systemic and environmental influences is typified by a family of two parents and six children – here called the Jones – who had been known to child protection social workers for about 12 years.[1] The family lived in conditions of extreme social disadvantage, including currently having a council house infested with rats. There had been persistent concern about home conditions, child neglect and, periodically, physical child abuse and sexual abuse, as well as domestic violence against Mrs Jones by her husband. The children had been in and out of care over the years. The eldest girl (13 years) was now in care due to concerns about neglect, physical abuse and sexual abuse. There were now control as well as care problems in that she and her eldest brother had begun to assault schoolteachers.

All of the children were viewed as almost completely lacking in boundaries and now exhibiting severe emotional, behavioural and educational difficulties. A report on the 12-year-old girl, for instance, stated that she regressed 'considerably [at times of serious marital conflict] especially in the area of toilet training'. She suffered from 'intermittent enuresis and encopresis both day and night despite toilet training at 2.5 years. Depending on what was happening in the family, the soiling would worsen or improve. She might soil 7/8 times on a bad day. ...She can be aggressive and will become moody when her mother corrects her.' It was noted that the four-year-old boy did not like to be separated from his mother. 'On visits, [name] is often inappropriately dressed and can be outdoors without any underwear on. Personal hygiene and physical care is poor' (case file). Mrs Jones was constantly washing clothes and furniture long into the night because of the children's bed-wetting and soiling. While she often found it hard to deal with the demands of six children, she consistently refused home help services and respite foster care.

A huge amount of intervention had gone into the family over the years. One report summarizes the 'various support and welfare services' offered to them as: 'psychological and psychiatric services, home help, child care, social work support, day fostering, residential care, speech therapy, environmental health, medical and nursing services and the housing department'. Despite this, the pattern over the years was of no improvement and even marked deterioration. Mr Jones has a history of alcohol abuse and self-destructive behaviour, having on various occasions, 'slashed his wrists and stomach, overdosed and had a number of admissions to [...] psychiatric hospital suffering from depression'. As a child he experienced emotional and physical abuse by his father and witnessed domestic violence. He has been violent to his wife and is believed to assume that she should be the sole carer of the children.

Problems engaging Mr Jones persisted over the years and he was rarely at home when social workers called. Attempts were made to get him to take more responsibility and one case conference noted that 'He is reported to supervise the children for half an hour per day to allow his wife some time to herself and he baby sits occasionally.' On one of the occasions when his wife left him and went to a refuge because of his violence he told the social workers that he would undergo treatment for his drinking and admitted that he had not taken enough responsibility for child care. A recent case conference epitomized the pessimistic view of the case in how legal action was being considered because 'a preventative approach to this multi-problem family is no longer tenable. In particular, the effects of Mr [Jones]'s alcohol abuse render all professional help impracticable.'

The research interview with her revealed that it was Mrs Jones herself who initiated contact with social services about 12 years ago to get help with her second child. 'I regret it now.' There wasn't much help around at the time, making parenting a matter of 'play by instinct and learn from your mistakes'. Overall, she regards the quality of social work she has received as uneven: 'Some of them have been alright and some of them have been shaggers.' Things got particularly bad when the children were received into care two years ago:

> Meetings that I had with management and social workers at the time, all their promises backfired on me. It's still difficult to talk about it. ... basically I was given a choice, choose my husband or the children.

And I said, naturally, the children. I was told that I would have to leave [home town] and [going to place] was arranged.

However, social services never came through on their side of the deal as the case never went to court. 'I suppose at the end of the day, it taught me not to trust management and not to trust social workers ever again. And, I don't to this day.' She claimed that there was no legitimacy whatsoever in social workers' concerns. A few years ago her husband did drink 'morning, noon and night' and would stay up for much of the night talking: 'drink talk'. But as far as she was concerned, far from being adversely affected, the children liked it because he gave them money when drunk. Nor was there any truth that there was violence: 'Well it wouldn't have been to the children, it would have been to me, but it was a lie.' Nor did she see any problem with her domestic routine or standards, choosing as she saw it to prioritize playing with the children over cleaning during the day:

> I think basically at the time [three years ago]…I preferred playing with the lads, because I knew [youngest] was my last child. I didn't care whether the table was dirty or the floor was dirty, because I knew eventually it would be done. Basically, I was enjoying my last child's babyhood to the very best that I could. And if that meant not doing the house until the night-time, so what? It's not a crime. There's worse crimes.

Mr and Mrs Jones had literally run social workers from the house. Her view of how she felt she was seen by professionals was: 'Probably that I'm a bitch! But then again I was told on the other side to get assertive and be more open, so! They didn't like me when I was quiet, they certainly don't like it if I don't agree with everything. And, I don't see why I should agree with everything with them.' She admitted to deliberately antagonizing social workers: 'I suppose in one sense to hurt them. But…I know I could never hurt them, the way they've hurted me so many times. It's just I suppose to get under their skin a small little bit and sometimes I'm glad I succeed.' Mrs Jones felt almost completely excluded by professionals from decision-making about her family. 'I've often waited three quarters of an hour to get into a Case Conference and I've complained about it. I've often knocked on the door and said well, if you're not out in two minutes, I'm going away and thank you very much. It's degrading. You wouldn't leave a dog outside the door would you?' Of the many attempts that were made to engage Mrs Jones over the years, the most recent was to introduce a psychologist. As the social worker explains: 'She has come from an abusive background ... Abused as a child as well. But she didn't take it [the psychologist] on board.' The problem, ultimately, as he saw it was 'lack of motivation to change'.

Mrs Jones' resistance and refusal to be a subject of welfare intervention appears in fact to be a product of a combination of her own (traumatic) biography and current intimate relationships, the impact on her psychological integrity of poverty and structural disadvantage, and a long history of dissatisfaction with the child care services on offer – which according to the social worker she constantly complained about:

> She is a pain. For a while my attitude was okay, leave her off. She and I got sucked in, I would say, by trying to address those issues that happened back then. Now 'I'm here to talk about this, I am not willing to talk about that, you know. I think myself I have got a little assertive with her. As a worker, I find it very difficult. Totally unpredictable, because she [mother] has her own attitude about social workers, because things have happened regarding other social workers in the past. We are implicated then, we are the same and there is no talking to her.

Such judgements by an exasperated social worker could be interpreted as pathologizing an extremely marginalized over burdened client. Yet, on one level, the social worker was merely reflecting back clearly what Mrs Jones herself said about how she deliberately tantalized professionals. At a deeper level, more complex, often destructive psychodynamic processes were at work. In getting 'sucked in' the worker became enmeshed in the interior world of the family, coming to symbolize for the parents a lifetime of abuse by authority figures. These highly charged emotional encounters with the family were, then, infused with transference and counter-transference. The notion of the client's 'transference' to the worker is summed up by Mattinson (1975) as the unconscious need 'to make the present relationship fit into the psychodynamic structure of a previous one'. As Agass points out (2002, p. 126), 'It is the worker's reactions to this transference which constitute the counter-transference. The crucial factor here is whether or not the worker can become aware of what is going on and use this knowledge to good effect, rather than simply getting caught up in the client's defensive system, which usually means getting drawn into some kind of "acting out".'

There is no doubt that Mrs Jones had some legitimate reasons to feel aggrieved at some of the responses to her and the family over the previous 12 years. What was striking about her was that in the research interview she regarded social services as never having done her anything but harm. This contrasted with some other parents in the study whose children had been taken into care or were at high risk of this happening, but who conceded that they had very real problems, even if they didn't always agree with the way professionals responded to them (see Ferguson and O'Reilly, 2001, Chapter 9). Mrs Jones made no such concession about her vulnerability. My hunch is that from the moment she first became involved with social services, she and social workers had become enmeshed in very powerful transference and counter-transference processes through which previous childhood experiences and insecure attachments were acted out (see also Howe *et al.*, 1999).

An illustration of the role of the social services in this can be seen in how the department had recently tried strategically to distance itself from the family even despite the social worker actually witnessing one of the children being hit:

> This is a difficult case. I'm sure that some of the decisions made by the [agency] would be questionable. Because one of the things that we would have done is kind of disarm ourselves from this family. I suppose the funny thing about it was that I would have observed this child being hit by the father and I have no doubt, judging from the other siblings, that they are getting abused. However in saying that, there is an overt attachment of the children to the parent, that you can't ignore either. They [the family] were very hostile to ourselves. The last time we went down there, they ran at another fella [social worker], the father ran out, ran after him and he had to jump into the car and off, you know.

Like all such cases it is run through with care and control struggles and dilemmas (Reder *et al.*, 1993). While the social work department has decided only to respond to crises (and will see the family if they come to the office), it is not clear just who is controlling who:

> I don't know are we better off out of it, than to be involved, you know? Because what are we going to achieve if we get in there? Take more control? Ok we have a thirteen-year old that has spoken about physical abuse, has made some comments that may allude to sexual abuse. Now we have to respect the idea this thirteen-year old is choosing not to live at home. That's a big decision for her to come to at a young age. Maybe we are totally wrong. Maybe we should be in there. How much are we, is our place as a [statutory agency] being

dictated by how these parents are towards us? Are we being determined by these parents, rather than losing our focus because the welfare of the kids is the most important thing.

The social worker at least poses the right question, even if he isn't sure of the answer – and knows there are no easy ones. Yet, the contradictions and splitting at the core of the social services' emotional relationship with the family are evident in how a decision had been made by the social work department to bring the police on their next visit to the Jones's home. 'We are saying that we need to show them where the control lies. Interview them with the police present. I think all along we were trying to relate with them in a kinda nicey way, so we wouldn't have to go to Court to take out a Care Order.' In an important sense, the inconsistent pattern of engagement and disengagement by social services was mirroring the same pattern of inconsistency of childcare provided by the parents, as well as the (conflictual) relationship *between* the parents. The professional response, then, stops short of the kind of psychodynamically reflective approach that is required to avoid the destructive characteristics of counter-transference and the professionals as well as the family act out unconscious dynamics in a manner which threatens the promotion of child safety and welfare.

On the most recent occasion, the two eldest children had been received into care and Mary (13) chose to stay there. She alleged physical and sexual abuse by her father and that her siblings were at risk from him also. According to the social worker 'With Mary we have been very child centred, we are very much listening to her, ensuring her protection, because she is clearly stating that she doesn't want to go home.' Access visits were 'difficult', exemplified by how the father actually assaulted the child during them. Tension also arose because Mary wanted to remain in care and not go home, which Mrs Jones could not understand. 'At the end of the day, we took on board her [Mary's] wishes in determining her access arrangements.'

For the most part Mary's narrative in the research interview concurs with the professional's in that she is generally positive about social workers, although she feels her present one is 'too calm'. She recognizes that she has 'been in trouble, way up, way over here like, and they've got me out of it', and is in no doubt whatsoever about her need for protection and to be in care:

They took me out of home and I shouldn't be there. That was the best thing, I thought about it. Because, I'd say I'd be dead by now if I was still living at home. I would be dead. I just would be dead, because I'd end up doing something stupid or something like that. So I'd either end up being killed or whatever by things I was doing. I wasn't doing anything that bad.

Mary has no desire to return home and does not think she ever will.

I don't have a life at home. There's no life for any young children there [name of neighbourhood], there isn't. The place was lovely once upon a time. I don't have any love for my mother and father. I do for my father, but even my father has hurt me more than my mother. I don't have any love for her. I said it to her one day, and I thought she was going to give me a slap across the face, but she understands, because she feels the same way about her mother.

The young person encapsulates clearly the inter-generational patterns of abuse, social exclusion and emotional chaos of which she is a survivor and within which social services are so deeply enmeshed. Mary felt no need to deal therapeutically with her feelings about all this, claiming: 'I am getting everything, that I want. I am spoilt I am. I do have a great life.' Here again, like in Chapter 6, we see how in late-modernity social intervention promotes contradictory outcomes of individualization within families: the young person regards her placement in care as an opportunity to both literally have a life and live a life of her own, while her mother in particular feels that her life has been taken from her by oppressive undemocratic social workers.

While I have been emphasizing psychodynamic processes, the family's social location remains highly significant. According to the public health nurse Mrs Jones felt 'intimidated by some medical professionals, feeling that they judged her by the manner of her dress and appearance along with the fact that she came from [name of estate]'. The impact of social exclusion was also apparent in how the home help service that went in did not work out because the mother 'resented another woman coming in' because it stigmatized the family.

The mother, father and, periodically, the children refuse to be active subjects of child protection, at least in the constructive sense of agency that dominates both the sociological literature on reflexivity and the social care discourse on service users. There is much evidence of knowledgeability about how they are governed but this 'cleverness' is put to use in a manner which mostly sabotages a better outcome for the family in terms of keeping the children, making the management of day-to-day life easier for the mother in particular, given the truly excessive demands of a violent partner and six children, and ultimately freeing them from social workers. They are their own worst enemies. The mother's destructiveness has its roots in her disadvantaged life circumstances, her past trauma (all relationships for her appear very difficult to sustain) and the corrosive impact of her anger and sense of disempowerment at the hands of the welfare system. Something similar can be said about the father, although I didn't get to know him personally because he failed to show up for an arranged interview. He evidently turned his traumatic life history into violence while drawing on the kind of patriarchal power that gives men the choice to withdraw from child care responsibilities and abuse their partners and was a significant danger and liability to his partner and children.

The capacities of individuals to care for children and their relationship to helping services are formed by the intersection of structural disadvantage and personal biography and how people adjust to adversity and cope with toxic experiences and relationships in their lives. This relates to the impact on the self of domination and the overt and hidden injuries of class, gender and racism and how these oppressions interact with both traumatic events, such as any abuse, and any protective factors, such as a consistent, supportive relationship in the person's life. Simply changing the life chances of service users and the way welfare services are delivered would not of itself be enough to turn such situations around. What the service user brings to (co)construction of the case and outcomes needs to be acknowledged and the psychodynamics of the social relations between workers and clients fully taken into account. A key variable concerns the (in)capacity of agency clients to accept help, even in conditions where extreme problems clearly exist for their children and themselves. At the extremes such people seriously harm and kill their children rather than surrender to the need for help (from what are perceived as persecuting agents). The research process itself is not immune from these processes, as mirrored by my own failed attempts to engage with some of these same clients, who agreed to meet for a research interview, but who, without explanation, just never showed up.

Clients/service users do not always stay fixed in the same position. Some in my sample who were initially resistant to intervention changed their views, to welcome it. This even occurred despite and because of the children being taken into care which, they said, brought them to a realization of the enormity of their problems and their need to change (see Ferguson, 2003a). Creative, reflexive agency in the sense of self-monitoring practices which are essentially good for the self, one's loved ones and society, is not a fixed, 'given' state but a process. We all take 'reflexive journeys' through life where the degree of knowledge we have about ourselves and our actions varies on a continuum between creative agency and non-reflexivity. Hoggett (2001) identifies three 'subject positions' in welfare: victim, own worst enemy, and creative, reflexive agent. What the present analysis shows is the complex reality that very often the most needy clients of services can occupy two or all of these positions at once. Abused women are victims/survivors and often their own worst enemy when it comes to self-care and being good enough parents, in a context where excessive demands are placed on them as mothers. This often arises, in part, *because* they are victims, but such awareness makes the social work task of child protection no less difficult.

'That sort of neglect smell': the symbolic dimensions of child protection

What gets played out between workers and families are not just psychological dramas. The 'social' dimension to the 'psychosocial' here contains a crucial symbolic element which provides a means into further analysing mobile, embodied child protection practices and relationships in terms of class, age, gender and ethnic relations. I now want to focus in more detail on this second 'expressive' dimension of child protection, the psycho-symbolic, as it has developed and manifests in late-modernity. While apparent in work with all forms of child abuse, the psycho-symbolic is most evident with respect to child neglect, because (as I argued in Chapters 3 and 4) of the centrality of dirt, disorder and smell to the symbolic orderings of modern child protection. The deeply expressive, emotional relationships in which professionals and families become embroiled involve ritualistic and symbolic exchanges which are crucial to understanding the meanings of child abuse, interventions, and how child protection is constituted within wider social relations of power.

We can immediately see how this manifests itself in deep struggles over boundaries, dirt, domestic order and definitions of good-enough parenting in cases like the Jones' which I am suggesting typify the multi-referred, multi-problem cases which dominate the high-risk concerns of child protection workers. Contrary to social workers' constant concern about hygiene and home standards, Mrs Jones did not see any problem with the home, about hygiene and home standards, making a conscious choice to play with the children and do cleaning at night. However, as she explained in the research interview, social workers 'didn't like it. The house not being done, at a relatively early time. ... I was content with it because I knew what I was doing. I knew that I was cleaning up the place properly at sort of eight or nine o'clock. I was quite happy, it was their problem, but they made it into a bigger one'. By her own account, the state of the house was 'Vicious. There would be clothes on the chair, the floor mightn't be swept all the time.'

> HF: *Were they passing judgement do you think?*
> Mrs Jones: Well! I've gone into their offices and I've seen their mugs on the table and everything and I wouldn't pass judgement on that.
> HF: *So this was some concern about neglect then was it?*
> Mrs Jones: Probably, but it was wrong, their heads get treated, they get bathed. So I think they should see beyond. Because I've often travelled in some of their cars and they've often been absolutely filthy, diabolical.

Here, in the midst of accounting for how she is framed by social workers as a dirty, neglectful parent, Mrs Jones is clearly aware of her 'low' social class position and turns it against the State and those who represent the 'high' culture that judges her. She articulates what I characterized in Chapter 4 as the 'Carnivalesque' spirit in how she throws symbolic filth back at her oppressors, admitting she knows how 'vicious' the home conditions are and claiming the social workers have little room to talk because of their own filthy offices and cars.

This helps to show how relationships between professionals and excluded agency clients involve fundamental issues to do with power. It is precisely such a fear of 'blaming the victim' or being seen to 'patholo-gize' the poor that appears to be behind the neglect by child protection scholars of the dynamics of interpersonal processes. The basis for this active repudiation of the psychological and symbolic is to be found in the radicalism of social work which began to emerge in the mid-1970s and the systematic attack on traditional structures and social boundaries that this involved. Social workers were among a group of new profes-sions which began to have influence in the 1970s which Bourdieu (1986, p. 366) calls 'the new cultural intermediaries', and Martin (1981) the 'expressive professions'.

The radical social work movement emerged in response to a profes-sion then dominated by social casework with its alleged tendency, under the influence of crudely imposed versions of theories such as psychoanalysis, to reduce all problems to the individual failings of clients. At the same time, social work was professionalizing and its training became embedded in the increasingly popular critical social sciences in the expanding university sector. Scorned as a method to control the poor and the oppressed, social work began to be seen as part of the problem rather than a possible solution to social ills. In a classic political cartoon of the time, two 'slum kids' hold a conversation: 'We've got rats', says one; 'Shit man', says the other, 'we've got social workers' (Pearson, 1975, 133). The crude neo-Marxist message was that state social work 'cooled out' the anger of working-class people blocking the revolutionary potential of political change. The radical social work movement helped engineer an inversion of values. Now it was the social workers, not their problem families who were shit; they were the 'social policemen' who couldn't be trusted.

The upshot was a loosening of the traditional classification schemes and boundaries between 'us' (professionals) and 'them' (clients/service users), of 'the boundaries set up to distinguish what is external to and what is internal to a collectivity' (Lash and Urry, 1987, p. 297). I showed in Chapter 5 how social workers live individualized lives and engage in types of 'body projects' which typify the new middle classes. Bourdieu characterizes the typical lifestyle preferences of such new cultural intermediaries – anti-psychiatry, anti-nuclear, dance, encounters, immigrants, Gestalt therapy, independent cinema, transcendental meditation, travel, trekking, vegetarianism, yoga, Zen – as an 'inventory of thinly disguised expressions of a sort of dream of social flying, a desperate effort to defy the gravity of the social field' (Bourdieu, 1986, p. 370). Above all, this represents an 'anti-institutional temperament' and a desire not to be classified or to classify others judgementally.

What happened in social work's transition to late-modernity is a destructuring which saw agency clients identified as being not only outside but *inside* of social work culture. The irony of radical social work's rejection of the relevance of the symbolic and interpersonal is that it was itself a deeply psycho-symbolic act. Responses typically involved expressions of a new identity politics which were premised on ways for social workers to show solidarity with excluded minorities and clients. In 1978, the first senior social worker from social services I ever met just happened to be a proudly out gay man. Among the team of social workers he supervised was a man who insisted on wearing woolly jumpers and jeans full of holes and whose hair and beard were long and often dirty. At first, I mistook him for a homeless client and wondered how he'd managed to get inside the office! This is precisely as he wanted it.

Radicals consciously dressed down to supposedly show support with and try not to alienate agency clients, leaving no doubt as to whose side they were on (Wilson, 1985).

If the actual numbers of radical social workers always appeared to be quite low, the impact of the radical impulse in social work education has been huge. By the 1980s and 1990s its focus had widened to concentrate not only on inequalities of class and poverty but other oppressions such as sexism and racism. Diversity and difference were to be *celebrated* not feared or excluded (Thompson, 1993; Dalrymple and Burke, 1995). This kind of critical awareness of tackling discrimination has been crucial in enabling social work to respond respectfully to the diverse needs of all social groups. Data from my study shows how families from marginalized groups are *in general* much more sympathetically treated today than under simple modernity with its powerful exclusionary dynamic and implicit forms of ethnic cleansing. Such radicalism, which has developed today into a significant critical social work paradigm (Fook, 2002; Healy, 2000), gave voice and shape to the kind of lifestyles and values which have become normative to an individualized 'self-culture' and living a life of one's own (Beck and Beck-Gernsheim, 2002). A commitment to such democratic practice in partnership with parents and children has increasingly been written into the law, in tandem with a growing emphasis on the need to 'refocus' child care systems away from child protection to provide family support to prevent children coming into care (DHSS, 1995).

But its by-product has been to help create a culture of social work and child protection riddled with tensions in how the values of allowing people to live a life of their own so often conflict with the requirement to use power in ways which ensure that parents promote the welfare of children. Anti-institutionalism sits very awkwardly with the requirement in child protection to stand for something solid, to represent and use authority in the interests of safeguarding children. The dangerous cost of simplistic demands to include agency clients within the social work group collectivity is exemplified in the one-dimensional, unproblematic portrayal of 'service users' in social work discourse. In fact, as I shall show, while considerable democratization has occurred in social work and child protection more generally, its habitus – which I showed in Chapters 4 and 6 refers to the embodied orientation middle-class professionals have to the world – is still pervaded by social class and lifestyle distinctions.

Nowhere are these tensions more evident and practice more morally questioned than with respect to neglect concerns in those families where women are clearly struggling to parent well in poverty and inadequate housing, home and child care standards are poor, there are addiction problems, violent partners, and so on. They are at the border-line between 'in need' and 'at risk'; between the need for family support and child protection. A case study involving a family I shall call the Browns provides a typical example of a confirmed neglect case which helps to illuminate these issues.[2] By the time of the referral included in my research study the case had been known to the social work depart-ment for four years. It was re-referred on four occasions during the 12-month follow-up period of the research, always regarding neglect. The mother, here called Jean Brown, had one child, Samantha, now aged five. Her partner, Paddy, was a shadowy figure who refused to engage with the services. The case was initially referred when Samantha was a year old by a GP requesting the social work department to 'investigate the social circumstances of the family'. The social worker made a home visit but did not gain admission, having to be satisfied with a conversa-tion with the grandmother through a closed door: 'I realised exactly what he [GP] meant by a very strange family. I mean it was like, almost like a time warp, like going back sixty years, strange.'

Samantha was hospitalized on five occasions before she was eight months old. There was consistent concern over the years that she was 'wild' and never allowed out of the house or to mix with other children. The social worker explains: 'she was strapped into her buggy during the day and subsequently was unable to walk until recently up to the age of three years approximately. She was on [formula milk] and not given any solid foods, she did not receive any stimulation in the home, does not mix with other children in the area and is terrified of any strangers com-ing into the house.' Now, the problem is not risk from starvation, as it was in the past, but obesity and poor nutrition. More knowledge about child development is used today as the basis to justify concerns for children. As the public health nurse remarked, 'she was very fat because she was sitting all the time and then dirty of course because they hadn't a clue how to deal with her.' The mother's 'own personal hygiene was very poor as well'. The home was 'very chaotic' and, latterly, the mother was suspected of being a prostitute. The child was also 'victimized in school' because she was dirty and smelly. According to the nurse: 'she would smell, you know that sort of neglect smell'.

Neighbours also put pressure on social services and environmental health because, as the family support worker explains:

> they weren't using their toilet and they were using buckets or pots or whatever and they were emptying them out the window. They [the neighbours] were concerned about rats and dumping all their rubbish

in the back. The house is just a tip, it's full of, it's like a time warp to go into the house actually.

Jean was regarded as extremely difficult to work with as she never meaningfully engaged with services offered to her. Her resistance was passive, as she always agreed to co-operate when the workers did get to see her. She was often suspected of being in the house and not allowing them in, and even a statutory Supervision Order which gave professionals a legal right of access to the child had not made access any easier. There was however a consensus among professionals that Jean did not 'wilfully' neglect the child and that her behaviour has to be seen in light of her own upbringing, which was similar to her own style of parenting: 'I think that she does love her in her own way, maybe to us a very strange way, but definitely she does love her' (social worker). The intervention aims were as simple as getting the mother to allow the child out of the buggy for long enough to walk and be physically stimulated.

Despite several case conferences and acknowledgement of high risk, the public health nurse felt that 'nothing was happening' and was frightened that the child 'would end up totally confused and unable to cope in the world'. Her main fear for the child (and society) was that she would end up mentally ill becoming a danger to herself and the community. But in her view social services were doing nothing to prevent such an outcome: 'So I was frightened I was actually very frightened by that'. Efforts were made though to prevent the child being taken into care, including the social worker personally taking her to school every morning. But the pressure from the community (the neighbours over whose fences the mother allegedly threw her rubbish) and from other professionals built up and even from within the social worker himself as he grew frustrated with the lack of change in the parenting. Thus, in the end, the social worker relented and the child was admitted to care where she remained after a successful application for a care order:

> hygiene is just one of the factors in a whole lot of things: how she behaved maybe towards her, towards the services, her attitude to bringing up the child, that she 'should be at home', 'she doesn't need to go to school she's fine', 'why does she need to mix with other children hasn't she got me,' you know that would be her response. And I suppose the other big factor at the time when it actually came to taking her into care was her going into town with her at night.

This puts into perspective well the place that the care of bodies and 'home conditions' has in such work today. Unlike the typical profile of the pre-1970s work I depicted in earlier chapters, dirt and disorder are in themselves no longer an immediate reason to take children into care. While practice remains no less embodied than it ever was, social workers have developed a disposition which permits a visceral response where they can sit in the dirt and smell and use their minds and a liberal knowledge base and ideological standpoint of empowerment and anti-oppressive practice to soften the assault on their senses. This is also apparent in how researchers who have accompanied social workers on visits to neglectful homes have expressed disgust at home conditions and the smell of practice which the social workers barely appeared conscious of (Dingwall *et al.*, 1983, pp. 58–61; Corby, 1987). Social workers no longer talk in explicit terms which express disgust towards families, but in the deodorized language of 'home conditions'. In late-modernity, the social work mind can now triumph over the body to some degree. The increased capacity of social workers to do this becomes clearer in comparison to other professional groups – like health visitors and public health nurses – whose personal and professional boundary formations, their habitus, remain more traditional and who typically place pressure on social workers to 'do *something*'.

Yet practice remains 'fleshy', sensuous and profoundly mediated by the senses for all that. Following Bourdieu (1977; 1986), this late-modern social work habitus continues to be an embodied way of being in the world which is pervasively related to lifestyle distinctions and class positions. This is evident in how children in such cases – like Samantha Brown – are now constructed as both victims *and* threats. Similar to the experiences of children in simple modernity (discussed in Chapters 3 and 4), they are still perceived as in danger due to the polluting presence of a style of parenting without acceptable boundaries, and as a contamination threat to the purity of the community and other children in terms of future risk (as criminals, prostitutes) (Morrison, 1997). While the removal of children is justified in (scientific) terms of impaired child development, the practice is constituted as much in terms of the symbolic as the rational. There occurs a powerful build-up of disgust and risk anxiety which culminates in the removal of the child as the internal logic of the practice surrounds purity and exclusion rituals. This can be seen in the persistence of the traditional pattern of the harmful impact on children of such parenting being about moral damage rather than just scientific evidence. The essential deviance of such families continues to be that they cause *moral* offence.

In fact, those professionals who got closest to this child spoke quite positively of her capacities. The public health nurse found that 'eventually she sort of trusted me and I bought her little bits and books and whatever and then I was able to take her up on my lap and she was surprisingly bright considering. I was very surprised, once I got her confidence, how good her ability to communicate was, she had a stutter but her speech was excellent and her comprehension'. The family support worker observed that 'I suppose from our limited contact with her it was obvious that while there was severe neglect and emotional abuse without a doubt and you know no stimulation, but for all that she was a child who seemed secure at home, funnily.' Yet, the powerful need to exclude the mother and family which built up within the lay and professional community resulted in the child's removal. This devastated the woman, who regarded her child as 'in prison'. Despite all the problems, 'she was her life, she was all she had. And this is what she kept telling us' (family support worker). To add further pain to the injury of separation, Jean was only allowed access to her child in care every six weeks. At least there is not the same scope today for professionals to make such decisions behind client's backs as existed in simple modernity as Jean complained through her solicitor about the limited access.

My point here is not to argue that such children are not *really* at risk, but to lay bare the embodied practices and the psycho-symbolic as well as scientific knowing which makes risk what it is. The notion, expressed by different workers, that working with the family was like being in a 'time warp' reflects how such families are viewed as being stuck in a different age ('sixty years ago'). In such a future-oriented practice as modern child protection, their failure to keep developing means moral decay, with potentially deleterious implications for the children and the community. Here we see the continued cultural power of the positioning of such families in terms of the 'grotesque body' of the excluded Other and contamination fears and disgust which I identified earlier in the book as being constitutive of modern child protection. The eventual removal of such children continues to constitute communal acts of purity and pollution rituals and through such exclusionary actions a kind of secular magic is enacted. This is not a rational process, or at least cannot be understood purely on rational terms, such as the scientific knowledge base which justifies taking children into care. There is a fundamental symbolic drama being played out. It is as if the community and the child protection system renews itself through these rituals of exclusion. All involved engage in a kind of collective shaking free, a cleansing of something, and a sense prevails that order has been restored.

At the heart of these interventions is the exercise of power: symbolic power (Bourdieu, 1986). De Montigny (1995) argues that negative associations between acrid smells and client's moral characters have been embedded in professional routines to become a common-sense aspect of organizational knowledge in social work. These common-sense practices are then in danger of routine application, rather than critical reflection on a case-by-case basis. Scourfield (2000, 2003) shows how perceptions of 'dirty, ill-fed children and untidy homes' are at the core of how child neglect is constructed in child protection today. Notions of dirt – understood not simply in terms of hygiene, but in Douglas's (1966) sense of 'matter out of place' – have an immense cultural power leading to an investigative focus on how children's bodies are maintained by mothers. But despite the rhetorical and symbolic importance of the child's body, as Parton *et al.* (1997) also show from their analysis of Australian and UK cases, and Buckley (2003) from her Irish research, social workers' attention is focused on parenting and most often mothering, which is judged according to expected standards and gender, as well as class and ethnic norms. The importance of the concept of symbolic power is that it goes beyond the notion of professional power as simply having statutory origins in the law and the state, to acknowledge also the cultural forms it takes. *Everything* about families, from the intimacies of what they eat, the decor and odour in their homes, to how they parent their children is part of professional judgement and moral evaluation.

How this occurs and the tensions involved in practising child protection in a democratic, anti-oppressive way are further amplified by a subsequent study I conducted (with Fergus Hogan) which included interviews with service users and child and family workers and explored their biographies, values and lifestyles, particularly with respect to gender and parenthood. Almost without exception, the professionals said they sought to have democratic relationships with their own partners and children. All of them believed that gender and age relations within the family had become more democratic and that fatherhood (the main focus of the study) had changed. Men in general were seen as more emotionally and practically involved with children and roles between partners more negotiated, all of which was regarded as being as it should be. The findings once again provide support for the impact of individualization processes on relationships that I discussed in Chapter 6. However, most of the professionals believed that these changes in gender and age relations were not equally distributed socially because they had not yet filtered down to the lower classes from which their client group is largely drawn. The dynamics of this perception is exemplified by one family centre worker:

> The families that come from here are very, very traditional. Even the food they eat is traditional. You know they haven't tried Chinese they

haven't tried Indian. There's the bacon and cabbage and spuds and stews and you know it's like taking families out of the, you know, 30 years ago. You know this particular part of society in general has changed but this group of families hasn't actually moved with the rest of it you know. I think society has changed I think because both parents are working you'd have to. You know what I mean. In other areas of life and stuff like I think women and girls are brought up different now as well you know. They're not brought up to sit at home they're brought up to have careers and things like that you know, there's aspirations around your daughters as well as your sons now, to have a life outside the home but that's not saying that everybody wants a life outside the home or anything like that, but you know. I don't think, girls aren't taken out of school early any more and boys left there. You know that type of thing doesn't happen any more, in most of society. Unfortunately for these people they don't go to school, they don't, they don't have the same traditions as people who may be middle class or who'd have better lives you know they've less chances and things like that you know. (Ferguson and Hogan, 2004)

Two things are particularly worthy of note here. On one level, there is a material basis to service user families' lifestyles, a particular habitus that is distinct from that of middle-class professionals. Poverty and the struggle for survival brings with it a particular functional orientation to the world where, classically, high culture's penchant for exotic meals is eschewed in favour of more economical bulky traditional food: 'meat and two veg' (Bourdieu, 1986). On the other hand, the processes at work are mythical and ideological in that expert perceptions of families reflect the exercise of symbolic power by middle-class professionals and the state. When interviewed in the research, the families regarded themselves as much more post-traditional and democratic in their values and practices than professionals allowed. We see, then, how a middle-class habitus – and the power inscribed in it to judge – reasserts itself in how contrasts are made between social professionals, families in general and client families who remain the dangerous, uncivilized Other requiring child protection.

Today, it is not simply a category of marginalized family, but the *individualized* Other who tends to be the focus of symbolic fears. A powerful element to this surrounds dangerous men and masculinities, as typified by constructions such as the 'paedophile priest' and other 'stranger danger' (Ferguson, 1995). Selective media attention to extra-familial child sexual abuse offenders has, ironically, shifted attention away from the family as a source of danger, despite the fact that most such abuse is perpetrated by persons known to the child. Scourfield speculates that in a cultural context where men 'as a problem' has gained increasing purchase in the media and where men who sexually abuse children are seen as universally deviant even within the humanist discourses of social work, giving men in general a bad name, pejorative discourses of masculinity have some value for staff in making social worker men seem all right, seem safe. 'The dangerousness of rough working-class men is implicitly contrasted with the respectability of other men (Hearn, 1990; Edwards, 1998), and male social workers themselves are among the respectable men' (Scourfield, 2003, p. 105). Thus, even within a commitment to democratic relationships, social workers continue in reality to construct identities – their own as well as agency clients – through practices of distinction, exclusion and 'Othering'.

As I showed in Chapter 3, the ways in which practice is mediated by the senses, especially smell and touch, creates a dynamic of detachment or engagement with children and families. The core consequence of this concerns the degree to which professionals can bring these processes to consciousness and literally get close to and meaningfully engage with children and their carers. Chapter 6 provided some positive examples of how such meaningful engagement can occur. In addition, some children (like Samantha Brown) clearly are protected despite the maintenance of a social distance – caused by professional detachment and/or client resistance – which means that the family's actual lived time and experience is never fully appreciated. For others, their suffering is completely missed by the system because such detachment results in a complete failure to engage with and literally get close to children.

A disturbing example of such processes and the influence of contamination fears on practice was the failure to protect eight-year-old Victoria Climbié, who died a horrendous death from brutal abuse (see Chapter 1). The inquiry into her death showed that Victoria was admitted to hospital on two separate occasions with suspicious injuries. Crucially, on the first of these admissions she was diagnosed by a consultant paediatrician as having scabies. While the inquiry adjudged this to have been an accurate diagnosis, the opinions of other doctors who suspected non-accidental injury were not given the same prominence as the scabies, especially by social services. Injuries were also missed because they were misinterpreted as marks from where Victoria scratched the infected area and as being old insect bites typical of someone who came from the Ivory Coast culture in which she was born and raised (Laming, 2003).

The latter was a culturally relativist and ultimately racist perception which had no basis in reality (Chand, 2003). Two social workers and a police officer, all independently of one another, refused to visit the home for fear of getting infected. At least one other social worker couldn't get away from Victoria quickly enough when she came to the office because of the scabies. Far from problematizing the distance this put between professionals and Victoria, the report describes the social worker's concern for her health and safety as 'understandable'.

This illustrates again that whole difficult area of primal fears and visceral experiences that, although they are central to child protection work, remain unspoken of. Victoria was a child on the margins. She had been brought to England at the age of seven by her Great Aunt from the Ivory Coast. Victoria was black and spoke in a foreign language, was homeless, incontinent, unkempt and smelly, and she wore a wig. Very early on in the case, soon after she first had contact with a social services department and some seven months before she died, she was actually described by the duty social worker who saw her as like one of the 'adverts you see for Action Aid' (Laming, 2003, p. 54). My suspicion is that Victoria was a child who generated mixed emotions and so far as professionals are concerned was hard to get close to.

This was not because of anything she herself did, but because of professionals' need to distance themselves from her. It felt safer to do so because they feared contamination by her and her family who were in effect constructed as a dangerous Other, and both literally and metaphorically handled carefully, or not at all. This was exacerbated at a social level by the persistent media demonization of asylum seekers and economic migrants which contributed to a context where Victoria and her carers were treated, in every sense, as outsiders in terms of their housing and wider needs. At the psychological level, direct contact with such 'outsiders' is experienced as a contaminating threat to the integrity of the self (Joffe, 1999). And if that individual, like Victoria, literally has an infectious disease then the drive to exclude is irresistible. Perhaps this helps to explain how, as the inquiry report into her death notes with cruel irony, while professionals refused to visit the home, they were content to let Victoria stay there in this apparently contaminating environment where she was gruesomely murdered.

The 'time warp' and other-worldliness of protecting children in (other's) space

Scourfield (2003) suggests that the 'rediscovery' of neglect can best be understood in the context of increased uncertainty and management of risk where it provides more tangible evidence of childhood adversity and parental deviance than other forms of abuse. But this should not distract from how child protection has *always* had psycho-symbolic dimensions and these are, I am arguing, becoming more intense. Our task is to render them visible (and smellable) in terms of how practice is constructed, goes on and is understood.

It is crucial to bear in mind that every aspect of the practices and encounters I have been analysing go on in movement, through mobilities. Their meaning can only be fully understood in terms of the dramatic speeding up of social life (Virilio, 1986). Mrs Jones's attack on the moral character of social workers through casting aspersions on their cars aptly reflects how the car has itself become a form of 'dwelling', an expression of the construction of a particular self. As Urry argues, the importance of the car to consumer lifestyles and identity formation is such that the nature of this 'dwellingness' has changed from 'dwelling-on-the-road' to 'dwelling-within-the-car'; the car as a 'home-from-home' (Urry, 2000, p. 191). Cars provide a comfort zone for professionals, a haven from the office politics and services users. In child protection work this has the added dimension of promoting personal safety through providing the means for a quick getaway when they are 'run out' of houses by hostile clients.

Cars also promote what in Chapter 5 I called 'instantaneous time' – the capacity and requirement to get instant information and act *immediately* – which I am arguing is taking over from clock time as the structuring principle of welfare organizations, and which conflicts dramatically with the 'lived time' of children and families' lives. Despite the best of intentions, the momentum is for cars to drive professionals, so to speak, away from a deeper connection with their (car less) clients. What is occurring then is a new configuration of space and time in child protection around 'dwellingness', mobilities, the body and the senses with which I want to conclude this chapter by examining further in terms of the practice of professional home visiting.

A good example of this is how, as we have seen, professionals describe the marginalized families they visit and their experience of stepping into their lives as having the quality of being in a 'time warp'. And sure enough, viewed across the 130 years of modern child protection traced in this book, the descriptions of such families do have a timeless quality, with their focus on dirt, chaos, disorder and the embodied disgust of workers. The notion of a 'time warp' expresses two key features of the experience of doing child protection. The first relates to *chronological* time and the implication that these marginal, dirty, uncivilized families have failed to move with and keep up with the times, that they are somehow 'out' of time. Second, 'time warp' relates to time as *practice* in the sense of acting 'in time'. Here 'time warp' expresses the routine underlying experience of home-visiting, the other-worldliness of stepping into someone else's domestic space. This can be understood in terms of making transitions and what anthropologists call 'liminality', which refers to an 'in between' state, a sense of normlessness that arises from moving from one state to another (Turner, 1969, 1974). As an engagement with time and space, practice goes on within and through symbolic systems.

Stepping across the threshold of someone's home – effectively into another world – is a classic entry into a liminal state. This applies to all kinds of homes, not just smelly, dirty ones as all interventions involve transitions: the crossing of a threshold, into the home, into the self and lived experience of the other(s). It is the most fundamental act or step that child protection workers have always taken, yet is the least well understood aspect of its practices and an absolutely crucial aspect of the context in which fateful moments get played out.

The notion of 'warped' time evokes the distortion of memory and perception that can occur when professionals make interventions into the home and how the needs of the vulnerable child requiring protection can seem to lose urgency within a liminal experience of space and time. Liminality tends to be a temporary stage which recedes once a sense of orientation to the new conditions and 'order' has been achieved. Thus, in effective child protection interventions, professionals are able to compose and hold themselves together on the actual visit, or get good enough supervision and support after the visit to enable them to go back and become child-safety centred (Munro, 2002). But liminality can exist on a sustained basis and last not only during the fateful moments of home visits, but for the long duration of a case. The child death scandal cases and inquiry reports provide many examples of social workers and other professionals seeming to consistently 'freeze' and lose memory and focus – especially on home visits – and rudimentary things just not getting done.

Following Bachelard (1969), it is necessary to understand domestic space, the home, as qualitative, sensuous and lived. Houses are lived through one's body and its memories. Classically, the home we dwelled in at birth and as children holds special meaning and memory traces. Bachelard (1969, p. 15) refers to a 'passionate liaison' between the body and this initial house. The home is a place which shelters imagination and daydreaming. Houses are experienced from day to day not simply in terms of the telling of our own story but through fantasy, image and memory. What Bachelard evokes is a sense of unpredictability and deep emotional and psychological resonance in our experiences of our own and others' homes. 'Through dreams, the various dwelling-places in our lives co-penetrate and retain the treasures of former days. And after we are in the new house, when memories of other places we have lived in come back to us, we travel to the land of Motionless Childhood, motionless the way all Immemorial things are' (Bachelard, 1969, pp. 5–6). He develops the notion of 'reverberation' as a way of describing the movement between the person and the house that disrupts any clear distinction between the two. Houses are within us and we reside in houses. The metaphor of reverberation suggests an immediacy in how the characteristics of houses are physically inscribed within us. Bachelard spatializes the temporality of memory. Houses are lived through one's body and its memories (Game, 1995, pp. 202–3). In homes we see 'the imagination build "walls" of impalpable shadows, comfort itself with the illusion of protection – or, just the contrary, tremble behind thick walls, mistrust the staunchest ramparts' (Bachelard, 1969, p. 5).

The vital importance of such arguments for child protection is that they 'dissolve the boundaries of time and space, of the social and the bodily, of past-present-future' (Urry, 2000, p. 118) – which is precisely what appears to happen once professionals step into the homes of clients. Visiting someone else's house evokes reverberations of all the memory traces and energies that constitute that home as a site of intimacy for that family. And it appears to evoke memories of one's own home and reverberations from one's own childhood that are carried within the body. Through memory of our own vulnerability, we risk becoming the (frightened) child at risk, or of creating an illusion of safe, protected childhood within these walls which may belie the reality of children's experiences. Little wonder, then, that remembering what you are fundamentally there for is such a problem for child protection workers and that the process of such forgetting is so deeply embodied that it is hard to remember and make sense of. Such an appreciation of the impact on practice of the client's home as qualitative, sensuous and lived is essential to reaching a deeper understanding of how 'free' professionals feel to move around and take control of investigations and just how easy it is to become literally immobilized in the space of the other. The 'land of Motionless Childhood' always threatens to become the space of motionless child protection.

A vital part of the context of this invariably involves trying to work with parents who are hostile to intervention and often intimidating and even actually violent towards professionals. The case examples used in this chapter again show the sheer difficulties professionals have in seeing children and working constructively with many families. Over the duration of its modern history, parental resistance and the scope and capacities they have to elude being properly seen or understood constitutes the most important single reason why child protection systems have failed to protect children in time. This is borne out by Stanley and Goddard's (2002) study of 50 cases of child abuse where children had been the subjects of a legal protection order, although all were living at home at the time of their study. They interviewed the workers from the 50 cases and recorded the extraordinary amount of violence and intimidation to which they had been subjected. Psychologically, they argue, workers become 'hostages' to their violent clients which seriously diminishes capacities to protect as they do not have relationships with children in any meaningful sense because abusers are controlling and orchestrating what happens.

What this points to is the deep emotional impact of child protection work on workers and their capacities to protect children. Everyone involved in this kind of work knows these feelings. That sense in which you are so preoccupied with your own safety and survival that the child's becomes an afterthought, where just getting out of the house alive or relatively unscathed becomes the defining criteria of a good intervention – but of course this is never made explicit. Or when not getting to see the child becomes not a source of concern, but a relief – in fact you have written to the family to pre-announce your visit not as a strategy to ensure they are there, but unconsciously to sabotage the visit by giving them a chance to be out, or hiding in the house when you call. And when you knock at the door and there's no reply, you skip back up the path and suddenly the world seems like a better place again, all because you don't have to struggle through yet another torturous session with angry parents or carers. Yet through it all, you keep going back as you feel drawn into a profoundly ambivalent relationship with the aggressive carer.

All of this has been enacted time and time again in the child death inquiry cases. In the Jasmine Beckford case (1985), for instance, social workers made over 50 abortive attempts to see Jasmine during the time that she was being systematically abused and murdered. Jasmine's mother and stepfather were often hostile to professionals and when the social worker did gain access to the home and Jasmine was present in the living room, the parents stage-managed the visit in a way that disguised Jasmine's fatal injuries being recognized (London Borough of Brent, 1985). The same pattern of conscious manipulation of social workers and their immobilization on home visits occurred in the Climbié (Laming, 2003) and other child death cases where, for example, the control of parents was such that the most workers have got were glimpses of children across rooms, or through the glass pane above a door (London Borough of Greenwich, 1987).

All of this points to the sheer vulnerability of the work and requires us to rethink what professionals really do get to see of the lives of children and families, what happens in child protection relationships and encounters and to theorize this in a much more rigorous way. Attempting this has been the central aim of this book and this chapter has shown the various ways in which late-modern child protection is constituted by the expressive dimension of psychological and symbolic processes. The experience of doing child protection work and the client's experiences of welfare interventions require a complex understanding of the nature of practice and human agency. A non-unitary theory of agency is required to do justice to the destructive as well as the constructive features of being human. This should include recognition of the impact of structural oppression and the biographical legacy of past and present trauma from abuse and other forms of perpetrated adversity.

I have argued that in late-modernity the rational mind does triumph over the body to a greater extent than was true prior to the 1970s. Yet, as I have tried to show, child protection remains no less embodied and sensuous an experience of time and space, both in how social class and lifestyle distinctions are constitutive of concepts of risk and social danger and in how the sense of smell and touch as well as sight and sound influence interventions. The psychological and symbolic processes I have outlined here are the essence of child protection as a form of bureaucratic late-modernism in that they are at the heart of its contingent, fateful character. When they cross the threshold into the domestic space and intimate lives of others, just like their counterparts going back to the nineteenth century, workers today have to come to terms with and literally make sense of what they see, smell, taste, hear; of just WHAT is going on here? It is in the complex interpersonal relationships and other-worldliness of practice in the time and space of others that the solid formations of policies and practice take on liquid forms and all that seems solid about child protection threatens, like children's lives themselves, to melt into air.

8
Liquid Welfare: Child Protection and the Consequences of Modernity

The consequences of modernity for child protection that I have traced in this book can be understood on a number of levels. Child protection, I have shown, is constituted by tangled networks of laws, procedures, offices, roads, cars, dwellings, children, adults, bodies, emotions and actions. My aim has been to try and do justice to the range of these networks, their complexity and effects. In particular I have sought to rethink child protection in terms of social theories of modernity, risk society, movement and the emerging sociology of mobilities, at the heart of which is the embodied social actor; the living, breathing, thinking, feeling professional going about their lives and everyday work.

It is easy to lose sight of the fact that a practice such as child protection is essentially about the human condition, relationships – past and present – and working with love, hate, ambivalence and how people go about living their day to day lives. Easy, that is, because most writing about it, and especially official reports and guidance but a good deal of social science too, treat it with a solidity and all-seeing power which belies the complexity of the lives with which it seeks to work and the partial ways in which it interfaces with those lives of others. Such observations take us to the limits of social science and the struggle to account for the human condition and intervention practices. Reviewing Graham Swift's novel *The Light of the Day*, which is about a disgraced police officer turned private detective, Hermione Lee (*Guardian Review*, 8th March 2003) comments:

And the moment of the crime itself remains obscure to us.
That's part of the point, though. You can sleuth all you like, as novelist or detective, and some things won't come to light. You can't lift up the

roofs of houses and see what's going on inside. How to explain the inexplicable things in life: the strangeness of love at first sight, love like a blow to the heart, love for the duration? One of the tender, hard questions the novel asks is how much can we watch over each other?

In many respects this book has been about the relentlessly hard, tender question of how can we 'watch over' children at risk? and how can this be done in the knowledge that children and families reside in homes and ways have to be found to protect them, to 'see what's going on inside', without being able to 'lift up the roofs of their houses'. Fundamentally, the book has explored how child protection became constituted as an experience of space and time and where the very basis of Western ideas about such watching over of children came from. I have traced the origins of the very idea that through social intervention children can and should be protected in time to key processes and practices that occurred across the 1870–1914 period, mapped the development of the ideology of protecting children in time across the twentieth century and examined its effects in practice, and theorized the nature of child protection as a modern, or 'late-modern' social practice. This has been necessary I have argued, because child protection has lost touch with its modern roots and failed to understand its (late-) modern(ist) character.

On one level, my aim of placing the dominant concerns and routines of contemporary child protection in a broader historical and sociological context and perspective has involved telling a story about the history of child abuse, key aspects of which have never been told – such as the sheer effort and struggles that have gone into keeping children alive and the fact that so many have died, and survived – in child protection cases. Beyond this descriptive approach, on a more analytical level the book has sought to theorize the nature of child protection practice in terms of its relationship to and the consequences of modernity and I now want to draw together the various strands of the argument and consider further how the book might contribute to the protection of children in better times.

Modernity under a positive sign: the creative achievements of child protection

I have argued in this book that understanding the nature of child protection is inseparable from reaching a more complete understanding of the nature of modern life, of 'modernity' itself. I have shown that the core consequence of modernity for child protection is that it is a form of 'bureaucratic (late-) modernism' which is constituted by three dimensions: the administrative domain of disciplinary, socio-legal powers; the aesthetic dimension in terms of experiences of time and space, creativity and emancipatory desire; and the psychosocial, 'expressive' realm of the intersection between the emotions, the body and the social and symbolic boundaries and practices which give meaning to everyday life and practices. In doing so, I have sought to correct for the dominant approach in child protection studies which is to fragment it and characterize its practices in one-dimensional ways.

Within this, across the Western world the administrative domain of instrumental reason has come to dominate how child protection is delivered and understood. This is reflected in the sheer dominance of concerns about so called 'system failures', especially those that result in the deaths of children in protection cases. It is not that we should not be concerned to investigate the reasons why children experience deaths that might have been prevented. The problem surrounds the assumptions and theoretical resources that are brought to bear in making sense of these cases and practices. In terms of an overall historical assessment of the nature and effectiveness of child protection today, in some crucial respects it has never been better. Professional action, as I have tried to show, *has* protected many children from death and other kinds of avoidable suffering as the extraordinary creativity of workers, policy makers, service users and ordinary citizens in 'constructing' cases has led to the discovery of new forms of abuse and ways to deal with them. The dramatically increased mobility of child protection across the twentieth century and the sheer capacity of its practices to cover space quickly together with a growing creative awareness of different forms of abuse suggest that, numerically, it certainly reaches more children today than ever. The core paradox of this history and of contemporary child protection is that, while problems undoubtedly exist within 'systems', the relentless focus on professional failure has arisen at a time when, overall, professionals are protecting more children than ever in time.

Once reached, I have tried to show how in late-modernity, in some crucial respects, child protection provides new opportunities for children and vulnerable adults and carers to gain protection from a much wider range of violence than was true in pre-modern times and even in the simple modernity that existed up to the 1970s. The kinds of changing awareness of serious physical abuse of children and child sexual abuse that I set out in Chapters 5 and 6 exemplify this. But in addition, these intervention practices are not simply about 'protection' in the limited (if vital) sense of promoting safety. In how they connect with a new context of individualization processes and the reflexive project of the self they provide opportunities for victims and survivors to engage in a new kind of life-politics where they are helped to make choices, plan their lives, develop a new narrative of the self, and to heal. I illustrated the positive scope of such life-political work in Chapter 6 in particular, in how sexually abused young people and women abused by violent male partners acting in critically reflexive ways in response to new awareness of abuse in the media and culture generally are able along with critically reflexive practitioners to co-construct meaningful intervention work which produces safety, healing and self-development.

A key defining feature of late-modern child protection is the way in which it promotes not only safe, but democratic relations within families (Giddens, 1998; Ferguson, 2001b). This is not to claim that it works like this all the time, or even perhaps most of the time. What I am arguing is that the key desired outcomes of child safety, healing and life-planning/life-political development occur when the three layers of child protection's modern character – the administrative, the aesthetic and the expressive – are made to work together in harmony. While a difficult and elusive balance to find, there is a noble modern tradition of work here that deserves to be honoured, celebrated and *developed*.

Time, space and the mobilities of child protection

But it rarely is. On the one hand, it is hard to acknowledge effective practices and even progress when it is known that too many children at risk are not even reported to services never mind protected (Chapter 6), and that child protection practices sometimes do chronically fail those that are reported and in general are struggling to protect well enough. On the other hand, however, the absence of an appropriate sense of perspective on the parameters of effective intervention work is in some measure due to the pervasive failure to understand history and the complex, multilayered sociological character of child protection within modernity.

A key consequence of modernity for child protection concerns the changing nature of risk. The relentless focus on professional 'failure' to protect means that scandal politics, social anxiety and the questioning of expertise has not only expanded into every aspect of child welfare services, but also shows no signs of abating. I have argued that this situation is best understood in terms of structural changes and the emergence of forms of reflexivity which constitute what Beck calls risk society. For Beck, risk society 'is a *catastrophic* society. In it the exceptional condition threatens to become the norm. ... In it the *state of emergency* threatens *to become the normal state'* (Beck, 1992, pp. 24–79, emphasis in original). A permanent state of emergency is precisely what has emerged in the area of child protection over the past three decades. Scandals and inquiries are examples of organizational responses which combine what Beck (1992, p. 78) calls 'the pretense of normality [with] the enabling power of catastrophes'. The organizing concern of the paradigm of risk society is *danger*. It produces an outlook which, as Beck says, is 'peculiarly *negative* and *defensive*. Basically, one is no longer concerned with attaining something "good", but rather with *preventing* the worst; *self-limitation* is the goal which emerges. The dream of the class society is that everyone wants and ought to have a *share* of the pie. The utopia of the risk society is that everyone should be *spared* from poisoning' (Beck, 1992, p. 49).

The point is not that there are no dangers. Child abuse deaths and the abduction, rape and murder of children, for instance, relate to very real human tragedies and reflect the kind of hazards that do exist for children in modern societies. But it would be mistaken to see this in terms simply of the emergence of overwhelming hazards to children, or as a reflection of declining professional standards and capacities to keep children safe. The challenge for child protection is to move beyond the impact of increased anxiety and self-limitations of risk society which now constantly threaten to paralyse workers and professional systems (Chapter 5) to reach a grounded analysis of the best practices that it is possible for professionals to achieve and what needs to be in place for them to happen (Ferguson, 2003b).

Giddens (1990) argues that expert systems fail for two main reasons: because of what he calls 'design faults', where problems are built into the very fabric of the system; and because of 'operator failure', due to a problem in the way practice is performed in the system, individually and collectively. I would add a third: because of the complex nature of human agency and the inability or unwillingness of (some) service users to accept that their children are at risk and in need of help. Most commentary which considers the possibility of 'design faults' in child protection examines how the system has been constructed in recent decades. In this book I have argued that such evaluations need to go as far back as to the nineteenth century to when the system first began to be constructed.

As I have suggested, the construction of an ideology and practice of protecting children in time, which was put in place by the first decades of the twentieth century, has in a real sense been a design 'achievement'. Yet, in some crucial respects, the very idea that children can and should be protected in time also amounts to a design *fault* and not merely of child protection systems, but of culture. The big problem, the faultiest part of the design, surrounds the prescriptive, 'should' part of the equation; the way in which the ideology of protecting children in time has developed into an over-anxious, edgy, blame-ridden absolute which is disconnected from consideration of the real conditions and complex relationships through which practice goes on. This is really about the triumph in the public domain and policy formation of the instrumentally rational features of child protection, of a way of seeing child protection which is built upon disciplinary power and a fantasy of total transparency of family life, the notion that there is a way of knowing all there is to be known about children and families if only we can prevent organizations from failing to do it. Implicitly, the story runs, it *is* possible to metaphorically 'lift up the roofs of houses and see what's going on inside'.

Yet, the reality has been quite different. I have traced a key historical moment early in the twentieth century when child protection practices developed nationally and internationally to cover space to a point where families had nowhere left to hide, and at least so far as the child protectors were concerned, the gaps in supervision practices through which families could escape had been filled. This same historical moment saw the social construction of the belief that children could and should be protected in time. The mystifications and optimism of science embedded this belief at the very same time as the social conditions for such total protection became more difficult. While the degree of supervision of vulnerable or marginal families increased the capacities of professionals to see children, their location in the private sphere of modern homes made such supervision fleeting and transitory. Little wonder then that the modern history of high risk child protection work is a story of 'liquid welfare', of mobile practices and constant movement, as professionals developed ever more sophisticated technological means to reach children and assess danger to them and families have ducked and dived so as to receive a service on their terms, or to avoid the clutches of professionals altogether.

In many respects, this infallible view of child protection was an illusion, a pure creation of the professional imagination. It was only, as I have shown, the active concealment of child death and troublesome information about agency failures to protect, in a context of significant social belief in progress and the benefits of science, which sustained the illusion of infallibility. For, in reality, families have always found ways of locating gaps and escaping the grasp of child protection workers and systems. Even as the net has tightened over the years and the work has focused ever more relentlessly upon encounters in the home, children are still apt to be lost sight of today as they are moved around within the family, neighbourhood and, increasingly, the world (Laming, 2003). With this, the 'gaps' and resistances to interventions manifest either in more subtle and creative psychosocial and symbolic ways, such as passive resistance, or in intimidation and violence towards workers.

The key implication of this is that all notions of infallibility in child protection need to be dropped, which is not the same as giving up hope. It means rather, having a grounded concept of the limitations as well as the possibilities, the opportunities and the risks of child protection work. It is because of this core tension between power and vulnerability and the fundamentally mobile nature of child protection practices that I have used the metaphors of 'solid' and 'melting', 'fluid' and 'liquid' to explore the constitution of child protection over time as a way of trying to do justice to the complex, multidimensional nature of its practices. From its modern beginnings 130 years ago, child protection has always been a mixture of solid and melting forms. 'Solid' captures the 'hard' or 'heavy' nature of the law and procedures, the bureaucracy that is at the core of child protection. It also refers to cultural forms and the belief systems that have held it together through forms of social relationships, trust and degrees of faith in science.

'Melting' and 'liquid' metaphors seek to capture the ephemeral, fleeting and contingent nature of child protection practices, and what happens when those solid bureaucratic forms are literally put into practice, when movement begins and action is taken to protect children. As the earliest child protection reformers and workers understood so well, in order for children to be protected it is necessary to act, to do something. At its core, in its engagement with children's and family's lives, by 1914, child protection had become a practice based on the implementation of the law through movement at speed and a fleeting, ephemeral and contingent experience. At the same time as notions of domesticity, the private domain and the 'home' took on their modern forms and meanings, getting to see the child and family became focused on the home visit. What professionals got (and continue to get) are snapshots of people's densely lived lives as they pass through them on hourly home visits, or through office interviews, consultations in hospitals and so on.

This experience of movement, speed and the constitution of the self is central to the very nature of child protection's modernity. As Bauman argues:

> The society which enters the twenty-first century is no less 'modern' than the society which entered the twentieth; the most one can say

is that it is modern in a different way. What makes it as modern as it was a century ago is what sets modernity apart from all other histori-cal forms of human cohabitation: the compulsive and obsessive, con-tinuous, unstoppable, forever incomplete *modernization*; the overwhelming and ineradicable thirst for creative destruction (or of destructive creativity, as the case might be: of 'clearing the site' in the name of the 'new and improved' design; of 'dismantling', 'cutting out', 'phasing out', 'merging' or 'downsizing', all for the sake of a greater capacity for doing more of the same in the future – enhancing productivity or competitiveness). (Bauman, 2000, pp. 28–9)

Since its late-nineteenth century beginnings, as we have seen, child protection has nourished itself on precisely this kind of dynamic energy and modernization impulse. The families it has typically dealt with are the 'refuse of modernity' (Baudelaire), those who capitalism's 'destruc-tive creativity' has cleared out of the way to make space for progress. The continuities between those late-nineteenth century SPCC social workers who tore across space, into communities and people's homes gathering dying children up in their mackintoshes and taking them to safety – or not (Chapters 2 and 3) – and the desire and actions of social workers today to help children and families and free them from suffering are striking. The greatest enemy of attempts to theorize child protection has been the treatment of it as if it were static and immobile in nature. Above all, in this book, I have tried to correct for this by showing how its linkages with modernity mean that child protection is an embodied experience of movement in time and space.

In an important sense, even the most static aspects of child protection are on closer examination not like that. Although fundamentally embedded in organizations, child protection work is a form of 'dwelling in mobility' (Sheller and Urry, 2003). First, getting to work involves a journey from home. Once there, workers occupy space – they dwell in the office – and in that workplace enquiries about families and inter- and intra-agency work may go on in apparently static ways in telephone conversations, meetings and other office routines. Yet it is a dwelling in mobility in that telephone or electronic contacts involve reaching across space to gather relevant information about a family. Case conferences always involve people who have travelled to the site of the meeting, with all the risks as well as opportunities involved in making such a move into another professional space and culture. And through it all there is the inescapable fact that at least one, some, or all of those pro-fessionals present will have to do a home visit, that is become mobile to see the child and family. In short, nothing in child protection is static. All is mobile.

Urry (2000) argues that social science, like social life itself, relies on the development of metaphors and the more rhetorically persuasive such metaphors are in how they capture the spirit of the times, the more meaningful the theory is. Thus, Urry's choice of the metaphors of *network*, *flow* and *travel* as the most appropriate to the opening years of the twenty-first century reflect the centrality of movement and mobilities to his vision of what social life fundamentally involves and sociology needs to be about. They have mass appeal because they resonate so well with everyday experience. The dominant metaphors accounting for and theorizing child protection on the other hand, have been determinedly solid, static, structural. Even the concept of risk which is so central to child protection today and which should fundamentally reflect notions of fluidity, uncertainty and ambiguity has been used metaphorically in solid terms to signify blame, prediction and social control. The absence of appropriate metaphors is an important reason why deeper understandings of the fluid, squelchy nature of child protection have failed to enter the public and professional imagination and is why we need to speak of it as a form of *liquid* welfare.

This is an important methodological as well as a theoretical point. In my use of a case study methodology in this book I have tried to show that a more complete study of intervention practices which does justice to the multilayered character of child protection involves analysing what gets done by the range of professional and lay actors involved in cases in particular social contexts to produce a universe of events, experiences, meanings and outcomes. It is then possible to see how statutory power ebbs and flows as laws and bureaucratic rules are turned into practices in the context of people's lives.

The notion of *flows* is crucial here. It seeks to do justice to how influence in intervention practices and the construction of cases moves in different directions. It is tempting to say that it 'flows both ways', that is between professional and client. In fact, it doesn't move in such a linear manner at all, but flows in and around different agencies, through parents and children and other significant persons in communities, through the media and culture and at all times through human persons, through bodies. As I showed in Chapter 6, a good example of such non-linear flows of power and information is the clear correlation that exists between child abuse becoming a public issue in a context of a newly emerged intimate citizenship (Plummer, 1995) and a regular topic of the 'confessional intimacy' of print media, radio and television programmes such as *Oprah*, and increased reporting of cases and a new politics of child protection in how victims/survivors are being empowered to influence powerful organizations, policy, practice and cultural perceptions.

This concept of non-linear flows of bureaucratic power and the generative power of human agency (Giddens, 1991) also helps us to think about social work and child protection in much more 'liquid' ways, as things that are, both figuratively and literally, 'hard to grasp'. We need to get away from the solid language of 'control', 'constraint' which typifies how practices are represented and understood and develop much more liquid metaphors and forms of language which can do justice to how children 'slip through the net' and the sense of uncertainty, riskiness of risk and things being inherently uncontrollable which characterizes the experience of child protection. This needs to include attention to experiences of time as well as space. As I showed in Chapter 7, the notion of 'time-warp' is a key metaphor used by professionals to describe the discontinuous lived experience of practice when in the homes of children and families, thus helping us to theorize time in non-linear, embodied ways.

Notions of heavy and liquid modernity also refer to changes over time in how social practices are shaped and experienced. Simple modernity which ran from 1914–70 was the epoch of 'heavy' modernity, when relationships between experts and lay people were hierarchical and, after a period of extraordinary public visibility of child protection case deaths when they were even viewed as a sign that child protection was working *well*, knowledge of such problems was repressed. The quality of reflexive modernity meanwhile is a 'liquid' modernity, where on top of the ephemeral, fleeting and contingent form that modern child protection has always taken since the routinization of home visiting by 1914, there is a new kind of fluidity to its practices. This, I have shown, arises from changes in the nature of (manufactured) risk where frontline professionals come to know that no matter what they do safety for children cannot be guaranteed, and the emergence of much more transient posttraditional individualized forms of intimate relationships.

Yet, while frontline workers no longer labour under the illusion of total protection that their predecessors in simple modernity did, the pressure on them to protect all children in time remains huge. Culturally, this arises from the impact on lay people's sense of ontological security of having to confront knowledge that systems fail and highly socially valued children suffer and die in a context where changes in the meaning of death mean that it constitutes a huge existential problem. Bureaucratically, within policymaking and the executive of the state, a belief in total protection persists – elements of that which Bauman (2000, p. 29) refers to as 'human affairs becoming totally transparent thanks to knowing everything needing to be known'. It co-exists with and gives rise to a blame culture which holds professionals to account for deaths when the state has to confront the painful truth of how total protection is not possible.

Yet, there is also evidence of a loss of faith in the future which is partly attributable to the growing displacement of clock-time by 'instantaneous time' (Chapters 5 and 7) in how the state manages human affairs. In organizational milieu where information can be accessed in an instant and advanced mobilities makes it possible for children to be physically reached in 'no time', the expectation of immediate protection in an everlasting present (where the future is *now*) takes shape. These are the changed social conditions within which it is possible for the disclosure of the death of a single child to cause public uproar and (demands for) reforms of entire systems.

The paradox of child protection in liquid modernity is that its 'liquidity' fully emerges at a time when organizationally it has never appeared more solid in terms of its bureaucracy and the deeply embedded nature of the law, procedures and performance management in trying to govern what professionals do. Parton is correct to argue that in what he calls post-modernity the state has become more instrumentally rational: 'If child abuse had previously been constituted as a disease, and thus a socio-health problem, the focus now was child protection, which was constituted as a socio-legal issue' (1991, p. 146). This reflects how in recent decades child protection has been reconfigured through the transmutation and renewed development of instrumental rationality. Yet, what requires equal emphasis is how its aesthetic and expressive domains have also undergone renewed development, such that as a social correlate of aesthetic modernism, child protection is now a social practice that includes a deepening of emancipatory reason and (aesthetic) undermining of calculative Enlightenment rationality. These patterns are expressed, for instance, in the importance of anti-oppressive values to social work and the increasing tendency for service users to demand and be given voice, and in the complex psychosocial struggles and experiences which I have shown always threaten to undermine child protection's solid administrative aims.

Viewed organizationally then, child protection today is literally 'top-heavy', but when viewed from the perspective of relationships and the actual work of home visiting and seeing children and carers, what goes on in 'private' has also developed. Both organizations/professionals and lay people/agency clients have become more knowledgeable about child protection to an extent that the struggles involved in it, the dangers as well as the opportunities, have magnified (Chapter 7). This means that in late-modernity child protection has become both more solid *and* more liquid in form. Organizations and professionals are desperately aware of their vulnerability, of risk *as* risk, and need to have clear procedures and accountability in place to ensure children are protected, while the more public disclosures about abuse and protection failures and elaborate the systems have become, the more knowledgeable and accomplished at resistance and reciprocity have service users had to become. Child protection exists then within a complex set of mobile transformations of 'public' and 'private' life in how as a network of rules, images, professional and lay bodies, emotions and practices, it flows through and around the media, and cultural, organizational and domestic spaces. As well as containing risks of failing and imposing oppressive interventions, it is the nature of these flows which opens up opportunities for effective child protection, healing and life-planning and which 'point to a proliferation of multiple "mobile" sites for potential democratization' (Sheller and Urry, 2003, p. 108).

Seen against this background, the striking thing about contemporary child protection is the degree to which it has come to be about fateful moments. And 'moments' here are meant quite literally in terms of the briefest encounters in time; snapshots of abused children's and their family's lives. For all the importance of coordinated inter-agency work, the difference between protecting children in time or not still hangs intensely on the management of the self during moments which always turn out to have fateful consequences, some of them fatal. While assessments of poor or tragic outcomes tend always to look to understand 'the *system* failure', a complete understanding can only be established by interrogating the flows of embedded relationships between public and private, organizations and families, offices and homes and the (mis)management of the fleeting, contingent encounters between professionals, parents and children which go to constitute the essence of what modern child protection is.

The better the design of the system and the more rigorous the training and discipline of those who operate it, the lower the risk of what Giddens calls operator failure. Operator failure is, however, ultimately ineradicable. So long as human beings are involved, the risk must be there (Giddens, 1990, p. 152). The case of child protection bears out the fact that the most important elements producing the unpredictability and riskiness of risk of modernity are *unintended consequences* and *reflexivity* (Giddens, 1990, p. 153). Irrespective of how technically efficient the system and its operators appear to be, the consequences of its introduction and functioning cannot be wholly predicted, especially since it takes place in the context of other systems and human activity in general. Responding to the lessons of the child death scandals impacted in such an unintended way that it helped create the conditions which led to further scandals in child sexual abuse work, which fed into still further radical doubt about professional trustworthiness in terms of the safety of children in care, and so on.

This shows too how reflexivity – the circularity of social knowledge (concepts, theories, findings) – 'does not simply render the social world more transparent, but alters its nature, spinning it off in novel directions' (Giddens, 1990, p. 153). Similar processes occur on a case-by-case level as the responses to professional interventions by family members can never be predicted. As I have shown, interventions also fail because of a lack of parental and sometimes children's co-operation. This may reflect problems in how the service provided isn't what the client wants or likes, but also the struggles vulnerable people have in forming healthy attachments and relationships, with professionals as well as their children.

In an important sense the dynamics of 'failure' are part of the norm of what child protection is about. That is to say, all interventions involve complex relationships and experiences which have to be worked through and have the potential to go wrong. As soon as human contact is made there is no telling how matters will end. There can never be risk-free intervention. Success and failure originate from the same fertile ground. My study typifies this in how in 11 per cent of the 319 case sample, children were known to have been re-harmed within a year of the initial referral in the study (Ferguson and O'Reilly, 2001, Chapter 10). Complex patterns of reciprocity and resistance pervade the work. A striking pattern, for instance, was the degree of 'closure' around themselves and their children that resistant clients maintained through avoidance of services. Such closure enables an emotional and physical boundary to be maintained which creates a distance between the family system and professional system, thus enabling the adult client to maintain control.

People like Anne Smith (in Chapter 5), Mr and Mrs Murphy (Chapter 6) and Mr and Mrs Jones and Mrs Brown (in Chapter 7) typified the high-risk client group in that they had significant unmet dependency needs, having invariably been abused as children, spent time in care, and in the case of the women were still experiencing violence from (ex)partners. Even in casework that has gone well and produced life-planning and therapeutic outcomes as well as safety, such as the case of Maureen (in Chapter 6), professionals are at constant risk of becoming overly drawn into attempting to meet the adult's dependency needs to the exclusion of attention to the children and *their* dependency needs, which limits attention given to the mother–child or father–child relationships (see also the vivid case examples and analysis in Buckley, 2003). Professionals need to be skilled at assessing the impact of past and present trauma, the possibilities for recovery, and be able to recognize when professionals and service users are engaging with one another in a meaningful way which openly takes account of the defences, psychosocial and symbolic processes which routinely come into play in such relationships.

This is where rational knowledge does help in the management of uncertainty and delivery of quality services. And there are encouraging signs that assessment frameworks are beginning to systematize approaches which place the gathering of information about child development, the dynamics of parent–child relationships and the apparent capacities of carers to change at the heart of practice (Howe *et al.*, 1999; Horwath, 2000; Munro, 2002). The logic and wisdom of this approach is to maximize understandings of the child and family when you do have them in your sights, thus making the 'passing moment' of contact endure as much as is humanly possible.

As the kinds of work done in the case studies featured in the later chapters of this book have shown, knowledge of what constitutes risk and how to recognize and intervene into different forms of abuse has developed significantly. So too has awareness of the need to practise in democratic, anti-oppressive ways, even if this is by no means always achieved in practice. The concepts I have used and developed in this book, such as reflexivity, individualization, fateful moments, help-seeking and life-planning are intended to advance further understandings of what is required in the achievement of child safe, democratic practices. Outcomes for children need to be assessed in terms of the promotion of their general welfare. Without the benefit of therapeutic services, the difficulties of abused children deepen over time, while improvements occur when work related to the abuse and its effects is provided (Farmer, 1997; MacDonald, 2001). The more that direct services intervene into children's distress and provide direct assistance to parents in the care and management of children, the more the children's welfare will be promoted and the ultimate goal of child safety and healing for parents as well as children can be achieved.

Failures to protect in time revisited: the tragedy of Victoria Climbié

What is striking, however, is the fragmenting of child protection and intensification of interpretations and policies which essentially regard it as a legal-rational activity. The dominant policy response across the Western world has been a rational-bureaucratic one of developing the law, procedures, audit, inspection and other forms of performance management. At its worst, even attempts to develop more systematic assessment frameworks in practice are being implemented in administrative ways where questions for families are used as management checklists to ensure something has been done, as opposed to guides to developing deep relationship work (Horwath, 2002). The evidence from my own study typifies the pattern which now appears universal across the Western world where professionals feel that they are hanging on by their fingertips to whatever freedom and capacities they still have to do constructive, creative work (Besharov, 1990; Howe, 1996; Parton *et al.*, 1997; Buckley, 2003).

The Laming report (2003) into the death of Victoria Climbié in the United Kingdom provides a compelling case study of how such texts and processes both help to focus attention on the urgency of the task of developing effective ways of protecting children and distort what is needed by positing one-dimensional, almost entirely rational solutions. It can be taken as an exemplar of how the issues are being addressed in Western countries. In its advocacy of the need for clearer accountability structures and management practices, it embodies the instrumentally rational strand of modernity, visions of administrative power and the fantasy of complete transparency of family life which I have traced in this book. But like all such texts it leaves out the other two, equally important, strands of child protection largely ignoring the aesthetic, and the psychological and emotional aspects of its practices. Yet embedded in the text is evidence and indicators which provide the basis for a different, more integrated and holistic reading of the case in terms of the three-fold nature of the consequences of modernity.

At the age of seven, Victoria was brought to England by her great aunt Marie Therese Kouao, from the Ivory Coast in the hope of a better life. Within a year she was dead with 128 separate injuries to her body, having been mercilessly abused by Kouao and her boyfriend Carl Manning. Clearly, like all such cases, serious legal-bureaucratic failings contributed to the failure to protect Victoria from appalling suffering. There was evidence of profound organizational malaise and an absence of leadership as exemplified by senior managers' apparent indifference to children's services, which were underfunded and neglected. Local child protection procedures were way out of date. This was compounded by major staffing problems and low morale among staff who were invariably over worked and 'burning out'. Frontline workers got little support or quality supervision and were uncertain about their role in child protection.

Extremely poor administrative systems existed for tracking referrals and case information. There was a consistent failure to engage with the child in any meaningful shape or form as a service user, while attempting to force Victoria's case into a bureaucratic definition of 'in need' as opposed to 'risk' but without any proper assessment of the child's needs. In effect, the child was treated as a legal and administrative *category* (Richardson, 2003). The focus throughout was on Kouao, Victoria's carer, as the client in the case. The report connects up well the experiences of frontline workers with poor management and a lack of accountability right up to the highest levels. We are left in no doubt that the workers involved were overworked and under-supported.

However, the power and excesses of the instrumentally rational way of seeing things is exemplified in the deeply worrying underlying premise on which the practice is interpreted and recommendations for change are based: the naïve idea that the way forward is 'doing the simple things properly' (Laming, 2003, p. 105), and 'doing the basic things well saves lives' (p. 69). This appears to refer to tasks such as speaking to other professionals about concerns, writing up case notes, reading faxes, files, or even reading the child protection guidelines, never mind following them, engaging with the child and challenging her suspected abusers, and doing home visits – none of which were adequately done in Victoria's case. A consistent finding of all such reports into child deaths is that what looked like straightforward tasks, just didn't get done. This requires us to in many ways explain the unexplainable.

Time and again we see in such reports well-intentioned, often very experienced professionals from all disciplines who simply can't explain their inaction in the face of evidence of marks and injuries. Things don't apparently come much simpler than writing up an observation in case notes. Yet, for instance, during one of Victoria's (two) stays in hospital in July 1999, on one occasion as many as five nurses observed Victoria's injuries while she was taking a bath. On another, a Nurse Pereira who was bathing Victoria was so disturbed by what she saw that she called in Nurse Quinn to observe the marks 'which she thought may have been caused by a buckle belt. She also noticed that Victoria's arm was bruised and swollen' (p. 266). Laming concludes from this:

> I have found it very difficult to understand why important observations of this nature were not recorded in the notes. Both Nurse Pereira and Nurse Quinn were aware that Victoria was a child about whom there were child protection concerns, and Nurse Pereira had seen fit the previous evening to make a note in the critical incident

log concerning the master–servant relationship between Kouao and Victoria. Nurse Pereira was frank enough to accept that she should have made a note of her observation that night. Nurse Quinn simply told me that she could not account for why she chose not to do so. (Laming, 2003, p. 266)

Similar examples could be given for social workers, the police, doctors and housing officials. Such cases reveal what Cohen calls 'the complex obstacles between information and action' (2001, p. 295). It is one thing to know about something, quite another to act on that knowledge. These professionals were caught in the midst of what Cohen calls 'the dynamics of knowing and not knowing'. They were bystanders before an appalling atrocity. They knew but they didn't know what was happening to Victoria and did nothing. Cohen refers to 'the essence of denial and bystanding' as 'an active looking away, a sense of a situation so utterly hopeless and incomprehensible that we cannot bear to think about it' (p. 194).

What leads professionals to this kind of paralysis lies in a combination of issues and processes which I have been detailing in this book: the aesthetic nature of child protection as a mobile practice which must engage with children on a fleeting, transient basis, severely limiting what can be known about them and creating a fluidity to how they are engaged with on the spot; the nature of risk anxiety and culture of organizations, their internal life and processes; and the embodied nature of practice, its mediation by the senses and the emotions, that is the symbolic processes and psychosocial dynamics of practice, including the unconscious denial of abuse and impact of service users and client–worker relationships on practice.

In retrospect, it became clear that Victoria's carers stage-managed the two visits the social worker made to the home, with the effect that Victoria appeared *from a distance* to be content. The worker never got close enough to touch or directly engage with her. Although Kouao never overtly threatened violence against any professional, she was described as being aggressive and menacing in her manner – 'difficult', 'forceful', 'manipulative'. Of equal importance in terms of the impact she had on people was what professionals observed of her relationship with Victoria, especially in terms of a so-called 'master–slave relationship', how Victoria would jump to attention and sometimes wet herself in Kouao's presence. In effect, not only was she 'master' to Victoria in a disastrous manner, but she and Manning dominated professionals, who in an important sense behaved like their 'slaves' or 'captors'. This amply demonstrates the fluid nature of power in child protection work. While service users who are socially excluded may be structurally relatively powerless in terms of the hierarchy of expert–client relationships, in practice they may be extremely powerful, not only in the child's life, but in their control and even abuse of workers (Stanley and Goddard, 2002).

Unconsciously, workers mirrored Victoria's feelings of terror and took up the 'servant' position they observed Victoria taking. The sense of helplessness, fear and discomfort workers felt was partly their own but also Victoria's. Crucially, this is an issue even if a particular client is not actually violent as workers bring their trauma from other threatening and abusive experiences with them into all the work they do. As a social worker in my study put it when asked about the impact of having to deal with a particularly violent and threatening male client, 'It depends on the day you're having. If you're quite in control of your day, you know, if this is the fourth person that's kind of verbally abusing you, you know it can be difficult. Whereas if he's the first one and the only one that day, you know, I could cope with it, or walk away from it.' But while the Laming report details the excessive caseloads of the social workers involved, it expressly does not assess the wider meanings and impact on them of the work that was being done in these cases.

Issues to do with identity, race and difference need to be central to this. In the London social services department which handled Victoria's case, as many as 60–70 per cent of children were, like Victoria, from homeless migrant families who had recently entered the country. As I argued in Chapter 7, the diagnosis of scabies was central to Victoria's abuse being missed and the distance that was maintained between her and professionals was underpinned by contamination fears and a whole tradition of such families being treated as the grotesque marginalized Other. Disgust and fear of the Other arise from a combination of social and psychological processes (Douglas, 1992; Joffe, 1999). Bauman observes that the 'ability to live with differences, let alone to enjoy such living and to benefit from it, does not come easily and certainly not under its own impetus. This ability is an art which, like all arts, requires study and exercise' (Bauman, 2000, p. 106).

Over the past 30 years, social workers have studied difference and have more than any other professional group endeavoured to make an art form out of tolerance and anti-oppressive practice. This democratizing impulse has undoubtedly led to more humane forms of practice than was evident in the era of simple modernity. On the one hand, there is more work – 'exercise' – to be done yet before social work can be considered fit enough to ensure children are protected and in ways that are democratic for them and their carers. On the other hand, social work finds itself being made to carry an intolerable burden where it is expected to do the dirty work that arises from a reconfiguration of public space and citizenship where negative policies and attitudes towards asylum seekers as an infecting Other means that fear of 'outsiders' is increasing (Bauman, 2000, pp. 108–9). In Victoria's case, these fears and exclusionary processes were exacerbated by Victoria literally having an infectious disease and the family were treated, in every sense, as outsiders in terms of their housing and wider needs.

As I have argued in this book, child protection is an embodied form of social action and one of the most significant and intriguing constants in its modern history is social workers' and other professionals' concerns with the smells, dirt, and the notions of disorder which surround the families who typically make up child welfare caseloads. Yet, since the emergence in the 1970s of critical perspectives in health and social care work, it has become much harder for professionals to admit to feelings of disgust and discomfort in working with families, as this would be to appear to judge and oppress people who are invariably already subordinated, rendering such honesty virtually taboo. Practice and ways of theorizing it have become deodorized.

This is exacerbated in a late-modern culture which places such an emphasis on deodorization and the clean and well presented body (Shilling, 1993), and where referring to how someone smells and disgusts us is the ultimate form of giving personal offence. Thus, none of the workers in Victoria's case appear to have discussed their contamination fears with colleagues, although one police officer did make efforts to raise it, but got little support. She simply failed to visit Victoria or to propose an alternative strategy for dealing with her fears. This painfully demonstrates the real dangers of workers not being able to discuss these fears and very uncomfortable feelings – which is precisely the kind of 'exercise' that workers need to get if they are to become consistently good at handling difference.

Lack of attention to these expressive processes in Victoria's case was compounded by various aspects of organizational culture. The social workers did not just have to deal with menacing and manipulative clients, but similar kinds of colleagues, including managers, and acted out distorted and abusive patterns with *one another*. The internal politics of the social work teams suggests that there was little comfort or release for the workers. One social worker recalled that the 'team was very divided, and there were a lot of deep conflicts. At times the working environment felt hostile, and it was not a comfortable place to work comfortably in.' There were allegedly 'two camps', with 'insiders and outsiders within the office'. Similar distorted relationships and communication extended to relationships between agencies: social workers were afraid to challenge doctor's opinions, while at least one team of social workers had it in for the police.

The very dynamics professionals had to routinely confront in families were embedded in the workplace also. This is no mere coincidence. As this book has shown, worker–client relationships are pervaded by psychosocial dynamics, such as transference and counter-transference. Professional systems and family systems become enmeshed and reflect one another and professional relationships come to mirror distorted and abusive relationships within families (Reder *et al.*, 1993). Lisa Arthurworrey, the social worker who had most contact with Victoria, actually referred to her Team Manager as 'the headmistress. I was a child who was seen but not heard, and had seen what had happened to those who challenged [her]' (p. 192). This was compounded by a one-dimensional performance management culture. Cases were just 'plonked on social workers desks', with no attention to the worker's needs, feelings, worries, or the degree to which the level of difficulty in the case reflected their experience or competence. One social worker referred to the culture of 'Conveyer belt social work' and how the 'ethos seemed to be particularly about getting the cases through the system and meeting the targets, meeting the statistics, getting them through the system' rather than 'doing the work that needed to be done' (p. 112).

Others spoke of the 'bombardment factor' of the relentless work that came into the office. As Lisa Arthurworrey, Victoria's social worker from the north Tottenham office told the inquiry: 'we always worked at a fairly cracking pace in north Tottenham' (Laming, 2003, p. 184). As I showed in Chapter 5, this reflects how there is a reflex flow to the work which demands that it needs to be done more and more quickly within the terms of what it is possible to make visible and measurable at an organizational level. So, having conquered space and developed their capacities to reach children physically, protecting children in time increasingly comes to be measured organizationally in terms of performance management targets aimed at pushing cases quickly through the system. The temporal structure of protecting children has come to be defined in terms of 'instantaneous time' (Urry, 2000) and 'instantaneity' (Bauman, 2000). Systematic time-targets are now set for the completion of investigations (within 24 hours) and comprehensive assessments (35 days in the United Kingdom, for instance) (DHSS, 2000).

Most worrying of all, organizational time has lost its connection with how time is lived and experienced in ordinary people's lives and with the rhythms of what is required if meaningful relationships between workers and clients are to be allowed to develop. Pressure to get cases 'through the system' creates a situation where attention, time and resources are diverted from doing in-depth, needs-driven work with children and families in ways which can promote child safety, welfare and healing. The soul is being squeezed out of the work, pulling workers and the entire system's attention away from understanding and developing the kinds of deep relationships with the self, children and carers that are required to do meaningful child protection and welfare work.

It is against all of this background that doing even 'the simple things' comes to seem enormously elusive and difficult. So you don't read the case file because you might have to confront yet more trauma; you don't make that crucial call to another professional, follow those guidelines or even read the procedures that are sitting on your desk. You don't engage with the child or ask the awkward questions of parents or carers. You know about the abuse, but you don't know. You don't visit the child or make any attempt to get close to her or him because unconsciously you fear contamination by their bodies and pain and they threaten to overwhelm you. You are just too busy trying to survive, defending yourself against the anxiety and perhaps over-identification with the perpetrator. And the upshot is a massive system failure, a dead child, and many other ruined careers and deeply traumatized lives.

Liquid practices: towards a critical theory of child protection without guarantees

> Recognizing the irreducible character of risk means having a critical theory without guarantees. Yet this recognition is also a source of liberation.
>
> Anthony Giddens (1994a, p. 21)

The Climbié tragedy provides a worst case example of what happens when all three strands of child protection's modernity are misunderstood and inadequately developed in practice. And it should be a warning to us of what might happen if attempts are made to improve child protection through critical attention to only one of those strands, the administrative. The way forward has to involve an integrated approach to child protection which gives equal attention to its bureaucratic, aesthetic and expressive dimensions. While the language of policy and practice is ever more 'solid', with its focus on structures, procedures, and the implication that practitioners somehow do – or should – have access to the totality of how children and families live, what it should be pointing up is the fluid, liquid character of the work and the implications of it being fundamentally about fateful moments. Moments don't get more fateful than when social workers or other professionals are in rooms with children who are seriously injured (or so it later emerges) but no direct engagement with the child establishes the risk and danger.

Yet, these moments have been poorly understood because analysis of child protection has been subjected to a massive overemphasis on the public domain, on organizations and inter-professional routines, as if children are protected without anyone ever having to leave their desks. It is possible to read most child protection texts today without realizing that most of the real action goes on at doorsteps and in people's homes. This reflects the utter decontextualization and deodorization of practice and ways of theorizing it. It is to miss the crucial sociological point that despite the increased capacities of child protection to be mobile and communicate with others without having to be physically co-present with them, it is a late-modern practice which epitomises the apparent compulsion to meet and talk which arises because of the depersonalizing properties of advanced communications (Urry, 2003). This requirement takes on its greatest significance in the meetings and talks between professionals and families that simply must go on if the actual well-being of children is to be established.

Bauman (2000) observes how a crucial dynamic in how power is imagined and exercised in late or liquid modernity is to the exclusion of any human contact at all. This for him is a crucial element of what makes modernity 'light' and 'liquid' in how governance is not tied down to any place or committed relationship requiring 'heavy' interpersonal resources. Analysts of child protection remain essentially focused on organizational forms *because they are palpably there* and they can gain easy access to them. Focusing on the much more ephemeral nature of practice and the actual relationships between workers and clients is by its very nature a more fluid, contingent thing to grasp. But it is only in understanding these liquid relationships and forms that the nature of what goes right and wrong in child protection can be properly understood.

Thus, despite the huge amount that has now been written about child protection, our knowledge of what is going on in social worker's and other professional's minds and bodies while in the course of doing the work, especially at the point of action of seeing children and parents, has been very limited. In part this reflects the sheer difficulties for social science of reaching into the depths of people's experiences at the moment when actions are being taken. As Boyne argues:

> Sociological explanation of reflexive consciousness at the point of action is hard to come by. Unedited cctv footage of street violence rarely reveals self-consciousness in action; while covert recordings of football hooligan reflection on skirmishes to come indicate disdain for or prohibition of analytical reflection. Methodological, cultural and ethical barriers to research on violence at the point of violence, or passion at the point of passion, mean that dramatists, lyricists, screenwriters, novelists and poets have the field pretty much to themselves.

Boyne argues that seeking explanation of reflexive consciousness at the point of action is a 'prime reason for holding the humanities and the social sciences squeezed together' rather than, as with so much of the sociological tradition, 'levering them further apart' (Boyne, 2002, p. 120). 'Levering apart' the integrated ways in which we need to understand the modern nature of social work and welfare practices is precisely what has happened in child protection.

My suggestion is that we need to start looking at child protection – as I have tried to do in this book – not just from the direction of the public into the private, but from the private outwards, from the vantage point of embodied experience (the 'smell of practice') and fateful moments. In other words, the mobile flows of practice and relationships and what happens when worker meets client, invariably by stepping across the threshold of their home and into their lives, should provide the core concerns for training, understanding practice and policy development. The fragment and all the glimpses of the totality that it contains needs to be placed at the centre of child protection studies.

This does not mean letting go of the importance of reaching as thorough a possible understanding of the totality of practice and how people live, including issues of poverty, stigma and social exclusion. The book has shown how child protection has always been most effective at times when social policy promotes healthy childhoods in general. Equally, some of the fiercest resistance to child protection in the past arose from its connections to highly stigmatizing forms of social provision such as the poor law. A concern with general forms of social provision and family support in terms of promoting child welfare needs to be at the heart of assessments of children's well-being, but should not at the same time distract from the particulars of what is needed to protect children from harm, which has been my primary concern in this book.

This means making sense of the impact of structural issues on families and of the law and organizational life through a primary focus on relationships. Nor is this to say that what goes on in the public domain is not important. It is profoundly so. Forms of organizational work such as record keeping and other form filling, supervision, and inter-agency meetings and discussions are vital to identifying children at risk and keeping them safe. But these areas are themselves pervaded by aesthetic and psychosocial processes as has been shown in some research into case conferences for instance (Bacon, 1988). There simply is no irrational free zone in such work. Everything in child protection reflects back (and forward) and flows through everything else.

This makes reaching an understanding of the aesthetic and expressive dimensions indispensable to good practice. What I am arguing against is the fantasy which pervades contemporary policymaking and the public imagination: that yet another re-organization of services alone is the key to promoting child safety. Tellingly, the government response to the Laming report into Victoria Climbié's death was to propose the 'biggest re-organisation of child protection services in 30 years' (the *Guardian*, 10 September 2003), but without paying systematic attention to the complexities of the relationships involved in the work (Department of Health, 2003).

Nowhere are the inherent irrationalities of child protection more evident than in approaches to children. While in principle at the centre of child protection, a remarkable feature of this history is the distance between children and professionals. In an important sense, the modern history of child protection is a story of the gradual encroachment by expertise on the body of the child to protect her or him from ever more intimate forms of abuse. Yet the project of getting close to children that this implies continues to be deeply problematic, and this is despite increased legislative duties to do so and exhortations by academics and child advocates (Butler-Sloss, 1988; Dalrymple, 2003).

The research evidence presented in this book suggests that, on the one hand, children generally are engaged with more today than ever before. Processes of individualization have set in place the conditions for children (like their parents) to have the opportunity to live 'a life of their own' in the sense of increased recognition of their rights to protection, to be heard and influence the course of their lives. This should not be mistaken for a general principle to cut them off from their families or heritage, but reflects how individualization means honouring family bonds and relationships in ways which give primacy to the rights of children to be respected as individuals. I have shown how the complexities of this are such that even within the same family/case, individual's perceptions of their interests and needs can be quite different. Thus it is no longer valid to speak to or about the experience of family members or 'service users' in a singular voice which claims to represent them all. The best work that is going on promotes democratic family relationships by recognizing and responding to the needs of individual children (and carers) within this complexity.

On the other hand, however, systematic distancing from children by professionals is severe and dangerous and is the aspect of contemporary child protection that appears most resistant to change. So persistent is this problem that it is clear that it is not simply a matter of rationally changing people's minds. There is something much more deep-seated going on in terms of an underlying generative structure to how children are viewed, which I have argued arises from a combination of a continuing legacy of poor law attitudes where children are not seen as the deserving poor and processes of social exclusion connected to social class, ethnicity and concepts of (good) citizenship and nationhood.

As Bourdieu argues, the truth of interactions is never solely to be found in the face-to-face encounter itself, and the characteristics of the situation. This is to 'forget that the interaction owes its form to the objective structures which have produced the dispositions of the interacting agents and which allot them their relative positions in the interaction and elsewhere' (Bourdieu, 1977, p. 81). Practices are constituted by wider historical and social processes which Bourdieu (1990) calls the 'structural moment'. The inherent problem surrounds a way of constructing families on the margins as the feared 'Other' in casework and the profoundly class-based nature of child protection where even the most discerning of democratic professionals are prone to reproduce differences according to the distinctions between their own habitus and that of agency clients. These deeply political yet personal psycho-symbolic dimensions place practitioners in a highly ambiguous position with respect to the engagement of their bodies and senses in whether or not they (literally) have contact with children and more generally in negotiating the contingent, fateful moments inherent to protecting children. The corollary of this concerns real problems in dealing with cases of suspected middle-class abusers and the emergence of a highly prescriptive yet cautious legalistic response to child sexual abuse in particular which results in poor outcomes for children and in bringing offenders to justice. Becoming aware of the influence of class, habitus and fields of interaction can at least give such processes a chance of being brought to consciousness as part of a re-visioning of the child in its social context.

This book has sought to correct for how the body and senses have gone unrecognized and largely undertheorized in social work and child protection (Peile, 1998; Tangenberg and Kemp, 2002). The exception is the powerful visual emphasis that I have shown is at the heart of modern child protection; its supposed SUPERvision. I have tried to go beyond the mind–body dualism that equates simply 'seeing' children as 'knowing' them in terms of cognition and the mind. As Shilling and Mellor (2001, p. 134) argue, 'Here the eye is taken as a natural corridor through which information passes to the brain for purposes of reflexive monitoring and evaluation, and subsequent incorporation into the routines of daily action.' However, as an embodied social practice child protection is a sensuous, fleshy practice in which all the senses are invoked. Smell and touch have always vied with sight and hearing in the sensuous hierarchy. I have also suggested that smell and attention to the 'smell of practice' can be taken as a useful metaphor for the contingent and unpredictable nature of child protection because of how it is especially through smell that practice is experienced through the body, provoking reactions that are particularly prone to unsettle the good premeditated intentions of professional interventions.

What is clearly needed are supportive systems that are 'expressively' aware, that routinely tune into the psychodynamic and symbolic properties and processes of practice. A crucial function of welfare organizations in late-modernity is to act as containers for social anxiety. When such organizations deal with risk of death and suffering they are placed under great pressure to manage their *own*, as well as others', anxiety. What practitioners need in such situations if they are to have a better chance of protecting children and of making democratic decisions which ensure welfare resources are delivered to children in need, is ways of 'holding' themselves to contain their anxiety. This does not only involve a capacity for intellectual insight and knowing how to assess children's well-being through the mind, but for deep engagement with what is going on in and through the body.

As I showed in Chapter 5, professionals already engage in late-modern lifestyles and 'body projects' which are oriented to help them gain mastery over their practical and emotional lives. Techniques to advance this need to move to the centre of organizational life. The impact of risk anxiety, fear, and even threat and violence on professionals is not inevitable. Much depends on how individuals adapt to it, the openness there is in teams and organizations to confronting it and dealing with feelings and the quality of supervision and support provided. Effective supervision requires considered attention to professional, administrative and personal issues (Fook, 1999, 2002). The worker's feelings need to be at the centre of this, not simply so their concerns for their own well-being can be addressed, but because their emotional experience provides crucial data about what children are feeling and experiencing. Attention must be given to these emotional and psychological dynamics right through organizations, from top to bottom.

One of the biggest deficits of education in child protection, and certainly of social work, is a failure to get to grips with the complexity of service users and the reality of involuntary clients as they are experienced in practice. Empathy, sensitivity, warmth, and the doctrine of 'unconditional positive regard' as espoused by the gentle counselling psychology of Carl Rogers are still consistently identified as what social work should be about in the context of practising in empowering anti-discriminatory ways. But these are deeply problematic in child protection work, especially given the preponderance of multi-problem, involuntary clients. Much more openness is required about the effects of human destructiveness, as well as resilience in this work. Full acknowledgement is required of the authoritative role and the *conflict* at the heart of such relationships. Practitioners need training to be what Barber (1991) calls *conflict managers* within an overall model of 'negotiated casework' which sets out what is non-negotiable – we must see and be able to engage with your children; be able to call unannounced, and so on – as well as negotiable.

This demonstrates the redundancy of one-dimensional critical approaches which emphasize the centrality of empowerment and emancipatory politics at the expense of life-politics. The key focus needs to be on what must be done in the minutiae of practice to promote the survival and well being of children and vulnerable carers; to enhance their practical and emotional mastery over their lives. We need to move beyond the deeply troubling way in which not only managerial but one-dimensional 'radical' approaches continue to negate attention to the self, the emotions, and the centrality of relationships (for instance, Garrett, 2003). This neglect of feelings and intimacy itself raises important questions about the fears and evasions which have driven so much of contemporary social work and child protection discourse (Cooper, 2002; Froggett, 2002).

Ultimately, we even have to be prepared to face the uncomfortable fact that any guarantees in protecting children are simply beyond the capacities of what human beings are capable of, even trained professional ones. The limits as well as the possibilities to human action need to accepted. The inability to face up to the impotence and sheer vulnerability of professionals as human beings is one reason why so much effort goes into trying to find ways to get the other, more technical bits of child protection right. What is needed is a critical theory of child protection without guarantees. Paradoxically, acknowledging this vulnerability can be a source of strength, a way of providing the type of preparation, supervision and support that social workers and other professionals truly need if children are to be protected as well as is humanly possible and if social work is to regain public trust and moral authority. As Andrew Cooper, a powerful advocate of therapeutic social work, has argued,

> [W]hat we [therapeutic social workers] are really skilled in, something that every one of us knows about, is the capacity for creative, subtle, evolving and balanced management of the complex relationship between desire, destructiveness, authority, freedom and choice. If we are experts in anything, I believe it is in this crucially important area, but our kind of expertise will not necessarily reassure others, because I think we are not prepared to collude with omnipotent solutions to risk in human affairs which say that 'It will never happen again'. The grim truth, which we know because we understand the impossibility of ever containing tendencies towards destructiveness, irrationality, disturbance and disorder is exactly that it will happen again. I am afraid that part of the reason why psychotherapy, and psychotherapeutic social work will always be ambivalently viewed both within the profession and by those beyond it, is that our message is not always a particular hopeful one. But, and I cannot stress the importance of this too greatly, it is an essentially truthful one. (Cooper, 2002, p. 12)

There is, then, no easy solution to the contemporary liquidity of child protection. In fact, the truth is that there is no solution *at all*, no way to make it rock solid. Breaking away from the excesses of managerialism and limited, unrealistic definitions of 'protection' has to involve 'confronting risk in a direct and engaged way, not expecting to create wholly controlled contexts of action' (Giddens, 1994a, p. 184). The theoretical resources and interpretative frameworks that are brought to bear on these issues will be crucial to how policy and practice are developed. What is required today is a more thoroughly reflexive modernity with regard to the new environment of trust and risk in child protection and an openness to opportunities as well as dangers which this period of development creates in our lives. We live at a time when huge potential exists for individual's lives and whole institutions to be transformed through the adoption of a radical reflexivity and critical reflection on the conditions of action. While certainly incomplete, this book has shown how genuine opportunities have arisen in late-modernity for children and adults to gain protection, healing and engage in life-planning. The extension of such opportunity to all children at risk is best advanced through an adaptive response which Giddens calls 'radical engagement'. This involves 'an attitude of practical contestation towards perceived sources of danger' (Giddens, 1990, p. 137). It is a stance which holds that, although we are beset by major problems, we can and should mobilize either to reduce their impact or transcend them. It is an optimistic outlook bound up with contestory action and critical self-reflection rather than simply a faith in rational analysis, or a cynical focus only on deficits and failures. It requires forms of discussion that learn from best practice, and develop risk awareness, management systems, therapeutic abilities and public discourse in ways that reskill professionals and lay people.

In many respects the project of revisiting the history and sociology of child abuse and protection outlined in this book has turned out to be an effort in promoting such reskilling. My hope is that the kind of reflexive experience it has pointed to and analysis it has provided can help us reach a deeper understanding of the nature of child protection, the underlying social conditions which shape its meanings and practices and point the way to more effective policies and practices in the context of the development of democratic relationships in the promotion of child welfare. In continuing to meet the life and death challenges of safeguarding children, a critical theory of child protection without guarantees can liberate us. It can do this even as, and because of how, professionals must keep on – as they have done for over a century – struggling to work at protecting more and more children in ever new times. And they must do this even as, and because of how the ambiguous, exhilarating, but so often tragic air of the smell of practice continues to blow hot and cold through them, and through us all.

Appendix 1

Primary sources used in the historical chapters, 1889–1950

The historical chapters of this book draw on case records and other primary sources held by the National Society for the Prevention of Cruelty to Children (NSPCC) whose practices covered the United Kingdom and Ireland. Behlmer (1982) includes analysis of casework practices based on a sample of 64 NSPCC case records for the York and Mid-Yorkshire Branch for the years 1898–1903. There are, however, many more surviving early NSPCC case records than Behlmer (1982, p. 168) states and draws upon. To my knowledge, NSPCC case records dating back to the 1890s are available for the York and Mid-Yorkshire Branch (many more records, in fact, for that locality than Behlmer refers to or uses); for the Coventry Branch; and for the Stockton and Thornaby Branch. I did not use the Coventry records in this study but focused on the York Branch and, in particular, the Stockton and Thornaby Branch case records for the 1889–1914 period. All numbered references to particular cases refer to the year of the case and the Stockton and Thornaby Case Record number on the file in the NSPCC archives. For example CR 19103262 refers to case record number 3262 in the year 1910.

In order to reconstruct extensive case histories on interventions for which no case records survive (hence no case record numbers are cited), I supplemented the use of NSPCC case records with material from newspaper accounts, local Police Court, and Poor Law records, especially those which detail the history of children taken into care. I conducted a full search of all child cruelty court cases that came before Stockton Police Court between 1889 and 1914 and of children's homes records for the same period. The bulk of the case-files survived did so because the Society had a preservation rule on cases involving legal proceedings. Therefore the sample is biased towards the most serious cases, which, by definition, ended up before the courts. I have been able to control for this bias by placing the cases that came before the courts in the context of all the casework done by the Branches. Local Branch Annual reports were the crucial sources in this regard. This study draws in particular on an exceptional series of surviving local annual reports for the Stockton and Thornaby Branch NSPCC.

Hundreds of NSPCC case records survive for the period after 1914. These cover many regions, and await the attention of historians, and I draw here on a sample of 45 of these that survive from the Stockton district for the period 1914–39.

I use these historical sources in the book to illuminate matters of general relevance to the construction of child protection.

Appendix 2

Data used in the study of contemporary child protection practices

The research study on which I draw here began in 1996 by gathering extensive data on all child care and abuse cases referred to three social work teams in the same region over a three-month sampling period, 1 April to 30 June 1996, which produced a core sample of 319 cases. The survey was conducted through a questionnaire that gathered data on every referral entering the system over the three month period. The aim of getting a 100 per cent sample of all the work done during the sampling period was achieved. Detailed information was gathered on every aspect of the referral/case, the decisions made and work done by the range of professionals involved. The 319 cases in the sample were then tracked over the following 12 months through to 30 June 1997. This involved the use of two methodologies. First, the outcomes – or 'case careers' – of each referral was analysed in terms of the types of 'abuse' and child care problems involved, the services provided, and the attempts that were made to promote the safety and welfare of the children. Second, an 'intensive' case-study method was employed and a sample of children, parents and the professionals who worked with them (involving, on average, three professionals per case) were interviewed during 1997 to establish their experience of practice and perceptions of how the system works, and the degree to which it promotes safety and welfare. This provided invaluable qualitative data to supplement the harder evidence gathered in the survey.

The qualitative dimension of the research adopted what I call an intensive case study approach, the aim of which was to examine the construction of cases and the work that went into them from the perspectives of the many actors involved. As many key actors as possible involved in the selected sub-sample of cases were interviewed using a semi-structured method. It was beyond the scope and the priorities of the research to qualitatively evaluate the direct processing of all the referrals/cases involved in the study. It was necessary, therefore, to design a sample which was representative of the typical concerns illuminated by analysis of all the referrals/cases involved. 32 cases – 10 per cent of the overall sample – were chosen for in-depth analysis (for a detailed breakdown, see Ferguson and O'Reilly, 2001, pp. 271–2). This process of theoretical sampling required careful analysis of the data, generating categories and building up the analysis from the bottom and was facilitated by creating 'case profiles' for every single referral in the study. The case studies used in this book are intended to represent practice in a way that provides for an extensive analysis of the meanings of safety and welfare in relation to different types of child abuse and child care problems. Those I have selected to use here represent examples which illuminate more general issues in the construction of child abuse and protection. **All names and other possible identifying characteristics have been changed in the case studies.**

Notes

2 Taking it Onto the Streets: The Discovery of Child Death and Birth of Child Protection, 1870–1914

1. This is based on a systematic search of newspapers in the north-east of England for the years 1879 and 1889.
2. On the sources from which such data on cases is drawn, see Appendix 1.
3. These figures have been compiled from: information contained in Stockton and Thornaby NSPCC *Annual Reports*, 1891–1914 (with the exception of 1898, for which the information has been gathered from a press report of the Branch A.G.M. for that year: cf, *North Eastern Daily Gazette*, April 30, 1898); NSPCC cases traced through Police Court records and NSPCC Case Records; and the records of Stockton, and Middlesbrough Poor Law Union Children's homes. Stockton and Thornaby Branch NSPCC Annual Reports provide figures on the numbers of children removed permanently from parental custody for each year up to 1903. They also give details of the numbers of children removed annually to the Children's Shelters until their closure in 1903. After 1903, more limited information is given in the NSPCC discourse on child removals and outcomes in cases. Each court case taken from the *Stockton Police Court Register* and each Case Record as followed up in the *Stockton Union Children's Homes Register of Children* and the children's histories in care after 1900 established the outcomes of placements for children.
4. This case study has been reconstructed from newspaper accounts, local Police Court records, and Poor Law records, as well as NSPCC sources (see Appendix 1).
5. These figures are based on an analysis of the Stockton and Thornaby NSPCC Branch.
6. This case study is based on a reading of the NSPCC case record, Stockton local Police Court records, and Poor Law Children's Homes records and newspaper reports.

3 The Smell of Practice: Child Protection, the Body and the Experience of Modernity

1. This case study is based on a reading of the NSPCC case record, Stockton local Police Court records, and Poor Law Children's Homes records and newspaper reports. See also Appendix 1.

4 From Day-to-Day Quietly and Without Fuss: Child Protection, Simple Modernity and the Repression of Knowledge of Child Death, 1914–70

1. Based on a Stockton NSPCC case record 19356669. See Appendix 1.
2. NSPCC Stockton and Thornaby case records. On the sources used here, see Appendix 1.

5 Child Physical Abuse and the Return of Death Since the 1970s: Child Protection, Risk and Reflexive Modernization

1. For further information on the study design and sampling, see Appendix 2.
2. This case study is based on interviews with a social worker, hospital consultant, public health nurse, family support worker and a reading of the case-file. While case study materials detail actual events and practices, some details have been changed to protect the anonymity of those involved. For a further note on sources, see Appendix 2.

6 Child Sexual Abuse and the Reflexive Project of the Self: Child Protection, Individualization and Life Politics

1. This case study is based on interviews with a social worker, the mother and father (separately), two of the children (separately) and a reading of the case-file. While the case study covers actual events and practices, some details have been changed to protect the anonymity of those involved (see Appendix 2).
2. This case study is based on interviews with the area social worker, court social worker, public health nurse, police officer, director of nursing, surgeon/head of accident and emergency, casualty sister, GP and the mother, and a reading of the case file. While the case study covers actual events and practices, some details have been changed to protect the anonymity of those involved (see Appendix 2).

7 Into Another World: Child Neglect, Multi-problem Families and the Psychosocial Dynamics of Late-modern Child Protection

1. This case study is based on interviews with a social worker, public health nurse, the mother and two children (separately) and a reading of the case-file. While the case study covers actual events and practices, some details have been changed to protect the anonymity of those involved (see Appendix 2).
2. This case study is based on interviews with the social worker, family support worker, and public health nurse and a reading of the case-file. While the case study covers actual events and practices, some details have been changed to protect the anonymity of those involved (see Appendix 2).

Bibliography

Adam, B. (1990), *Time and Social Theory*, Cambridge: Polity.

Adam, B. (1995), *Timewatch: The Social Analysis of Time*, Cambridge: Polity.

Adam, B. (1996), *Timescapes of Modernity*, London: Routledge.

Agass, D. (2002), 'Counter transference, supervision and the reflection process', *Journal of Social Work Practice*, 16(2): 125–33.

Allen, A. and Morton, A. (1961), *This is Your Child: The Story of the National for the Prevention of Cruelty to Children*, London: Routledge and Kegan Paul.

Aries, P. (1974), *Western Attitudes Toward Death: From the Middle to the Present*, Baltimore: John Hopkins University Press.

Babcock, B. (1978), *The Reversible World: Symbolic Inversion in Art and Society*, Ithaca: Cornell University Press.

Bachelard, G. (1969), *The Poetics of Space*, Boston, MA: Beacon Press.

Bacon, R. (1988), 'Counter-transference in a case conference: resistance and rejection in work with abusing families and their children', in G. Pearson, J. Treseder and M. Yelloly (eds), *Social Work and the Legacy of Freud: Psychoanalysis and its Uses*, Basingstoke: Macmillan.

Bailey, V. and Blackburn, S. (1979), 'The Punishment of Incest Act 1908: a case-study of law creation', *Criminal Law Review*, 707–18.

Bailey, R. and Brake, M. (1975), *Radical Social Work*, London: Edward Arnold.

Bakan, D. (1971), *Slaughter of the Innocents*, San Francisco.

Bakhtin, M. (1968), *Rabelais and his World*, Cambridge Mass: MIT Press.

Balloch, S., Pahl, J. and McLean, J. (1998), 'Working in the social services: job satisfaction, stress and violence', *British Journal of Social Work*, 28: 329–50.

Barber, J. (1991), *Beyond Casework*, Basingstoke: Macmillan.

Baudelaire, C. (1965), *The Painter of Modern Life and other Essays*, translated & edited by Jonathan Mayne, London: Phaidon.

Bauman, Z. (1990), *Modernity and Ambivalence*, Cambridge: Polity.

Bauman, Z. (1992), *Mortality, Immortality and Other Life Strategies*, Cambridge: Polity.

Bauman, Z. (1993), 'The sweet smell of decomposition', in C. Rojek and B. Turner (eds), *Forget Baudrillard?* London: Routledge.

Bauman, Z. (2000), *Liquid Modernity*, Cambridge: Polity.

Bauman, Z. (2002), 'Individually together', Foreword to U. Beck and E. Beck-Gernsheim (eds), *Individualization*, London: Sage.

Bauman, Z. (2003), *Liquid Love*, Cambridge: Polity.

Bean, P. and Melville, J. (1989), *Lost Children of the Empire: The Untold Story of Britain's Child Migrants*, London: Unwin.

Beck-Gernsheim, E. (2002), 'Life as a planning project', in E. Beck-Gernsheim, *Reinventing the Family: In Search of New Lifestyles*, Cambridge: Polity.

Beck, U. (1992), *Risk Society: Towards a New Modernity*, London: Sage.

Beck, U. (1994), 'The reinvention of politics: towards a theory of reflexive modernization', in U. Beck, A. Giddens and S. Lash (eds), *Reflexive Modernization*, Cambridge: Polity.

Beck, U. (1995), *Ecological Politics in an Age of Risk*, Cambridge: Polity.

Beck, U. (1997), *The Reinvention of Politics*, Cambridge, Polity.

Beck, U. and Beck-Gernsheim, E. (1995), *The Normal Chaos of Love*, Cambridge: Polity.

Beck, U. and Beck-Gernsheim, E. (2002), *Individualization*, London: Sage.

Beck, U., Bonass, W. and Lau, C. (2003), 'The theory of reflexive modernization: problematic, hypotheses and research Programme', *Theory, Culture and Society*, 20: 1–33.

Behlmer, G.K. (1982), *Child Abuse and Moral Reform in England 1870–1908*, Stanford: Stanford University Press.

Bell, Lady F. (1907), *At The Works: A Study of a Manufacturing Town*, London: Virago edition, 1985.

Bell, S. (1988), *When Salem Came to the 'Boro: The True Story of the Cleveland Crisis*, London: Pan Books.

Bell, V. (1993), *Interrogating Incest: Feminism, Foucault, and the Law*, London: Routledge.

Benjamin, W. (1973), *Charles Baudelaire: A Lyric Poet in the Era of High Capitalism*, London: New Left Books.

Berman, M. (1983), *All That is Solid Melts into Air: The Experience of Modernity*, London: Verso.

Besharov, D. (1985), ' "Doing something" about child abuse: the need to narrow the grounds for state intervention', *Harvard Journal of Law and Public Policy*, 8: 539–89.

Besharov, D. (1990), 'Gaining control over child abuse reports', *Public Welfare*, 48: 34–9.

Bosanquet, H. (1874), *A Handy Book for Visitors of the Poor in London*, London: Charity Organisation Society.

Bosanquet, H. (1973), *Social Work in London: 1869–1912*, London: Harvester Press, 2nd edn.

Bourdieu, P. (1977), *Outline of a Theory of Practice*, Cambridge: Cambridge University Press.

Bourdieu, P. (1986), *Distinction: A Social Critique of the Judgement of Taste*, London: Routledge.

Bourdieu, P. (1990), 'Codification', in P. Bourdieu (ed.), *In Other Words: Essays Towards a Reflexive Sociology*, Cambridge: Polity.

Boyne, R. (2002), 'Bourdieu: From class to culture: In Memoriam Pierre Bourdieu 1930–2002', *Theory, Culture and Society*, 19(3).

Briggs, A. (1963), *Victorian Cities*, London: Penguin.

Brown, A. and Barrett, D. (2002), *'Knowledge of Evil': Child Prostitution and Child Sexual Abuse in Twentieth Century England*, Devon: Willan Publishing.

Bryant, G.A. and Jary, D. (2001), 'The body, self-identity and social transformation', in G.A. Bryant and D. Jary (eds), *The Contemporary Giddens: Social Theory in a Globalizing Age*, Basingstoke: Palgrave.

Buckley, H. (1996), 'Child abuse guidelines in Ireland: for whose protection?', in H. Ferguson and T. McNamara (eds), *Protecting Irish Children: Investigation, Protection and Welfare*, Special Edition of *Administration*, Vol. 44, No. 2, Dublin: Institute of Public Administration.

Buckley, H. (2003), *Child Protection Work: Beyond the Rhetoric*, London: Jessica Kingsley.

Burgess, A. (1997), *Fatherhood Reclaimed: The Making of the Modern Father*, London: Vermillion.

Butler-Sloss, Lord Justice, E. (1988), *Report of the Inquiry into Child Abuse in Cleveland 1987*, London: HMSO.

Campbell, B. (1988), *Unofficial Secrets: Child Sexual Abuse, The Cleveland Case*, London: Virago.

Cannadine, D. (1981), 'War and death, grief and mourning in modern Britain', in J. Whaley (ed.), *Mirrors of Mortality: Studies in the Social History of Death*, London: Europa.

Cawson, P., Wattam, C., Brooker, S. and Kelly, G. (2000), *Child Maltreatment in the United Kingdom*, London: NSPCC.

Chand, A. (2003), 'Victoria Climbié, Child protection and issues in working with ethnic minority families', paper given to the *Beyond Laming* Conference, 10th June 2003, Bristol: University of the West of England.

Chaney, D. (2002), *Cultural Change and Everyday Life*, Basingstoke: Palgrave.

Classen, C. (1993), *Worlds of Sense*, London: Routledge.

Classen, C., Howes, D. and Synnott, A. (1994), *Aroma: The Cultural History of Smell*, London: Routledge.

Clyde, J.J. (1992), *The Report of the Inquiry into the Removal of Children from Orkney in February 1991*, Edinburgh: HMSO.

Cohen, S. (1985), *Visions of Social Control*, Cambridge: Polity.

Cohen, S. (2001), *States of Denial: Knowing about Atrocities and Suffering*, Cambridge: Polity.

Cohen, S. and Scull, A. (eds) (1983), *Social Control and the State: Historical and Comparative Essays*, Oxford: Martin Robertson.

Colwell Report (1974), *Report of the Committee of Inquiry in the Care and Supervision Provided in Relation to Maria Colwell*, London: HMSO.

Cooper, A. (2002), 'Keeping our heads: preserving therapuetic values in a time of change', *Journal of Social Work Practice*, 16(1): 7–13.

Corbin, A. (1988), *The Foul and the Fragrant*, Berg: Leamington Spa.

Corby, B. (1987), *Working with Child Abuse*, Milton Keynes: Open University Press.

Corby, B. (1993, 2002), *Child Abuse: Towards a knowledge Base*, Milton Keynes: Open University Press, 2nd edn, 2002.

Corby, B., Doig, A. and Roberts, V. (2001), *Public Inquiries into Abuse of Children in Residential Care*, London: Jessica Kingsley.

Cooter, R. (ed.) (1992), *In the Name of the Child: Health and Welfare, 1880–1940*, London: Routledge.

Cox, P. (1996), 'Girls, deficiency and delinquency', in D. Wright and A. Digby (eds), *From Idiocy to Mental Deficiency: Historical Perspectives on People with Learning Difficulties*, London: Routledge.

Crowther, M.A. (1981), *The Workhouse System, 1834–1929*, London: Batsford.

Crowther, M.A. (1988), *British Social Policy 1914–1939*, London: MacMillan.

Dalrymple, J. (2003), 'Professional Advocacy as a force for resistance in child welfare', *British Journal of Social Work*, 33: 1043–62.

Dalrymple, J. and Burke, B. (1995), *Anti-Oppressive Practice, Social Care and the Law*, Buckingham: Open University Press.

Daniel, B. and Taylor, J. (1999), 'The rhetoric versus the reality: a critical perspective on practice with fathers in child care and protection work', *Child & Family Social Work*, 4: 209–220.

Daunton, M. (1983), *House and Home in the Victorian City: Working-class Housing, 1850–1914*, London: Routledge and Kegan Paul.

Davies, K. (1990), *Women and Time: Weaving the Strands of Everyday Life*, Aldershot: Avesbury.

Davin, A. (1978), 'Imperialsim and motherhood', *History Workshop Journal*, 5: 9–65.

Davin, A. (1988), 'Little women: the childhood of working-class girls in late 19th century London', Paper presented to the *B.S.A. conference on History and Sociology, Edinburgh University*.

Deacon, A. and Mann, K. (1999), 'Agency, modernity and social policy', *Journal of Social Policy*, 28(3): 413–35.

Dean, M. (1994), *Historical Sociology, Foucault and Genealogy*, London: Routledge.

De Montigny, G.A.J. (1995), 'The power of being professional' in M. Campbell and A. Manicom (eds), *Knowledge, Experience and Ruling Relations: Studies in the Social Organisation of Knowledge*, Toronto: Toronto University Press.

Demos, J. (1985), 'Child abuse in context: an historian's perspective', in J. Demos (ed.), *Past, Present and Personal*, Oxford: Oxford University Press.

(DHSS) Department of Health and Social Security (1982), *Child Abuse: A Study of Inquiry Reports 1973–81*, London: HMSO.

(DHSS) Department of Health and Social Security (1988a), *Protecting Children: A guide for Social Workers Undertaking a Comprehensive Assessment*, London: HMSO.

(DHSS) Department of Health and Social Security (1988b), *Working Together: A Guide to Inter-Agency Co-operation for the Protection of Children from Abuse*, London: HMSO.

(DHSS) Department of Health and Social Security (1988c), *Diagnosis of Child Sexual Abuse: Guidance for Doctors*, London: HMSO.

Department of Health and Social Security (1991), *Child Abuse: A Study of Inquiry Reports 1980–1989*, London: HMSO.

(DHSS) Department of Health and Social Security (1995), *Child Protection: Messages from Research*, London: HMSO.

(DH) Department of Health (2000), *Framework for the Assessment of Children in Need and their Families*, London: Stationary Office.

Department of Health (2003), *Every Child Matters*, London: Stationary Office.

Dennis, R. (1984), *English Industrial Cities of the Nineteenth Century: A Social Geography*, Cambridge: Cambridge University Press.

Dienhart, A. and Dollahite, D. (1997), 'A generative narrative approach to clinical work with fathers', in A. Hawkins and D. Dollahite (eds), *Generative Fathering: Beyond Deficit Perspectives*, London: Sage.

Dingwall, R. Eekelaar, J. and Murray, T. (1983), *The Protection of Children: State Intervention and Family Life*, Oxford: Basil Blackwell.

Dobash, R.E and Dobash, R.P. (1992), *Women, Violence and Social Change*, London: Routledge.

Dodd, N. (1999), *Social Theory and Modernity*, Cambridge: Polity Press.

Donzelot, J. (1979), *The Policing of Families*, London: Hutchinson.

Douglas, M. (1966), *Purity and Danger: An Analysis of the Concepts of Pollution and Taboo*, London: Routledge and Kegan Paul.

Douglas, M. (1970), *Natural Symbols: Explorations in Cosmology*, London: Barrie and Jenkins.

Douglas, M. (1992), *Risk and Blame: Essay in Cultural Theory*, London: Routledge.

Driver, E. and Droisen, A. (eds) (1989), *Child Sexual Abuse: Feminist Perspectives*, Basingstoke: Macmillan.

Dublin Branch NSPCC Reports 1889–1955, London: NSPCC archives.

Dubowitz, H. and Newberger, E. (1989), 'Pediatrics and child abuse', in D. Cicchetti and V. Carlson (1989), *Child Maltreatment: Theory and Research on the Causes and Consequences of Child Abuse and Neglect*, Cambridge: Cambridge University Press.

Durkheim, E. (1964), *The Division of Labour in Society*, New York: Free Press.

Dyhouse, C. (1978), 'Infant mortality in England 1895–1914', in C. Webster (ed.), *Biology, Medicine and Society, 1840–1960*, Cambridge: Cambridge University Press.

de Mause, L. (1976), 'The evolution of childhood', in L. de Mause (ed.), *The History of Childhood*, London: Souvenir Press.

Edwards, J. (1998), 'Screening out men: or "Has mum changed her washing powder recently"?', in J. Popay, J. Hearn and J. Edwards (eds), *Men, Gender Divisions and Welfare*, London: Routledge.

Edwards, S., Lohman, S.M. and Soetenhorst-de Savornin, J. (1994), 'The impact of "moral panic" on professional behaviour in cases of child sexual abuse: an international perspective', *Journal of Child Sexual Abuse*, 3(1): 103–26.

Elias, N. (1985), *The Loneliness of Dying*, Oxford: Basil Blackwell.

Elliott, A. (1996), *Subject to Ourselves: Social Theory, Psychoanalysis and Postmodernity*, Cambridge: Polity Press.

Engels, F. (1969), *The Condition of the Working Class in England in 1845*, London: Panther.

Farmer, E. (1997), 'Protection and child welfare: striking the balance', in N. Parton (ed.), *Child protection and Family Support: Tensions, Contradictions and Possibilities*, London: Macmillan.

Farmer, E. and Owen, M. (1995), *Child Protection Practice: Private Risks and Public Remedies*, London: HMSO

Featherstone, B. (1999), 'Taking mothering seriously: the implications for child protection', *Child and Family Social Work*, 4(1): 43–54.

Ferguson, H. (1990), 'Rethinking child protection practices: a case for history', in The Violence Against Children Study Group, *Taking Child Abuse Seriously*, London: Routledge.

Ferguson, H. (1992), 'Cleveland in history: the abused child and child protection, 1880–1914', in R. Cooter (ed.), *In The Name of The Child: Health and Welfare, 1880–1950*, London: Routledge.

Ferguson, H. (1994), 'Child abuse inquiries and the report of the Kilkenny incest investigation: a critical analysis', *Administration*, 41(4): 385–410.

Ferguson, H. (1995), 'The "paedophile priest": a deconstruction', *Studies*, 84(335).

Ferguson, H. (1996), 'Protecting Irish children in time', in H. Ferguson and T. McNamara (eds), *Protecting Irish Children: Investigation, Protection and Welfare*, special issue of Administration, Dublin: Institute of Public Administration.

Ferguson, H. (2000), 'Ireland', in B. Schwart–Kenney, M. McCauley and M. Epstein eds, *Child Abuse: A Global View*, Westport, CT.: Greenwood Press.

Ferguson, H. (2001a), 'Social work, individualisation and life politics', *British Journal of Social Work*, 31: 41–55.

Ferguson, H. (2001b), 'Promoting child protection, welfare and healing: the case for developing best practice', *Child & Family Social Work*, 6: 1–12.

Ferguson, H. (2003a), 'Welfare, social exclusion and reflexivity: the case of child and woman protection', *Journal of Social Policy*, 32(2): 199–216.

Ferguson, H. (2003b), 'Outline of a critical best practice perspective on social work and social care', *British Journal of Social Work*, 33: 1005–24.

Ferguson, H. (2003c), 'In defence (and celebration) of individualization and life politics for social work', *British Journal of Social Work*, 33: 699–707.

Ferguson, H. and O'Reilly, M. (2001), *Keeping Children Safe: Child Abuse, Child Protection and the Promotion of Welfare*, Dublin: A&A Farmar.

Ferguson, H. and Hogan, F. (2004), *Strengthening Families Through Fathers: Issues for Policy and Practice in working with vulnerable fathers and their families*, Dublin: Research Report for the Department of Social, Community and Family Affairs.

Fido, J. (1977), 'The charity organisation society and social casework in London 1869–1900', in A.P. Donajgrodski (ed.), *Social Control in Nineteenth Century Britiain*, London: Croom Helm.

Finkelhor, D. (1984), *Child Sexual Abuse: New Theory and Research*, New York: Free Press.

Finnegan, F. (1979), *Poverty and Prostitution: A Study of Victorian Prostitutes in York*, Cambridge: Cambridge University Press.

Fook, J. (1999), 'Critical reflectivity in education and practice', in B. Pease and J. Fook (eds), *Transforming Social Work Practice*, London: Routledge.

Fook, J. (2002), *Social Work: Critical Theory and Practice*, London: Sage.

Foucault, M. (1977), *Discipline and Punish: The Birth of the Prison*, Harmondsworth: Allen Lane.

Foucault, M. (1979), *The History of Sexuality*, Vol. 1, London: Penguin Books.

Franklin, B. (1989), 'Wimps and bullies: press reporting of child abuse', in P. Carter, T. Jeffs and M. Smith (eds), *Social Work and Social Welfare Year Book 1*, Milton Keynes: Open University Press.

Fraser, N. (1989), *Unruly Practices: Power, Discourse and Gender in Contemporary Social Theory*, Cambridge: Polity Press.

Frisby, D. (1982), *Sociological Impressionism: A Reassessment of Georg Simmel's Social Theory*, London: Heinemann.

Frisby, D. (1984), *George Simmel*, London: Heineman.

Frisby, D. (1985), *Fragments of Modernity: Theories of Modernity in the Work of Simmel, Kracauer and Benjamin*, Cambridge: Polity Press.

Frisby, D. and Featherstone, M. (eds) (1997), *Simmel on Culture*, London: Sage.

Froggett, L. (2002), *Love, Hate and Welfare: Psychosocial Approaches to Policy and Practice*, Bristol: Policy Press.

Frost, N. and Stein, M. (1989), *The Politics of Child Welfare*, Brighton: Harvester Wheatsheaf.

Frykman, J. and Lofgren, O. (1987), *Culture Builders: An Historical Anthropology of Middle-Class Life*, New Brunswich, NJ: Rutgers University Press.

Furedi, F. (2001), *Paranoid Parenting*, London: Penguin.

Gamarnikow, E. and Purvis, J. (eds) (1983), *The Public and the Private*, London: Heinemann.

Game, A. (1995), 'Time, space, memory, with reference to Bachelard', in M. Featherstone, S. Lash and R. Robertson (eds), *Global Modernities*, London: Sage.

Garland, D. (1981), 'The birth of the welfare sanction', *British Journal of Law and Society*, 8: 29–45.

Garland, D. (1985), *Punishment and Welfare: A History of Penal Strategies*, Aldershot: Gower.

Garland, D. (1990a), 'Frameworks of inquiry in the sociology of punishment', *British Journal of Sociology*, 41(1): 1–15.

Garland, D. (1990b), *Punishment and Modern Society: A Study in Social Theory*, Oxford: Clarendon Press.

Garrett, P. (2003), ' "The trouble with Harry", Why the "new agenda of life politics" fails to convince', *British Journal of Social Work*, 33: 381–97.

Gibbons, J., Conroy, S. and Bell, C. (1995), *Operating the Child Protection System*, London: HMSO.

Giddens, A. (1984), *The Constitution of Society*, Cambridge: Polity.

Giddens, A. (1985), *The Nation State and Violence: Volume 2 of a Contemporary Critique of Historical Materialism*, Cambridge: Polity.

Giddens, A. (1987), *Social Theory and Modern Sociology*, Cambridge: Polity.

Giddens, A. (1990), *The Consequences of Modernity*, Cambridge: Polity.

Giddens, A. (1991), *Modernity and Self-Identity: Self and Society in the Late Modern Age*, Cambridge: Polity.

Giddens, A. (1992), *The Transformation of Intimacy*, Cambridge: Polity.

Giddens, A. (1994a), *Beyond Left and Right: The Future of Radical Politics*, Cambridge: Polity.

Giddens, A. (1994b), 'Living in a post-traditional society', in U. Beck, A. Giddens and S. Lash, *Reflexive Modernization*, Cambridge: Polity.

Giddens, A. (1998), *The Third Way: The Renewal of Social Democracy*, Cambridge: Polity.

Gilmour, A. (1988), *Innocent Victims: The Question of Child Abuse*, London: Michael Joseph.

Gordon, L. (1986), 'Feminism and social control: the case of child abuse', in J. Mitchell and A. Oakley (eds), *What is Feminism?*, London: Blackwell.

Gordon, L. (1989), *Heroes of Their Own Lives: The Politics and History of Family Violence, Boston 1870–1960*, London: Virago.

Gorer, G. (1965), *Death, Grief, and Mourning in Contemporary Britain*, London: Cresset Press.

Gorham, D. (1978), 'The "maiden tribute of Babylon" re-examined: child prostitution and the idea of childhood in late Victorian England', *Victorian Studies*, 21(3): 353–87.

Guérer, A. (1993), *Scent: The Mysterious and Essential Powers of Smell*, London: Chatto and Windus.

Harris, R. and Webb, D. (1987), *Welfare, Power and Juvenile Justice*, London: Tavistock.

Harvey, D. (1985), *Consciousness and the Urban Experience*, Oxford: Basil Blackwell.

Harvey, D. (1989), *The Condition of Postmodernity: An Enquiry into the Origins of Cultural Change*, Oxford: Basil Blackwell.

Hawkins, A., Christiansen, S.L., Pond Sargent, K. and Hill, E.J. (1995), 'Rethinking fathers involvement in childcare: a developmental perspective', in W. Marsiglio (ed.), *Fatherhood: Contemporary Theory, Research and Social Policy*. London: Sage.

HDAR, Hartlepools and District NSPCC (1935), *Annual Report*, London: NSPCC archives.

Healy, K. (2000), *Social Work Practices: Contemporary Perspectives on Change*, London: Sage.

Hearn, J. (1990), ' "Child abuse" and men's violence', in The Violence Against Children Study Group *Taking Child Abuse Seriously*, London: Routledge.

Hearn, J. (1998), *The Violences of Men*, London: Sage.

Hendrick, H. (1992), 'Child labour, medical capital, and the school medical service, c 1890–1918', in R. Cooter (ed.), *In the Name of the Child: Health and Welfare, 1880–1940*, London: Routledge.

Hendrick, H. (2003), *Child Welfare: Historical Dimensions, Contemporary Debate*, Bristol: The Policy Press.

Herman, J. (1992), *Trauma and Recovery*, London: Pandora.

Herman, J. and Hirschman, L. (1981), *Father–Daughter Incest*, Cambridge, MA: Harvard University Press.

Heywood, J.S. (1959), *Children in Care: The Development of the Service for the Deprived Child*, London: Routledge and Kegan Paul, 3rd edn (1978).

Hinshelwood, R.D. and Skogstad, W. (2000), *Observing Organisations: Anxiety, Defence and Culture in Health Care*, London: Routledge.

Hoggett, P. (2001), 'Agency, rationality and social policy', *Journal of Social Policy*, 30(1): 37–56.

Hoggett, P. (2000), *Emotional Life and the Politics of Welfare*, Basingstoke: Macmillan.

Holman, B. (1988), *Putting Families First: Prevention and Child Care*, London: MacMillan.

Holway, W. (2001), 'The psycho-social subject in "evidence-based practice" ', *Journal of Social Work Practice*, 15(1): 9–22.

Hooper, C.A. (1992), *Mothers Surviving Child Sexual Abuse*, London: Routledge.

Horwath, J. (2000), *The Child's World: Assessing Children in Need*, London: Department of Health.

Horwath, J. (2002), 'Maintaining a focus on the child? First impressions of the *framework for the assessment of children in need and their families* in cases of child neglect', *Child Abuse Review*, 11(4): 195–213.

Housden, L. (1955), *The Prevention of Cruelty to Children*, London: Cape.

Howe, D. (1992), 'Child abuse and the bureaucratisation of social work', *Sociological Review*, 40(3): 491–508.

Howe, D. (1996), 'Surface and depth in social work practice', in N. Parton (ed.), *Social Work, Social Theory and Social Change*, London: Routledge.

Howe, D., Brandon, M., Hinings, D. and Schofield, G. (1999), *Attachment Theory, Child Maltreatment and Family Support*, London: Macmillan.

Irish Society for the Prevention of Cruelty to Children (1958, 1976), *Annual Report*, Dublin: ISPCC.

Jackson, L. (2000), *Child Sexual Abuse in Victorian England*, London: Routledge.

Jackson, S. and Scott, S. (1999), 'Risk anxiety and the social construction of childhood,' in D. Lupton (ed.), *Risk and Sociocultural Theory: New Directions and Perspectives*, Cambridge: Cambridge University Press.

James, A. and Prout, A. (1990), *Constructing and Reconstructing Childhood: Contemporary Issues in the Sociological Study of Childhood*, London: Falmer Press.

James, A., Jenks, C. and Prout, A. (1997), *Theorizing Childhood*, Cambridge: Polity Press.

Jamieson, L. (1998), *Intimacy*, Cambridge: Polity.

Jay, M. (1986), 'In the empire of the gaze: Foucault and the denegration of vision in twentieth-century French thought', in D. Couzens Hoy (ed.), *Foucault: A Critical Reader*, Oxford: Basil Blackwell.

Jenks, C. (1996), *Childhood*, London: Routledge.

Joffe, H. (1999), *Risk and 'The Other'*, Cambridge: Cambridge University Press.

Jones, G. Stedman (1971), *Outcast London: A Study in the Relationship between Classes in Victorian Society*, Oxford: Clarendon Press.

Jordan, B. and Jordan, C. (2000), *Social Work and the Third Way: Social Policy as Tough Love*, London: Sage.

Kahan, B. and Levy, A. (1991), *The Pindown Experience and the Protection of Children: The Report of the Staffordshire Child Care Inquiry*, Stoke: Staffordshire County Council.

Kempe, C.H. (1976), 'Keynote Address', *National Symposium on Child Abuse*, Dublin, 5 May 1976, Dublin: NSPCC Archives.

Kempe, C.H., Silverman, F.N., Steel, B.F., Droegemueller, W. and Silver, H.K. (1962), 'The battered child syndrome', *Journal of the American Medical Association*, No. 181: 17–24.

Kempe, R. and Kempe, H. (1978), *Child Abuse*, London: Open Books.

Kern, S. (1983), *The Culture of Time and Space, 1880–1918*, Cambridge, MA: Harvard University Press.

Kirkwood, A. (1993), *The Leicester Inquiry 1992*, Leicester: Leicestershire County Council.

Kitzinger, J. (2003), 'Creating discourses of "false memory": media coverage and production dynamics', in P. Weaver and S. Warner (eds), *New Feminist Stories of Child Sexual Abuse: Sexual Scripts and Dangerous Dialogues*, London: Routledge.

La Fontaine, J. (1990), *Child Sexual Abuse*, Cambridge: Polity.

Laming, H. (2003), *The Victoria Climbié Inquiry*, London: Stationary Office.

Lash, S. (1987), 'Modernity or modernism? Weber and contemporary social theory', in S. Whimster and S. Lash (eds), *Max Weber, Rationality and Modernity*, London: Allen and Unwin.

Lash, S. (1994), 'Reflexivity and its doubles: structure, aesthetics, community', in U. Beck, A. Giddens and S. Lash, *Reflexive Modernization*, Cambridge: Polity.

Lash, S. (2002), 'Individualization in a non-linear mode', Foreword to U. Beck and E. Beck-Gernsheim, *Individualization*, London: Sage.

Lash, S. and Friedman, J. (eds) (1992), 'Subjectivity and modernity's other', in *Modernity and Identity*, Oxford: Blackwell.

Lash, S. and Urry, J. (1987), *The End of Organised Capitalism*, Cambridge: Polity.

Lash, S. and Urry, J. (1994), *Economies of Signs & Space*, London: Sage.

Lefebvre, H. (1991), *The Production of Space*, Oxford: Blackwell.

Levitas, R. (1998), *The Inclusive Society? Social exclusion and New Labour*, Macmillan: Basingstoke.

Lewis, J. (1980), *The Politics of Motherhood: Child and Maternal Welfare in England, 1900–1939*, London: Croom Helm.

Lindsay, D. (1994), *The Welfare of Children*, New York: Oxford University Press.

London Borough of Brent (1985), *A Child in Trust: Report of the Panel of Inquiry Investigating the Circumstances Surrounding the Death of Jasmine Beckford*, London: Borough of Brent.

London Borough of Greenwich (1987), *A Child in Mind: The Report of the Commission of Inquiry into the Circumstances Surrounding the Death of Kimberley Carlile*, London: Borough of Lambeth.

Lull, J. and Hinerman, S. (1997), 'The search for scandal', in J. Lull and S. Hinerman (eds), *Media Scandals: Morality and Desire in the Popular Culture Marketplace*, Cambridge: Polity.

Lupton, D. (1999), *Risk*, London: Routledge.

MacDonald, G. (2001), *Effective Interventions for Child Abuse and Neglect*, Chichester: John Wiley and Sons.

Mahood, L. and Littlewood, B. (1994), 'The "vicious girl" and the "street-corner boy": sexuality and the gendered delinquent in the Scottish child-saving movement 1850–1940', *Journal of the History of Sexuality*, 4: 549–78.

Martin, B. (1981), *A Sociology of Contemporary Cultural Change*, Oxford: Basil Blackwell.

Marx, K. and Engels, F. (1888), *The Communist Manifesto*, London: Foreign Languages Press.

Mattinson, J. (1975), *The Reflection Process in Casework Supervision*, London: Institute for Marital Studies, Tavistock Clinic.

Mattinson, J. and Sinclair, I. (1979), *Mate and Stalemate*, Oxford: Oxford University Press.

McGee, H., Garavan, R., de Barra, M., Byrne, J. and Conroy, R. (2002), *The SAVI Report: Sexual Abuse and Violence in Ireland*, Dublin: Liffey Press.

McGrath, K. (1996), 'Intervening in child sexual abuse in Ireland: Towards victim-centred policies and practices', in H. Ferguson and J. McNamara (eds), *Protecting Irish Children: Investigation, Protection & Welfare*, Dublin: Institute of Public Administration.

McGuinness, C. (1993), *Report of the Kilkenny incest investigation*, Dublin: Government Stationary Office.

McKay, S. (1998), *Sophia's Story*, Dublin: Gill and Macmillan.

McKeown, K., Ferguson, H. and Rooney, D. (1998), *Changing Fathers? Fatherhood and Family Life in Modern Ireland*, Cork: Collins Press.

MDAR, *Middlesbrough and District Branch NSPCC Annual Reports*, 1902–60, London: NSPCC Archives.

Mellor, P. and Shilling, C. (1993), 'Modernity, self-identity and the sequestration of death', *Sociology*, 27(3): 411–32.

Menzies, I. (1958), 'The functioning of social systems as a defence against anxiety. A report on a study of the nursing service of a general hospital', in I. Menzies Lyth (ed.) (1988), *Containing Anxiety in Institutions. Selected Essays Volume One*, London: Free Association Books.

Mills, A.J. (1989), 'Gender, sexuality and organisation theory', in J. Hearn, D.L. Sheppard, P. Tancred-Sheriff and G. Burrell (eds), *The Sexuality of Organization*, London: Sage.

Milner, J. (1993), 'Avoiding violent men: the gendered nature of child protection policy and practice', in H. Ferguson, R. Gilligan and R. Torode (eds), *Surviving Childhood Adversity: Issues for Policy and Practice*, Dublin: Social Studies Press.

Milner, J. (1996), 'Men's resistance to social workers', in B. Fawcett, B. Featherstone, J. Hearn and C. Toft (eds), *Violence and Gender Relations, Theories and Interventions*, London: Sage.

Monckton, Sir Walter (1945), *Report on the Circumstances which led to the Boarding-out of Denis and Terence O'Neill at Bank Farm, Minsterly and the Steps taken to Supervise their welfare*, HMSO, Cmd. 6636.

Morrison, B. (1997), *As If,* London: Granta.
Morrison, T., Erooga, M. and Beckett, R.C. (eds) (1994), *Sexual Offending Against Children: Assessment & Treatment of Male Abusers,* London: Routledge.
Munro, E. (2002), *Effective Child Protection,* London: Sage.
Murray, C. (1996), *Charles Murray and the Underclass: The Developing Debate,* London: Institute of Economic Affairs.
Nava, M. (1988), 'Cleveland and the press: outrage and anxiety in the reporting of child sexual abuse', *Feminist Review,* 28: 103–21.
National Society for the Prevention of Cruelty to Children (1904, 1910, 1914, 1960), *Inspector's Directory,* London: NSPCC Archives.
National Society for the Prevention of Cruelty to Children (1988), *Annual Report,* London: NSPCC.
NEDG, *North-Eastern Daily Gazette* newspaper, 1879–1914, Middlesborough County Library.
New South Wales Child Death Review Team Report (1997), *Annual Report,* 1996–97, Sydney.
Nelson, B.J. (1984), *Making an Issue of Child Abuse,* Chicago: Chicago University Press.
Nelson, S. (1987), *Incest: Fact and Myth,* Edinburgh: Stramullion.
Nettleton, S. (1988), 'Protecting a vulnerable margin: towards an analysis of how the mouth came to be separated from the body', *Sociology of Health and Illness,* 10(2): 156–69.
Packman, J. (1981), *The Child's Generation,* London: Blackwell and Robertson.
Parr, J. (1980), *Labouring Children,* London: Croom Helm.
Parr, R. (1919), *How Much is a Baby's Life Worth?* London: NSPCC Archives.
Parton, N. (1985), *The Politics of Child Abuse,* London: Macmillan.
Parton, N. (1991), *Governing the Family: Child Care, Child Protection and the State,* London: Macmillan.
Parton, N. (1996), 'Social work, risk and the blaming system', in N. Parton (ed.), *Social Work, Social Theory and Social Change,* London: Routledge.
Parton, N., Thorpe, D. and Wattam, C. (1997), *Child Protection, Risk and the Moral Order,* London: Macmillan.
Pearson, G. (1975), *The Deviant Imagination: Psychiatry, Social Work and Social Change,* London: Macmillan.
Percival, T. (1911), *Poor Law Children,* London: Shaw and Sons.
Peile, C. (1998), 'Emotional and embodied knowledge: implications for critical practice', *Journal of Sociology and Social Welfare,* 25: 39–59.
Pinchbeck, I. and Hewitt, M. (1969, 1973), *Children in English Society,* London: Routledge and Kegan Paul, 2 Vols.
Pleck, E. (1987), *Domestic Tyranny: The Making of American Social Policy against Family Violence from Colonial Times to the Present,* Oxford: Oxford University Press.
Plummer, K. (1995), *Telling Sexual Stories: Power, Change and Social Worlds,* London: Routledge.
Pollock, L. (1983), *Forgotten Children: Parent–Child Relations from 1500–1900,* Cambridge: Cambridge University Press.
Radbill, S.X. (1973), 'Children in a world of violence: a history of child abuse and infanticide' in C.H. Kempe and R.E. Hefler (eds), *The Battered Child,* Chicago: University of Chicago Press, 2nd edn.

Raftery, M. and O'Sullivan, E. (1999), *Suffer the Little Children: The Inside Story of Ireland's Industrial Schools*, Dublin: New Island Books.

Reder, P., Duncan, S. and Gray, M. (1993), *Beyond Blame: Child Abuse Tragedies Revisited*, London: Routledge.

Reder, P. S. and Duncan, S. (1999), *Lost Innocents: A Follow-up Study of Fatal Child Abuse*, London: Routledge.

Richardson, N. (2003), 'The Victoria Climbié inquiry', paper given to the *Beyond Laming* Conference, 10th June 2003, Bristol: University of the West of England.

Richardson, R. (1989), *Death, Dissection and the Destitute*, London: Penguin.

Rojek, C., Collins, S. and Peacock, G. (1988), *Social Work and Received Ideas*, London: Routledge.

Rorty, R. (1980), *Philosophy and the Mirror of Nature*, Oxford: Blackwell.

Ross, C.J. (1980), 'The lessons of the past: defining and controlling child abuse in the United States' in G. Gerbner, C.J. Ross and E. Zigler (eds), *Child Abuse: An Agenda for Action*, New York: Oxford University Press.

Rothman, D. J. (1980), *Conscience and Convenience: The Asylum and its Alternatives in Progressive America*, Boston: Little Brown.

Rowntree, B.S. (1901), *Poverty: A Study of Town Life*, London: Nelson.

Ruddick, M. (1991), 'A recepticle for public anger', in B. Franklin and N. Parton (eds), *Social Work, the Media and Public Relations*, London: Routledge.

Scheper-Hughes, N. (ed.) (1987), *Child Survival: Anthropological Perspectives on the Treatment and Maltreatment of Children*, Dordrecht, Holland: Reidel.

Schoenwald, R.L. (1973), 'Training urban man: a hypothesis about the sanitary movement', in H.J. Dyos and M. Wolff (eds), *The Victorian City*, London: Routledge and Kegan Paul, Vol. 2.

Scourfield, J. (2000), 'The rediscovery of child neglect', *Sociological Review*, 48(3): 365–82.

Scourfield (2001), 'Constructing women in child protection work', *Child and Family Social Work*, 6(1): 77–87.

Scourfield, J. (2003), *Gender and Child Protection*, Basingstoke: Palgrave.

Scourfield, J. and Welsh, I. (2003), 'Risk, reflexivity and social control in child protection: new times or same old story?', *Critical Social Policy*, 23(3).

Seale, C. (1998), *Constructing Death: Sociology of Dying & Bereavement*, Cambridge: Cambridge University Press.

Sennett, R. (1970), *Families Against the City: Middle-Class Homes of Industrial Chicago 1872–1890*, Cambridge, MA: Harvard University Press.

Sennett, R. (1974), *The Fall of Public Man*, Cambridge: Cambridge University Press.

Sgroi, S. (1998), 'The McColgan case: increasing public awareness of professional responsibility for protecting children from physical and sexual abuse in the Republic of Ireland', *Journal of Child Sexual Abuse*, 8(1).

Sheller, M. and Urry, J. (2003), 'Mobile Transformations of "Public" and "Private" Life', *Theory, Culture and Society*, 20(3): 107–25.

Shilling, C. (1993), *The Body and Social Theory*, London: Sage.

Shilling, C. and Mellor, P. (2001), 'Embodiment, structuration theory and modernity: mind/body dualism and the repression of sensuality', in C. Bryant and D. Jary (eds), *The Contemporary Giddens: Social Theory in a Globalizing Age*, Basingstoke: Palgrave.

Shorter, E. (1976), *The Making of the Modern Family*, London: William Collins.

Smith, C. (2001), 'Trust and confidence: possibilities for social work in "high modernity"', *British Journal of Social Work*, 31: 287–307.

Smith, C. (2002), 'The sequestration of experience: rights talk and moral thinking in "late modernity"', *Sociology*, 36(1): 43–66.

Soja, E. (1985), 'The spatiality of social life: towards a transformative retheorisation', in D. Gregory and J. Urry (1985), *Social Relations and Spatial Structures*, London: Macmillan.

Soothill, K. and Francis, B. (2002), 'Moral panics and the aftermath', *Journal of Social Welfare and Family Law*, 24(1): 1–17.

Stallybrass, P. and White, A. (1986), *The Politics and Poetics of Transgression*, London: Methuen.

Stanley, J. and Goddard, C. (2002), *In the Firing Line: Power and Violence in Child Protection Work*, London: Wiley.

STAR, *Stockton and Thornaby Branch NSPCC, Annual Reports*, 1890–1960, London: NSPCC Archives.

Stedman Jones, G. (1971), *Outcast London*, Oxford: Oxford University Press.

Steedman, C. (1992), 'Bodies, figures and physiology: Margaret McMillan and the late-nineteenth century remaking of working class childhood', in R. Cooter (ed.), *In the Name of the Child: Health and Welfare 1880–1940*, London: Routledge.

Stein, M. (1993), 'The abuses and uses of residential child care', in H. Ferguson, R. Gilligan and R. Torode (eds), *Surviving Childhood Adversity: Issues for Policy and Practice*, Dublin: University of Dublin, Social Studies Press.

Stockton MOH (1910), *Report of the Medical Officer of Health for Stockton-on-Tees*, Stockton-on-Tees library.

Stone, L. (1977), *The Family, Sex and Marriage in England 1500–1800*, London: Weidenfeld & Nicholson.

Summit, R.C. (1988), 'Hidden victims, hidden pain: societal avoidance of child sexual abuse', in G.J. Wyatt and G.J. Johnson Powell (eds), *Lasting Effects of Child Sexual Abuse*, London: Sage.

Swift, K. (1995), *Manufacturing 'Bad Mothers': A Critical Perspective on Child Neglect*, Toronto: University of Toronto Press.

Tangenberg, K.M. and Kemp, S. (2002), 'Embodied practice: claiming the body's experience, agency, and knowledge for social work', *Social Work*, 47(1): 9–18.

Taylor, C. and White, S. (2000), *Practising Reflexivity in Health and Welfare: Making Knowledge*, Buckingham: Open University Press.

Taylor-Gooby, P. (1999), *Risk, Trust and Welfare*, Basingstoke: Palgrave.

Thomas, N. (2002), *Children, Family and the State: Decision Making and Child Participation*, Bristol: Policy Press.

Thompson, E.P. (1967), 'Time, work-discipline and industrial capitalism', *Past and Present*, 36: 57–97.

Thompson, N. (1993), *Anti-Discriminatory Practice*, London: Macmillan.

Thoburn, J., Lewis, A. and Shemmings, D. (1995), *Paternalism or Partnership? Family Involvement in the Child Protection Process*, London: HMSO.

Thorpe, D. (1994), *Evaluating Child Protection*, Buckingham: Open University Press.

Thrift, N. (1983), 'On the Determination of Social Action in Time and Space', *Environment and Planning D: Society and Space*, 1: 23–57.

Thrift, N. (1990), 'The making of a capitalist time consciousness', in J. Hassard (ed.), *The Sociology of Time*, London: Macmillan.

Titterton, M. (1992), 'Managing threats to welfare: the search for a new paradigm of welfare', *Journal of Social Policy*, 21(1): 1–23.

Turner, V.W. (1969), *The Ritual Process: Structure and Anti-Structure*, London: Allen Lane.

Turner, V.W. (1974), *Dramas, Fields and Metaphors*, Ithaca, NY: Cornell University Press.

Urquart, J. and Heilmann, K. (1984), *Risk Watch: The Odds of Life*, New York: Facts on File.

Urry, J. (2000), *Sociology Beyond Societies: Mobilities for the Twenty-first Century*, London: Routledge.

Urry, J. (2003), 'Social networks, travel and talk', *British Journal of Sociology*, 54(2): 155–75.

USABCAN (United States Advisory Board on Child Abuse and Neglect) (1995), *A Nation's Shame: Fatal Child Abuse and Neglect in the United States*, Washington, DC: Department of Health and Human Services.

Virilio, P. (1986), *Speed and Politics*, New York: Semiotext(e).

Walkowitch, J. (1980), *Prostitution and Victorian Society*, Cambridge: Cambridge University Press.

Waller, P.J. (1983), *Town, City and Nation*, Cambridge: Cambridge University Press.

Walter, T. (1991), 'Modern death: Taboo or not taboo', *Sociology*, 25: 293–310.

Walter, T. (1994), *The revival of Death*, London: Routledge.

Ward, A. (1995), 'The "matching principle": exploring connections between practice and training in therapeutic child care: part 1 – therapeutic child care and the holding environment', *Journal of Social Work Practice*, 9(2): 177–89.

Wattam, C. (1997), 'Is the criminalization of child harm and injury in the interests of children?', *Children and Society*, 11: 97–107.

Wattam, C. and Parton, N. (1999), 'Impediments to implementing a child-centred approach', in N. Parton and C. Wattam (eds), *Child Sexual Abuse: Responding to the Experiences of Children*, London: Wiley.

Weeks, J. (1980), *Sex, Politics and Society*, London: Longman.

Weindling, P. (1992), 'From isolation to therapy: children's hospitals and diptheria in *Fin De Siecle* Paris, London and Berlin', in R. Cooter (ed.), *In the Name of the Child: Health and Welfare, 1880–1940*, London: Routledge.

Wexford and District NSPCC (1922), *Annual Report*, London: NSPCC Archives.

Whaley, J. (ed.) (1981), *Mirrors of Mortality: Studies in the Social History of Death*, London: Europa.

Whimster, S. (1987), 'The secular ethic and the culture of modernism', in S. Whimster and S. Lash (eds), *Max Weber, Rationality and Modernity*, London: Allen and Unwin.

Wilkinson, I. (2001), *Anxiety in a Risk Society*, London: Routledge.

Williams, F. and Popay, J. (1999), 'Balancing polarities: developing a new framework for welfare research', in F. Williams, J. Popay and A. Oakley (eds), *Welfare Research: A Critical Review*, London: UCL Press.

Williams, F., Popay, J. and Oakley, A. (eds) (1999), *Welfare Research: A Critical Review*, London: UCL Press.

Williams, G. and Macreadie, J. (1992), *Ty Mawr Community Homes Inquiry 1991*, Monmouth: Gwent County Council.

Williams, P. (1987), 'Constituting class and gender: a social history of the home', in N. Thrift and P. Williams (eds), *Class and Space: The Making of Urban Society*, London: Routledge and Kegan Paul.

Williams, R. (1973), *The Country and the City*, London: Chatto and Windus.

Wilson, E. (1985), *Adorned in Dreams: Fashion and Modernity*, London: Virago.

Wise, S. (1995), 'Feminist ethics in practice', in R. Hugman and D. Smith (eds), *Ethical Issues in Social Work*, Routledge: London.

Wolff, L. (1988), *Postcards from the End of the World: An Investigation into the Mind of Fin-de-Siecle Vienna*, London: Collins.

Woodroffe, K. (1962), *From Charity to Social Work in England and the United States*, London: Routledge and Kegan Paul.

Wright, P. (1987), 'The social construction of babyhood: the definition of infant care as a medical problem', in A. Bryman, B. Bytheway, P. Allatt and T. Keil (eds), *Rethinking the Life Cycle*, London: MacMillan.

Wyatt, G. and Higgs, M. (1991a), 'The medical diagnosis of child sexual abuse: the paediatrician's dilemma', in S. Richardson and H. Bacon (eds), *Child Sexual Abuse: Whose Problem? Reflections from Cleveland*, Birmingham: Venture Press.

Wyatt, G. and Higgs, M. (1991b), 'After the diagnosis: everyone's dilemma', in S. Richardson and H. Bacon (eds), *Child Sexual Abuse: Whose Problem? Reflections from Cleveland*, Birmingham: Venture Press.

Zigler, E. and Hall, N.W. (1989), 'Physical child abuse in America: past, present and future', in D. Cicchetti and V. Carlson (eds), *Child Maltreatment: Theory and Research on the Causes and Consequences of Child Abuse and Neglect*, Cambridge: Cambridge University Press.

Zelizer, V. (1985), *Pricing the Priceless Child: The Changing Social Value of Children*, New York: Basic Books.

Index

abandonment 34
abduction 196; fears 143, 146
abuse 19, 37; alleged 5, 142, 147;
attempts to protect from risk of
43; brutal 185; changing meanings
attached to 4, 12; children in care
9, 100, 107; contemporary discourse
on 15; continuity and change in
constructions of 21; curious
decline in public interest in 80;
deaths 4–5, 6, 7, 8, 86; definitions
of 72; dirty, dangerous Others
121, 165; disappearance of public
interest in 105; discovery/
rediscovery of 24, 108; dramatic
increases in numbers of reported
cases of forms of 111; effects 101;
emotional 109, 112, 116, 139, 168;
history of 25; identification,
investigation and management of
4; institutional 102; inter-
generational patterns of 173;
judgements as to what constituted
95; mental 144; merciless 206;
months of 7; new forms of 158,
194; numbers taken into care 12;
ongoing disclosures of 9; past,
remembering/forgetting 101;
possible to prevent 3; protecting
from 100; rediscovery of 122;
responses to particular forms of
13; safety from 10; scientific
knowledge of 17; secondary 142;
serious 133; social obligation of
protecting 50; substance 116;
suspected 45, 54, 63, 67, 109, 123,
159, 160; systematic 100, 101,
102, 190; transformations in the
nature of 106; unconscious denial
of 208; *see also* physical abuse;
sexual abuse
academic interest 5
acceptable behaviour 29

access 12, 140, 172; legal right of
180; limited 182; struggles
113–14; supervised 143
accidents 103
accommodation 27; cultural and
professional 74
accountability 121, 132, 203; better,
need for 8; embodied metaphor
for 133; lack of 103, 207; state
6, 109
'acting in time' 188
acting out 171, 172; distorted and
abusive patterns 210
Adam, B. 126
addiction 114, 115, 149, 166, 179
administrative powers 10, 13, 17, 19,
43, 73, 77, 106, 132, 206;
consequences of modernity for
contemporary child protection in
relation to instrumental rationality
107; development of 50;
emergence of 52; increased scope
of 87; new 53; turned into
practices 136
adversity 92, 100, 106, 164, 187,
191; how people adjust to 174
'Advice Sought' cases 92
aesthetic realm 13, 14, 18, 52, 53,
72–3, 105, 106, 215; modernism
15, 202; sensibility 10, 136
affluent neighbourhoods 36
Agass, D. 170
age 62, 71, 175, 183; clearly
defined 53; differences 126;
roles 137
agency functions 52, 53; putting
into practice 15
agency reports 11, 99
AIDS 129, 130
alcohol/alcoholics 113, 124, 142,
144, 168
allegations 45, 64, 74, 77; writing off
as 'unsubstantiated' 5

240